God Knowable and Unknowable

GOD
KNOWABLE
AND
UNKNOWABLE

EDITED BY ROBERT J. ROTH, S.J.

New York

Fordham University Press

1973

© Copyright 1973 by FORDHAM UNIVERSITY PRESS

All rights reserved.

LC 77–188274

ISBN 0–8232–0920–2

Printed in Monotype Bembo and Perpetua;

Manufactured in the United States of America

The inspiration for this book is our colleague

ELIZABETH G. SALMON

who has been appointed Professor Emeritus after 36 years of devoted service to Fordham and its students. Professor Salmon has been particularly interested in questions about God and metaphysics, and she has written, taught, and lectured on these topics. It is no accident, then, that we have chosen as the theme of this book "God Knowable and Unknowable."

Nor is it by chance that in honoring Professor Salmon her colleagues have been brought together, as it were, within the pages of a book. By her wisdom, graciousness, and thoughtfulness, she has often brought us together in mind and purpose when differences on academic or philosophical issues threatened to separate us. As Professor Emeritus, Elizabeth Salmon will continue to be a center of unity and inspiration.

THE CONTRIBUTORS

W. NORRIS CLARKE, S.J.

Professor
Fordham University

JOSEPH V. DOLAN, S.J.

Associate Professor
Fordham University

JOSEPH DONCEEL, S.J.

Professor Emeritus
Fordham University

KENNETH T. GALLAGHER

Professor
Fordham University

ROBERT O. JOHANN

Professor
Fordham University

QUENTIN LAUER, S.J.

Professor
Fordham University

GERALD A. McCOOL, S.J.

Associate Professor
Fordham University

ROBERT C. NEVILLE

Visiting Associate Professor
State University of New
York College at Purchase

ROBERT J. O'CONNELL. S.J.

Professor
Fordham University

VINCENT G. POTTER, S.J.

Associate Professor
Fordham University

JOSEPH D. RIORDAN, S.J.

Assistant Professor
Fordham University

ROBERT J. ROTH, S.J.

Professor
Fordham University

ALEXANDER VON SCHOENBORN

Assistant Professor
University of Texas
at Austin

CONTENTS

vii

Preface

THIS COLLECTION OF ESSAYS is intended to be a contribution to the lively contemporary dialogue about God. In spite of the "God is Dead" theology, serious discussion about God and the reach of human reason goes on as intensely as ever. The great questions about God's existence, nature, attributes, and relation to the world are still with us and are as challenging and controversial as ever, no matter how new the garb in which they appear. The present essays represent the tradition of positive effort to ascend by reason to the ultimate Mystery which is the source of all being, meaning, and value.

The essays fall into two main groups. One is historical and includes original reflections by contemporary philosophers on the classical philosophers in order to bring out their contributions to the above questions. The book is in effect a dialogue with past thinkers, sometimes in agreement and sometimes in disagreement, but always with the attempt to see something which may have been missed. From Plato to the present, we witness human reason struggling to give expression to what is meant by the deity. The picture which is painted is that of a "God Knowable and Unknowable," a God of light and shadow, of clarity and obscurity. The essayists have attempted to catch something of this picture, still in the making, as it emerges in the works of the philosophers discussed.

The other is more speculative and problem-oriented, striving to come to grips with old questions in their new setting and to build bridges between different traditions which have been taken too long as irreconcilably diverse or opposed. The volume is thus also a dialogue with contemporary thinkers representing process philosophy, transcendental philosophy, existentialism, pragmatism, moral positivism, and Eastern and Western philosophies of religion.

Moreover, in history the philosopher has seldom remained completely aloof from theology. Plato had a good deal to say about the deities of Greek religion, and Hegel was much influenced by the Christian view of God. Though Thomas Aquinas continues to be considered as a theologian, he also stands in his own right as a philosopher, and as such he looked to philosophy for guidance in his search for the meaning of God.

On the current scene, there is a growing interest in philosophical theology. Like their medieval counterparts, contemporary theologians continually find themselves being forced back to metaphysics and epistemology. This is true even within those theological traditions which make a sharp distinction between faith and reason. Consequently, careful attention is being given to the process philosophy of Whitehead, for example, who in the eyes of many provides a metaphysical framework within which to rethink traditional positions about God's nature and His relation to the world.

This volume, then, can help in this enterprise. The historical essays do this indirectly by showing how past philosophers brought into focus problems about God and how they made steps toward their resolution. The speculative essays attempt more directly to apply metaphysics and epistemology to questions about theism in both an Eastern and a Western context.

In their efforts to deal with the reach and limits of reason in relation to the ultimate Known-Unknown, our essayists enter into dialogue with many streams of ancient and contemporary thought, both philosophical and theological. Hence the complementarity of the historical and speculative sections. But they also enter into dialogue with each other. All the contributors have or had been members of the Department of Philosophy of Fordham University for some years. They have engaged in discussion and debate over many philosophical issues. For the first time they have had the opportunity in a sustained way and without interruption or counterargument to indicate how they view philosophers and philosophy on the question of theism.

Now that they have brought their views out into the open, perhaps the debate has only really begun, and we can expect that heated argument will continue far into the night!

In all this, it is hoped that the reader has not been forgotten, for in the last analysis the book is written for you. May it in some small way provide clarification of problems, enlargement of vision, and especially inspiration to dialogue on your own with past and present philosophers and with your own fellow-philosophers on the ever-fascinating question of "God Knowable and Unknowable."

ROBERT J. ROTH, S.J.

God Knowable and Unknowable

I

The Unknown Socrates' Unknown God

ROBERT J. O'CONNELL, S.J.

"REALLY, SOCRATES," Hippias exclaims, "what a creature! Please tell me who he is." And who indeed is this anonymous objector to whom Socrates keeps referring, one who would never be content with Hippias' answers about the essence of beauty? "You would not know him," Socrates assures him, "even if I told you his name."[1] And sure enough, when finally Socrates admits that the annoying questioner is himself, "the son of Sophroniscus," Hippias fails to recognize his identity.

Only a playful sally, one is free to think; an instance of Plato's dramatic art. Yet, read in a certain mood, such playful sallies can jolt the mind with sudden, tragic revelation; and the time is past when philosophers can confidently slice the *Dialogues* into "dramatic" and "philosophic" passages, as though the first had no bearing on the import of the second. The tragic trouble was, as Plato is artfully reminding us, that people did know Socrates' name, yet failed to know the man. Beneath the playful sally gapes the chasm of irony; Hippias' impatience with this troublesome man is not entirely unlike the slow-burning fury of an Anytos, who knew enough to wait his moment and finally mount that deadly trial depicted in the *Gorgias*, in which a pastry-cook like Hippias prosecutes the doctor before a jury of children who simply do not understand what the doctor is about. Or, put another way, they—whether Anytos or Sophist or ordinary Athenian—did not know the "real" Socrates.

One way of looking at Plato's philosophic quest, it has been suggested, would be this: his works, in a series of touches both dramatic and dialectical, gradually unfold to view what it meant to Plato to have come to know this "older friend" of his, "our companion, Socrates."[2] It will be my intention to try this approach here and at the end to suggest that knowing Socrates meant coming to know something of that mysterious personage he often refers to simply as "the God." Something of that personage: for "the father and maker of all this universe is past finding out, and even if we found him, to tell of him to all men would be impossible."[3] For here the problem is even deeper than that of knowing the genuine reality of a man; we are ignorant not only of the nature of the gods, but even of the "names they give themselves," their true names.[4] Piercing the mystery of the unknown Socrates may bring us some way toward, but never to a fully contenting insight into, the Unknown God.

THE SOCRATES PLATO KNEW

Plato's earliest efforts to fix the identity of Socrates must deal with a series of misidentities which have been foisted upon him. The *Apology* depicts a man on trial for his life, endeavoring to show his judges that they have him confused with Anaxagoras, with a caricature from Aristophanes, with the Sophists, with oligarchic Spartan sympathizers, even with the young bloods who found his elenctic method a cruelly amusing toy for the deflation of their elders. Plato may likely have had another series of misidentifications to deal with as well; the current, competing portraits of his dead master, issued by parties who, whether knowingly or not, painted his manners and features much after their own image.[5] No doubt that charge can to some extent be retorted, for Plato's portrait of Socrates is definitely Plato's. We must take him as confiding to us what it meant for *him* to know the man. And yet, not everyone can equally come to know the intimate reality of everyone else; there must be some interior resonance between the individuals involved, something "congenial" (οἰκεῖον) between them, as the *Lysis* suggests, which predisposes them to that reciprocal communication which burgeons into friendship.[6]

That predisposition must include a readiness to be challenged by Socrates, to be convicted, where appropriate, of one's ignorance. A Meno, full of his own conceited pseudo-learning, can learn little or nothing from Socrates of the "virtue" the man not only inquires about, but embodies. A Lysis, on the other hand, a Charmides, even a doughty Laches, can endure the withering fire of his questioning, admit their ignorance, and through the darkness of ἀπορία dimly sense that knowing Socrates was a living approach to gaining acquaintance with the paradigms of human excellence they had not managed to enclose in definition—and perhaps were never really meant to. For such as these the process of honest dialogue yields something richer than knowledge—or better, yields some measure of the kind of knowledge which, in Plato's thinking, was constitutive of virtue. For Socrates embodies not only the spirit of honest inquiry, but the very excellence which each particular dialogue is inquiring about: an excellence one gains insight into at the price of admitting, not only ignorance, but the precise kind of ignorance which goes with not possessing the excellence in question as fully as one might, as fully as Socrates did.

All of this, once again, represents Plato's personal view of his master; the Socrates we meet in the *Dialogues* is very much Plato's Socrates. But then, we must be prepared to find a certain measure of Plato himself in the Socrates he exhibits to us—and not only in Socrates, but in various other characters Plato the dramatist brings to life. This partial identification with his dramatic creations we should reasonably expect to be especially marked in cases in which Plato's artistic empathy takes a heightened form. We must not be surprised to uncover thinly disguised autobiographical elements, traces of the youthful Plato himself, in the Callicles of the *Gorgias*, for instance, in the Alcibiades of the *Symposium*, or in the young Theaetetus of the later works. Their spiritual adventures he saw, at least partly, as mirror-images of his own. "This is what Socrates did to *me*," Plato is discreetly confiding to us, "how he challenged me, my life, my ambitions and my values; and because I let him, consented to his doing so, this is what I came to *see*."

THE TEACHING AND THE MAN

He came to see a man who refused to let his words be one thing, his life another. Socrates' refusal in the *Apology* to change his manner of speaking to suit the unspoken desires of his jurors is tantamount to a refusal to become unfaithful to himself, to become another man from what he had always, in word and act, claimed and shown himself to be. The manner of his discourse is seamlessly one with the manner of his life: the style is the man. Again, the substance of his discourse is the inner substance of the man himself; friendship, σωφρο-σύνη, piety, and courage are not abstractions "out there" which he talks about; they are, in harmonious unity, the inner reality of the man himself. To accuse Socrates of impiety, of corrupting the youth, is never to have known what piety and authentic care of the soul truly are—is never to have known *him*.

What has been said so far may sound much like an embroidery on Friedländer's reminder that Socrates was, for Plato, the "place of the Forms." But for all the truth of Friedländer's insight, it seems to me from one point of view unilateral and incomplete. The absence, in his introductory volume, of a chapter on "God" (or "the gods") may be thought initially symptomatic of that inadequacy.

SOCRATES: PLACE OF THE GODS

For in one of the dramatic episodes where all the above themes weave together most strikingly, Plato speaks of his master as the place for encountering, not "Forms," but "gods." Again, we start with his manner of discourse: words, "simple words," Alcibiades admits, and yet "what an extraordinary effect his words have had upon me—and still do."[7] His talk is about common things, pack-asses and black-smiths, shoemakers and tanners; "he always seems to be saying the same old thing in just the same old way."[8] But the relation between the man's discourse and the objects of that discourse is perfectly anal-ogous to that between the man's interior reality and the divine world he embodies. We must compare him with those Silenus statues, unattractive to the point of being almost ugly, until you split them down the middle and there behold the "little figures of the gods" inside.[9]   As for his words, his ideas and arguments, the same comparison holds: open them up, and no one else's are so godlike, so rich in images of virtue.[10]   The teaching and the man are one. But the teaching is not only about the moral virtues, such that it might lead us to what Plato comes to call the ideal Forms; it treats of those moral virtues as disclosing a divine world, a world (to wrench the phrase of Thales) quite literally "full of gods."

GODS AND FORMS: THE PERSONAL AND IMPERSONAL

At this point we encounter a disjunction in Platonic teaching which must frankly be admitted—that between the personal gods and the seemingly impersonal Forms. Some have been tempted to forge an identity between the Forms, or between that Form of Forms which may be the Good, the Beautiful, or the One, and the God or gods. Others have found themselves compelled to point out that this identity, whatever may be said of later Platonic thinkers, was never forged by Plato himself.

The "gods" for Plato's forebears and contemporaries were unquestionably personal beings; the Forms, including the Forms of moral excellence, seem to remain in Plato's thought impersonal entities, transcendent and unchanging, unresponsive to man's striving to imitate, participate in them, embody them in the stuff of living. The eventual relation Plato sets up between them is suggested as early as the *Euthyphro*, in which Socrates asks whether piety is what the gods deem so, or do they, rather, deem it so because it *is* so:[11] are not the gods, like the demiurge of the *Timaeus*,[12] ruled by, subordinated to, these eternal standards which preside over all true judgment, even (or better, especially) divine? Shocking, Brochard admits,[13] to a twentieth-century man, habituated by centuries of Christianity's insistence that nothing can be superior to God; and yet, for the Greeks, even Zeus was not considered master of Destiny. Above the Gods, then, there held sway over our universe some inexorable, impersonal law—call it Δικη, 'Αναγκη, Λογος, what you will—which all, even divinities, must submit to and cannot overmaster. It has been suggested that this subordination of the personal to the impersonal is what permitted the term θεῖος to come to mean, for Greeks emerged from the mythological age, not "divine" or "godly" in the personal sense, but "enduring," "indestructible."[14] So one might apply the term to the fundamental element of the cosmos, and Thales has his leave to say that "all things are full of the gods" and mean no more than that everything is constituted of water. The divine as fundamental element underlying all, or the divine as the overarching law presiding over all—the insight remains in one important respect analogous; in either case, the cosmos is ruled by the impersonal. Hence it should come to us as no surprise, the argument runs, that Plato from first to last subordinates the personal gods to the impersonal Forms.

I do not mean to contest the fact that, as far as what he "said," even as far as what he consciously meant to say, Plato appears to fit the above description. But that description of his system (if system it may be called) has been vigorously contested; partly, to be sure, from a post-Platonic Christian standpoint; but partly, too, from the encouragement drawn from the Neoplatonists and their attempts to mend this nagging divorce between the personal and impersonal character of our universe. Such attempts to reduce a systematic tension which Plato himself never reduced may quite properly be accused of trying to get at the "back of Plato's mind," of attempting to explore, not what he did say, but what he might, or could, or should have said.

THE TENSION BEFORE PLATO

And yet, such attempts to read the back of Plato's mind need not draw encouragement uniquely from post-Platonic thought. Even before his time, poets and philosophers had vaguely experienced the scandal of placing the impersonal over the personal in the guidance of cosmic affairs. Gilson seems quite right in pointing out that, whatever our modern sense of logic would compel Thales to say, Thales himself seems to have stepped back from actually saying that "water" was "god."[15] The equation is, in Brochard's term, too "shocking"—and not only to the twentieth-century Christian; it seems to have been too shocking for the Greeks themselves. And so we witness a series of signal-flares locating a profound unsettlement in the Greek religious consciousness: the persistence of a "personal" piety alongside the "reflective" piety which demythologization would alone seem to warrant;[16] Aeschylus' and Sophocles' dramatic endeavors to link the gods, both old and new, with Δική; Hecuba's tormented prayer to the power which "mounts the world, whosoever you be, Zeus-named, nature's necessity, or mortal mind," but at all events the last "mystery of man's knowledge."[17] All those signals echo Xenophanes' insistence that our human modes of representing the God who is "one, supreme among gods and men" are radically defective,[18] as well as Heraclitus' dark hints that his Logos and Zeus may in the end be one.[19] For the wonder of personal existence in the world, there must be personal accounting; the tensions in pre-Platonic Greek attitudes toward the Absolute seem to stem from an acknowledgment, however dim, of this perennial human insight.[20]

THE PERSONAL IN PLATO

And something of that insight lurks at the heart of the religion Plato encountered in the mystery of Socrates' life and death. In the *Apology*,[21] he portrays his master as appealing to the mythic figure of Achilles, the symbol of courageous manliness—ἀνδρεία—to illuminate his sense of dutiful fidelity to the mission the "god" had laid upon him, even in the face of death. The appeal is to the soldier's sense of αἰδώς, of shame, reverence, and duty, and Socrates grounds the reasonableness of his response on a great "hope" (ἔλπις),[22] something very like a "faith" (πίστις),[23] that his death will come about not through the workings of some mechanical, impersonal law (ἀπ' αὐτομάτου) but exactly in a world where gods exist and are mindful of, responsive to, the good and evil which men do.[24]

Later, when faced with the very antithesis of his moral attitude in the Callicles of the *Gorgias*, Plato invokes this same triad. He has Socrates elicit from his youthful opponent what remains in him of this sense of shame, the shame which even Callicles must implicitly admit is natural, not merely conventional. The shame in question is, again, that which intervenes when man confronts his manhood's crucial test of bravery or cowardice in face of death.[25] And finally, Socrates concludes, the difference between them is said to lie in Callicles' belief that we live in a chaos, while the older man holds firmly to the belief that we live in a "cosmos"[26] and, if the final myth of judgment is to be taken seriously ("You, I suppose, will consider

it μῦθος, but I consider it λόγος,. . . the actual truth": ἀληθῆ ὄντα²⁷),
a "moral cosmos" at that. Now if we choose to honor Dodds' sug-
gestion²⁸ that there is in Callicles much of the younger Plato, and
Friedländer's claim that the same must be said of Alcibiades,²⁹ then
a connection leaps swiftly to mind: one of Alcibiades' most devastating
admissions is that Socrates, that "place of the gods" whose courage
in the face of death he has already admiringly portrayed, made him
feel positively "ashamed," indeed, was the only man who ever could
make him feel ashamed.

To this sense of shame or duty in the face of death, and to the moral
cosmos it implies, we shall return shortly. But before doing so, we
must try to understand why Plato did not go straight at those implicits but, if the term may be excused, got sidetracked.

THE TRIUMPH OF EUDAEMONISM

For Plato never really explored the personal character of God (or,
the gods) so deeply as he did the nature of the Forms. This has been
attributed to a defective sense of the personal, more generally characteristic of Greek thought. It has, as well, much to do with the obvious
unacceptability of the anthropomorphic portraits of the Olympians:
one may regret the lack of "warmth" in Plato's divine realm, as
Armstrong rightly does, and still understand it—who would choose
to enshrine the warmth of Zeus' lusts and Hera's jealous rages?³⁰

Yet we come even closer home by tracing the development of
Plato's central concern: to elaborate reflectively a world in which
Socrates' life, death, and the faith which grounded his unshakable
fidelity would all make sense.

That world, we saw, must be a "moral cosmos." ˙ In the terms
Socrates uses in the *Apology*, it must be a world in which doing the
right, the honorable deed, will ultimately prove profitable and
advantageous to the doer. A Kantian might properly complain that
Plato draws no clear distinction between *Pflicht* and *Neigung*, between
the disinterested sense of duty and the quite conceivably unrelated
desire for happiness. And yet, there are signs that Plato could briefly
entertain that distinction. The very way Socrates frames the appropriate question for a man in his plight suggests this: the good man,
or perhaps better, the good-and-beautiful man, the καλός κ' ἀγαθός,

will in certain circumstances ask not what redounds to his advantage or loss, but only what is the noble or ignoble—the beautiful or shameful—thing to do.[31] The purification of the question about Justice which Glaucon and Adeimantos force upon him in the second book of the *Republic* compels Socrates to defend that virtue as having intrinsic value apart from any rewards or punishments which might be meted out to the just man either by his fellow-men or by the gods.[32]

And still, Plato's deeply entertained conviction that ours is a moral cosmos seems to have persuaded him to think this distinction in the last analysis inoperative. Socrates' faith in an afterlife is largely dependent upon a conviction that the "good" or profitable is basically identical with the "right" or noble. So, nothing will satisfy him, after having answered Glaucon and Adeimantos and their question in the terms in which they posed it, but to turn in his tracks and to cast doubt on the legitimacy of the question itself: the just man *will* be rewarded, normally by men, but by the gods infallibly and always.[33] A world in which this was not so would be, for him, badly out of kilter, more a Calliclean chaos than a cosmos. This was the very belief which subtended the Athenians' implied objection to the righteousness of his life, and, far from questioning it, Plato has Socrates assume its validity in replying to their objection.[34] Surely, certain notions of the gods and of their manner of dealing with men must be purified, and to this task the Plato of the *Republic* sets himself; but they are notions would make the gods imperfect, even immoral, and therefore not the gods appropriate to a genuinely moral cosmos.[35]

This underlying belief in the equation between the morally right and the humanly good, in the coincidence between acting nobly and achieving ultimate εὐδαιμονία, may partly excuse the Plato of the *Protagoras* and the *Gorgias* for what may strike us as an obstinate exploitation of a linguistic muddle—he seems to feel that he has full warrant for taking advantage of his adversary's unexamined confidence that whatever is καλόν is ἀγαθον, whatever is αἴσχρον is κακόν, and vice versa.[36]

That same belief may have made him feel entitled to develop his theory of Forms more from the eudaemonistic than from the deontological side. He does not feel the need for presenting the Good, which eventually presides as ultimate touchstone for right moral activity, constantly and explicitly in that guise which constitutes it a normative law upon man, a ground of obligation in the strict deontological sense. It sufficiently suits his purpose to consider it mainly from the eudaemonistic side, whereby it stands as τέλος, end to be envisaged, desired, and quested for, the ultimate criterion of what is good *for*, to the true "profit and advantage" of, man.[37]

THE DRIFT TOWARD THE IMPERSONAL

But that Good must also make possible an objective moral knowledge which delivers man from the skepticism and relativism of the Sophists. Plato is determined that such "orthodoxy," such right opinion as could guide an Athenian in the ways of virtuous activity, must be examined and "pinned down" by causal reasoning, at least by the philosophic segment of the community,[38] that the faith and hope which sustained Socrates, not only during his trial, but throughout his life, could by philosophic method be transformed into the insightful grasp of ἐπιστήμη. The object of that ἐπιστήμη must, in its turn, be unchangeable, beyond all flux, immune from the whimsy and arbitrariness which characterize the performances of Euthyphro's gods. Even the gods, then, must measure their actions, including their judgment of and response to men's actions, by this objective, and impersonal, standard.

At this juncture in his career, then, Plato finds himself compelled to cast his philosophic net more widely than the Sophists, by and large, had ever cared to do. The question of the good for man must take on no less than cosmic dimensions; it forces him to deal with problems as large as the One and the Many, Being and non-Being, Change and the Unchanging. His determination to "know," on the other hand, invites him to deal with this spectrum of issues with the tools of "reason," often furnished him by geometricians and mathematicians, in a sustained effort to test the extent to which even the radically personal, mythic, and seemingly irrational, daemonic features of his primordial Socratic experience might yield to the workings of the demonstrative understanding.

But this widening of his problematic, and the adoption of a series of methods to deal with it, exacted their price. The logical, the demonstrative, quasi-mathematical modes of "reason" may not, after all, be the most appropriate means of understanding the dimension of the personal. To his credit, Plato never loses complete sight of that possibility, never abandons the resort to myth, the acknowledgment of the daemonic and irrational elements embedded in his experience of Socrates' existence. But he tempts us, I submit, to underplay the contribution made to his theory of Forms by modes of thought which are far more mythic and aesthetic than logical, and thus to view the Forms as the impersonal objects of an impersonalizing reason, dealing with the relatively impersonal problems of order and disorder, being and change, in the universe as a whole.

GODS AND FORMS: DYNAMIC AND STATIC

I do not mean to suggest that Plato ever completely loses sight of what I take to be his original intention—to show forth the beauty and value of Socrates' life against the setting of a moral cosmos. On the contrary, I hope to point out that Plato regularly revisits this shrine of his youthful conversion, and what occurs when he does so. But at the mid-point of his development, the "gods" tend to be assigned other tasks besides that of guaranteeing the personal and moral character of our world. Plato is confronted with the need to explain such physical and metaphysical features of the universe as the changing and the dynamic on the one hand, the stable and static on the other. And, as Brochard,[39] Grube,[40] and others have claimed, though the Forms continue to account for stability, the gods (and soul) begin more and more to account for the dynamic side of things. It is significant, however, that the gods are never deprived of their original role. To the very end, as we shall have occasion to see, Plato vigorously attacks an "atheism" defined in any terms which would deprive them of it.[41] There is, from first to last, a "moral" side to the god-question, and Plato never loses touch with it.

THE PROBLEM OF KNOWLEDGE AND VIRTUE

To trace that moral side of the question, we must begin again where any study of Plato must, with the underpinnings of human moral action. Consider it as Plato frames it in his eudaemonistic register: if the Good be the ultimately Desirable for man, and insight into it can be gained by the lucid clarities of reason, one can understand the confidence with which Plato's Socrates can claim that a man who truly "knows" the good would infallibly choose it. It would be eminently unreasonable for him to do otherwise. What the reasonable man will look for, on this supposition, is some science of the good, a kind of ethical calculus, quasi-mathematical in nature.[42]

The conclusion is problematical, surely, and its problematic character was pointed out as early as Plato's own time.[43] For what grounds would anyone have for being genuinely "ashamed" of not achieving the Good? This objection to a (presumed) cardinal point in Plato's ethical theory has been repeatedly urged and variously answered. On the face of it, if the Good be no more than the ultimately desirable for man, then the man who fails to achieve it does so out of ignorance; he is guilty of no more than a mistake, a ἁμαρτία in the original sense. The question is only begged by saying that his ignorance itself is culpable, for no genuine moral duty can exist to know an ultimate Good which is *merely* the ultimate Desirable: the imperative, as Kant would say, may be conditional, but never categorical. Of all this, I have already indirectly suggested, Plato was more than dimly aware. I mean now to develop the proposition that each time he revisits his early Socratic experience, a complementary series of aspects regularly emerges to suggest what the "back of Plato's mind" meant by knowing, by the Good, and by the antecedent belief in moral cosmos required for genuine moral insight to arise.

Developing that proposition will involve showing that each time the moral side of Plato's theology emerges into view, there is some telltale sign of the "faith" he drew from meditating on Socrates' death, along with the sense of shame, reverence, duty he experienced in encountering his master. In each case, Plato finds himself forced to acknowledge the elements of the mythic, the daemonic, the apparently irrational, which pervade any such interpersonal encounter and so implicitly to warn us that logical, demonstrative modes of thought are by no means all the weapons the complete philosopher must possess in his arsenal—particularly when approaching the mystery at the heart of man's universe.

As far back as the *Laches*, Plato's triad of courage, dutiful shame, and their connection with the death-situation—all so central to the *Apology*, as we have observed—surfaces clearly. As the dialogue proceeds, courage seems well on the way to being the correlate of the reflective man's reasonable estimate of what is truly "terrible" or fearful: δεῖνον.[44] Death, which seems the ultimately terrible reality for the soldier (and, Socrates reminds them, for the man in peace as well), is obviously on the scene.[45] But the back of Plato's mind is active; the suggestion has been made that courage involves, beyond an attitude of reasonability, a certain mysterious strength of "heart."[46] The suggestion may seem to have been shelved; but with all such parenthetical asides, one has to watch for its reappearance in another guise.

To grasp the "royal art" which marks the excellence proper to man, the old and venerable Protagoras is made to suggest, one may begin from either μῦθος or λόγος; the messages of both are at one.[47] And one of the key features of political virtue, his myth suggests, is the sense of "reverence" (again, αἰδώς) which permits men to live together in communion among themselves and in union with the gods.[48] His λόγος goes on to spell out the rightness of praise and blame for failure in this sort of virtue, implying that the "knowledge" which guides man's moral conduct may well be somehow different from the technical knowledge presiding over the other arts.[49] In the face of Socrates' persistent questioning he is eventually compelled to assent that knowledge is the key to all the virtues, and yet, even here he makes a significant exception: and the anomalous exception is precisely courage.[50]

Later, it does not seem any lack of logic on Callicles' part, so much as a defect in natural "feel" for our world as cosmos, which roots his opposition to Socrates. Courage, be it noted, is the one thing he most respects, but he has not plumbed the implicits of that regard for courage—the sense of "shame" which lies, after all, so close to a sense of duty, even of natural reverence.[51]

The *Symposium* opens on a related note: Phaedrus' speech extolling love underlines the shame a lover would feel in playing the coward before his beloved.[52] The note is temporarily submerged as Pausanias' shallow musings warn us of the cynical, conventional rationalizations such feelings of shame may disclose; it seems to disappear entirely as Socrates himself leads us up the ladder of loves to a Beauty which bears all the earmarks of a vast oceanic impersonality. If we know, the thesis seems to be, if only we reflect upon what attracts us in every concrete instance of beauty in the world of our experience, we would see that this supreme Beauty is the true object of our heart's desire. The atmosphere is slightly tinged with mysticism—with all the hues of daemonic irrationality—but it can be argued that the "philosophic" nature of the ascent, the eudaemonistic cast of the quest, remains relatively intact. Until Alcibiades enters.

What is remarkable about Alcibiades—and I am suggesting that Plato was, in some hidden compartment of his mind, aware of this in a painful way—is that he stands as existential contradiction to the thesis that the reasonable man is inevitably the virtuous man, that knowledge is virtue, even if the knowledge takes the peculiar form it must if it is at once knowledge of the virtues Socrates discoursed about and knowledge of those virtues as undivorced from Socrates as their personal embodiment. For one thing is plain: Plato portrays Alcibiades as "knowing" Socrates, indeed, as warning the others that he knew him in a way they never got to know him! And yet, his intimate knowledge of the man as "place of the gods" was not sufficient to deter him from his life of wastrel, timeserver, and eventual traitor to Athens. Of all this, when now he stands before Socrates, he feels ashamed.

Plato, then, never trusts himself entirely to the line of eudaemonistic, depersonalizing thought to which his widened problematic and experiments with method tempt him. A case in point: why does the searing critique of popular religion in the *Republic* not dispense him once and for all from the need for these Homeric gods? In strict logic, the Forms alone would seem to answer to his problem, providing stable, objective criteria for what is good for man and state alike; and the dialectical ascent of reason to a glimpse of the Good appears for a time to assume a purely mathematical cast.[53] And yet, when the philosopher eventually catches sight of the intelligible Sun, that Sun is far from static; it is hailed as productive source of being as well as of intelligence.[54] And if we interpret his vision from the analogous locus of the *Symposium*, it is easy to suspect that it "burst upon him" in a way not fully accounted for by the disciplined character of the ascent.[55] From their side, the gods threaten to take on something quite akin to the stable nature of the Forms: to be perfect, they too must be beyond change.[56] The personal and impersonal "ultimates" of Plato's world almost promise to merge.

Part of the reason for all this may be that Plato's parenthetical remark that the citizens of his *Republic* are to honor gods and parents, and (the connection is suggestive, and reminiscent of old Protagoras) to value their friendship with one another,[57] betrays a deep-running preoccupation after all, one which emerges afresh from his encounter with Socrates, and one to which the Forms, if their changeless impersonality is to remain intact, cannot reply. Nor can utterly changeless gods.

Enter Phaedrus once again, and once again in the context of a discussion of friendship, love: that great "irrational" in human life. The ostensibly reasonable ways of trying to understand the friendship-relation have long since been tested in the *Lysis*, and (apparently) to no avail. Now the enthusiastic Phaedrus is oddly thrilling to Lysias' calculatingly "reasonable" argument that the beloved should never lose his head over his lover.[58] And it is Socrates, whose earlier remarks on Ion's demonic enthusiasm seemed hardly flattering then, who now comes to the defense of enthusiasm, possession by the daemon of love, indeed, of losing one's reasonable head; the possession in question, then, betrays a divine dimension. Significantly, the central burden of his argument must be couched in myth, a myth featuring those very Homeric gods from whom the *Republic* should logically have freed us.

The central portion of the work recalls the core of Alcibiades' speech; it portrays the encounter of a lover and his beloved. Immediately the lower and higher portions of the lover's nature are brought into activity; the inferior part is stung with desire for union with, possession of, the beloved, the higher part resists this desire. But on what grounds? Not, this time, the grounds we should have looked for from the *Symposium*: not a "higher" ἔρως fighting with the lower, a superior form of desire, that is, and mobilized by the insight of what the lover truly wants. On the contrary, the lover is "afraid" (ἔδεισε), falls backward "in reverence" (σεφθεῖσα); he retreats from the encounter in "shame and wonder" (αἰσχύνη, θάμβος), and

from that time on follows his beloved "in reverence and awe" (αἰδου-
μένην τε καὶ δεδινῖαν).[59]

Throughout this central section of his myth, then, Plato repeatedly
evokes the sense of αἰδώς, but "duty," "respect," "shame" have
now become too feeble to translate that polyvalent term. It points
to nothing less than the sense of religious mystery without which,
he seems to be saying, the mystery of human friendship, love, and
mutual reverence would remain inexplicable. The *Lysis'* treatment
of this phenomenon had ended with the arch hint that lover and
beloved must share something "congenial" with one another;[60] now
at last the nature of that congeniality stands revealed; the mysterious
kinship which makes them responsive to each other comes, Plato
now tells us, from their having followed the same "god" in their
pre-existence in the overworld. They "recognize" each other as
bearing the imprint of that allegiance. But that recognition depends
on how much they give themselves to the enthusiastic insight which
comes with divine possession; and the gods in question are the old
Homeric gods: purified, demythologized to some extent, but still
indispensable to the kind of world the youthful Plato found disclosed
to him when, years before, he encountered Socrates.

THE LATER WORKS

The rest of the story is familiar. Not only in his subsequent works,
but even in the *Phaedrus* itself, the gods remain distinct from, and
apparently subordinate to, the unchanging, impersonal Forms.
Arguments which would establish some identity between Forms
and Gods must rest on *obiter dicta* of a near-parenthetical sort. This
much has to be admitted when it comes to what Plato actually
"said."

But those *obiter dicta*: need they represent only lapses in which
Plato momentarily lost firm grip on his "system"? To the thinker
driven to extend rather than merely purvey the thought of Plato,
they may be taken, rather, as a series of further signal-flares, locating
points where some nagging dissatisfactions persist in Plato's mind.
He may not, after all, have been perfectly content with the settlement
he overtly came to on the issue of gods and Forms. That manner of
treating his parenthetical "lapses," furthermore, may find itself justi-

fied if those lapses bear to each other clear traces of the family resemblance we have been exploring above.

Take, for instance, the startling remark about Beauty in the *Phaedrus*: unlike the Forms of Wisdom and Goodness, it is directly manifest to sense-experience.[61] The mind is tempted to convert this seeming exception into a rule: are the Forms, after all, much less the termini of logical, abstractive thought, much more the ideals projected from an aesthetic experience? That temptation only becomes stronger when one reflects that here, in the *Phaedrus*—as in the *Symposium* and *Apology*—the self-manifestation of Beauty occurs in the context of an interpersonal relation, one in which the beauty glimpsed both in and beyond the beloved elicits a sense of awe and reverence.

But if Beauty be taken as the ultimate metaphysical correlate of this crucial sense of shame, awe, and reverence, an equation suggests itself: it may be Plato's pregnant term for denoting that personal quality pervading what merely seems to be the mindless, mechanical web of physical happenings, transforming them into the order and harmony of a "moral cosmos." It then becomes understandable why that quality of our universe should disclose itself most powerfully when a "congenial" person encounters another whom he is invited, and consents, to revere.

So the artful way in which Plato draws the character—and even the unprepossessing outer appearance—of Theaetetus: young though he was at his encounter with death, he bore himself with a wisdom and a courage which brook comparison with Socrates' own.[62] So, too, his breathtaking reply to the venerable "Stranger" in the *Sophist*. Asked, in effect, whether the world he beholds is but a fabric of mindless, mechanical occurrences, or the product of "divine craftsmanship" working with "reason and art," he first answers that, young as he is, he finds himself shifting from one opinion to the other. Are such basic options, Plato seems to be asking, ever really decided by cold reason, mathematically measuring the "evidence"? One must think now of the youthful Plato himself, catching fitful sight of the divine world disclosed in and through his "old companion" Socrates; otherwise, Theaetetus' answer sounds like little more than an abdication to emotional unreason. "At this moment, looking at your face, and believing that you hold that these things have a divine origin, I too am convinced."[63]

Is it mere happenstance that in this same dialogue, the previously unchangeable world of "true being" is forced to admit into its company "change, life, soul, and understanding"? Otherwise it would stand immutable, "in solemn aloofness"—unresponding, we may translate, incapable of response to man's cry that the arena of our actions be a "moral cosmos."[64]

No, I would submit, not mere happenstance, but the dramatic emergence to Plato's consciousness of what had, years before, flamed forth from his own encounter with that other "Stranger," the unknown Socrates.

To account for the reverence which came over him then, Socrates must not only discourse about, he must embody in his person the "divine world" of moral excellence he uncovered to view. So too with the gods: they cannot inspire us with awe and shame—a response which Plato invariably connects with *personal* encounters—unless they too, the shimmering background of our Socratic encounters, not only consult and revere, but embody the very Forms of cosmic beauty which preside as normative upon our moral activity. Who would be "shamed" at not having achieved the Good as merely the ultimate, impersonal, unresponsive Desirable for man? No one. But if the Good be Beauty, and Beauty be the secret name for that divine craftsmanship which lays claim upon our reverence, then Beauty can be Some One, and before that Some One the man who refuses reverence may rightly be ashamed.

But then, in some mysterious depth, gods and Forms must be identical. Only once, granted, does Plato lapse into actually referring to the Forms in this way. But the reference is couched in the very aesthetic terms we have been exploring. The "father and creator" is depicted as beholding the "creature he had made" as the "created image of the eternal gods": τῶν αἰδίων θεῶν . . . ἄγαλμα.[65] Again, though, it may not be sheer coincidence that the phrase occurs in the *Timaeus* where he warns us that the "father and maker of this universe is past finding out."[66]

For if he exists, this artist of our universe must be "found out" through reverent contemplation of his ἄγαλμα, the embodied disclosure of his divine craftsmanship. But for disclosure to occur, the physical and metaphysical features of our universe must be regarded as constantly pervaded by the personal aura which makes them features of a genuinely moral cosmos.

THE LAWS

This exigency is repeatedly suggested by the theology of the *Laws*. Here for one last time the aging Plato addresses himself to the central problem which Socrates bequeathed him as the heart of his unremitting concern: that of assuring the conditions on which the community of man might live together, in justice and mutual reverence, valuing their friendship with each other and with the gods. It should be no surprise that Plato feels it necessary to devote the whole of book ten to the theological orthodoxies—buttressed with death-penalties—which he views as indispensable underpinning for the values of his model city.

The dogmatic content may seem minimal, but Plato means to stay with the essential. And the essential remains what it had been for the Socrates of the *Apology* and the *Euthyphro*. He never once contested the right of Athens to prosecute him for atheism, if atheist he truly was. But atheism is not limited to disbelieving in the existence of the gods; one may believe that they exist, but are indifferent to the good and evil men do; or, one may consider the gods as susceptible to being bribed by men. This last form of "atheism" Plato clearly views as the most dangerous and reprehensible of the three: for nothing could be more destructive of the notion—so dear to Socrates and to his great disciple—that ours is, after all is said, a moral cosmos.

For the Plato of the *Laws*, the Forms almost seem to have receded from view. As partial result, the gods are in one respect closer, they are the spirits who order the majestic movements of the astral world, movements manifest even to sense.[67] But they are closer, too, in another way: parents and elders now must be regarded—and revered—as ἀγάλματα of the divine at home with the human.[68] This twin emphasis on the aesthetic mode of access to the divine backdrop of human affairs seems suggestively consonant with Plato's way of bringing his citizens to a lived awareness of the cosmic harmony their city's harmony imitates and embodies; the musical education of the *Republic* has blossomed into the civic θεωρίαι—pageants, spectacles, contemplative delights for mind and eye alike—in and through which the spirit of the city's ideals are meant to make entrance into the soul entire.[69]

And yet, though the gods may be closer, the "father and maker" remains past all finding out. Even in the aesthetic register, the symbolized divine must be grasped not only in, but beyond, all its sensible embodiments; our knowledge of God must constantly be safeguarded from degeneration into emotional effusion seduced by the lures of deceptive immediacy. And so the city's guardians must still submit to a long and arduous process of education; mathematics, dialectic, the exacting processes of abstract thought still remain indispensable.[70] For it always remains true that the Father lies beyond all our easy dichotomies of dynamic and static, mutable and immutable, personal and impersonal; at the furthest outreach of a thought which strives to do justice to both reasonable and irrational, to discipline and enthusiasm, logic and myth, abstract clarities and aesthetic apprehensions, eudaemonistic desire and deontological reverence. The God of whom, a long tradition assures us, we remain in the end far more ignorant than knowing. Socrates' Unknown God.

NOTES

1. *Greater Hippias*, 290DE. All translations of Plato are taken from *The Collected Dialogues of Plato*, edd. Edith Hamilton and Huntington Cairns (New York: Pantheon, 1963). I have introduced occasional modifications of my own, consulting the Greek.

2. See Paul Friedländer, *Plato: An Introduction* (New York: Harper Torchbook, 1958), p. 129. The whole chapter is worth consulting in this connection.

3. *Timaeus*, 28E.

4. *Cratylus*, 400D.

5. See Anton Hermann Chroust, *Socrates: Man and Myth* (Notre Dame: University of Notre Dame Press, 1957) for these divergent portraits.

6. *Lysis*, 221E.

7. *Symposium*, 215DE.

8. *Ibid.*, 221E.

9. *Ibid.*, 215B.

10. *Ibid.*, 221D-222A.

11. *Euthyphro*, 10A.

12. *Timaeus*, 28B.

13. V. Brochard, *Études de philosophie ancienne et de philosophie moderne* (Paris: Vrin, 1926), p. 98.

14. See G. M. A. Grube, *Plato's Thought* (Boston: Beacon Hill Press, 1958), pp. 150-51.

15. Étienne Gilson, *God and Philosophy* (New Haven: Yale University Press, 1959), pp. 2-4.

16. See André M. J. Festugière, *Personal Religion Among the Greeks* (Berkeley: University of California Press, 1960), pp. 1-36.

17. *The Trojan Women*, II, 884-86. Translation taken from *Greek Tragedy*, edd. David Grene and Richard Lattimore (Chicago: University of Chicago Press, 1960), II, with my modifications.

18. Fragment 23. Translation taken from *Early Greek Philosophy*, ed. Milton C. Nahm (New York: Appleton-Century-Crofts, 1964), p. 85.

19. Fragments 19, 28, 36, 65.

20. For a more comprehensive treatment of all these issues, see Werner Jaeger, *The Theology of the Early Greek Philosophers*, trans. E. S. Robinson (Oxford: Clarendon Press, 1947).

21. *Apology*, 28CD.

22. *Ibid.*, 40C.

23. *Ibid.*, 41CD.

24. *Ibid.*, 41D. See René Mugnier, *Le sens du mot θεῖος chez Platon* (Paris: Vrin, 1930), pp. 17-18.

25. *Gorgias*, 494E-499A.

26. *Ibid.*, 508A.

27. *Ibid.*, 523A.

28. In his excellent Introduction to the *Gorgias* (Oxford: Clarendon Press, 1959), pp. 14; 30-34.

29. *Op. cit.*, p. 133.

30. A. H. Armstrong, "Platonic *Eros* and Christian *Agape*," in *Downside Review*, 79 (1961), 110.

31. *Apology*, 28B.

32. *Republic*, 357A-367E.

33. *Ibid.*, 580BC.

34. *Apology*, 28B. Note that Socrates does not question the supposition that *if* death be the greatest of evils, the fact that his line of action has led him here indicates that his actions must, in the moral sense, have been "evil."

35. *Republic*, 377B-388C.

36. The exploitation is implicit in *Protagoras*, 352A-359E, becoming explicit toward the end; it is bolder in *Gorgias*, 474C-477A. In all this, of course, something must be allowed for Plato's use of irony.

37. It must not be forgotten that there is also a normative, as well as a creative side to the "Good," neither of which can be accounted for entirely from the eudaemonistic side.

38. *Meno*, 97D-98A.

39. *Op. cit.*, pp. 95-112.

40. *Op. cit.*, pp. 150-71.

41. See especially the *locus classicus* in *Laws*, x, entire; cf. *Republic*, 364CE.

42. *Protagoras*, 356C-357A; *Gorgias*, 508A; cf. the mathematical cast of the education of the guardians in the *Republic*.

43. See E. R. Dodds, *The Greeks and the Irrational* (Berkeley: University of California Press, 1951), pp. 186-87.

44. *Laches*, 195A.

45. *Ibid.*, 191CD.

46. *Ibid.*, 192BC.

47. *Protagoras*, 320C. Cf. *Meno*, 81AB, where Socrates is made to approve of this move from myth to logos.

48. *Protagoras*, 322AC.

49. *Ibid.*, 324E-325D.

50. *Ibid.*, 349D.

51. It should be clear that the Greek root for "shame," "shame-ful," and "reverence" is the same.

52. *Symposium*, 178D-179A.

53. *Republic*, 522C-534E.

54. *Ibid.*, 517C.

55. *Symposium*, 210E-211A.

56. *Republic*, 381BC.

57. *Ibid.*, 386A.

58. See Josef Pieper, *Enthusiasm and the Divine Madness*, trans. Richard and Clara Winston (New York: Harcourt, Brace & World, 1964), pp. 3-28, for a brilliant commentary on the thrust of this dialogue.

59. *Phaedrus*, 254BE.

60. *Loc. cit.* (note 6).

61. *Phaedrus*, 250D.

62. *Theaetetus*, 142A-144D.

63. *Sophist*, 265CE.

64. *Ibid.*, 249A. It would be an error to claim this as arguing for Plato's identification of the dynamic with the static in his world of true being; and yet, it should not be ignored that a dramatic reversal of earlier principle has been effected: change, and the dynamic properties which accompany it (in the best understanding we can have of change), has been admitted to the realm of the really real.

65. *Timaeus* 37C. See Grube, *op. cit.*, p. 152*n*2.

66. *Ibid.*, 28E.

67. *Laws*, 899B; 966E-968A. Cf. 821B.

68. *Ibid.*, 931A.

69. *Ibid.*, 653A-665C; 771A-772D; 799A-804B.

70. *Ibid.*, 747B; 817D-822C; 961C-968A.

2

God, Intellect, and Avicenna

JOSEPH D. RIORDAN, S.J.

NEXT TO THE "I am the Lord, thy God" of Judaism and the "I believe in God" of Christianity, the third great revealed religion of the West has inscribed its own sacred words: "There is no God but Allah." In the wake of Jewish and Christian speculation about the God they believed in and the meaning of belief, Islam too has provided a dramatic spectrum of the resources of philosophy, Greek or otherwise, in coming to terms with the perennial philosophical problem of the knowability of God. Indeed, the ability of a philosophy to deal responsibly with this problem has been used as the criterion of an authentic philosophy. S. H. Nasr, for example, though not dealing explicitly with the problem of God, contrasts Western philosophy with truly Islamic philosophy and finds the former a tragic story because of its inability to distinguish between intellect and reason.[1]

Even this brief reference raises many questions. *Is* there something which can be called Western philosophy? Is there a Muslim point of view in philosophy? Above all, what is intellect and what is reason, and why talk about a confusion? Moreover, any attempt to deal with any one of the above questions raises more problems: medieval *intellectus* and *ratio*, Kant's *Verstand* and *Vernunft*, the death of philosophy in the West with Averroës, its subsequent fortunes in the East, positivism, the possibility of metaphysics, philosophy and faith, etc.

Nonetheless, some preliminary clarifications can certainly be attempted. Western philosophy from Ockham to the present may be described under a rubric like "The Role of Reason": reason as dialectic; reason as the empirically valid; reason as the enemy of religion, of subjectivity, of personalism, of existentialism, etc. The "reason" which Nasr deplores is that which manifests itself in contemporary forms of positivism, secularism, and materialism, and the intellect (which he also calls understanding) he extols is the basis of metaphysics at the heart of Islamic doctrine.

It might seem at this point that such a view is precisely what one should expect. In view of the fact that Islamic philosophical thought was influenced by Greek philosophy, and medieval Western philosophy was influenced by both Avicenna and Averroës, is it not very natural for a contemporary Muslim philosopher to endorse an interpretation of the intellect which was also found in medieval Christian philosophy and which was lost in the empirical emphasis of modern Western philosophy? It is, but only if certain qualifications are kept in mind.

The "Greek" philosophy referred to, for example, is not homogeneous and includes elements derived from Aristotelian, Platonic, and Neoplatonic thought. Moreover, it was not felt that there was any particular difficulty in making all these elements consistent. A second important qualification concerns elements of philosophical insight which were already in the possession of Islam at the time of its exposure to Hellenistic thought. Corbin and Nasr have insisted on this point in appreciating and presenting Islamic meditation.[2] Koranic interpretation and philosophy are looked upon as supporting each other, and a common source of both is sought in ancient Iranian thought. Finally, one cannot expect without investigation that the words intellect and reason will have the same meanings for Nasr and for the medieval philosophy of Western Europe—and this sets the stage for the present inquiry. In view of the sources mentioned by Nasr, what are the threads which have become intertwined in his notion of intellect? Are there any similarities between this notion and any current views in Western thought? How useful can this notion be in throwing some light on the vast philosophy-and-faith problem of our own era?

For reasons which will be presented later, the complex thought of Avicenna will be the focus of our attention, but history and the history of ideas have contrived to put Averroës in such a unique position as far as sources and influence are concerned that we shall begin with him . It will be recalled that Nasr credits (if that is the word) Averroës with a decisive role in setting European philosophy on the path to a tragic end.[3]

A familiar reading of Islamic philosophy emphasizes three events: a high point in Avicenna, the destruction of Avicenna (and philosophy) in the East by Algazel (al-Ghazālī), a final flowering of philosophy in Spain in the writings of Averroës—and then the end. If the familiar reading is questioned, it involves the admission that something did indeed die in the East with Algazel's critique, but something survived and is still flourishing. What that "something" is becomes the object of a second controversy, and the topic of this paper is at the heart of it.

Corbin and Nasr make it very clear that the word "philosophy" as ordinarily used in the West does not adequately represent their field of interest; words like "doctrine," "meditation," "metaphysics," and, of course, "intellect" are preferred.[4] This is true wisdom (hikmah) and this is also, in substance, the field cultivated by the mystics of Islam, the Sūfis; but, once again, there are differences. Distinctions have been attempted with the help of designations like the following: philosophy, also called rationalistic, utilizing argumentation and logical thought-processes; Sūfism, which emphasizes gnostic experience, intuition, and poetic imagination.[5] The picture is blurred by the fact that there are various combinations of the foregoing elements and no unanimity in the use of certain terms. Nonetheless, with full realization that even a clarification of the meaning of intellect for the various thinkers and students of Islamic philosophy will by no means suffice to define their positions (since other elements may or may not be added), some progress may be hoped for.

As the foregoing pages have suggested, Nasr's remark does not refer to an isolated corner of philosophy, but seems to go to the heart of the problem of the knowability of God—indeed, the very meaning of philosophy in Europe and in Islam. His statement has two parts, a negative one (condemnation of the neglect of *intellectus* in the West, with Averroës singled out for much of the blame), and a positive one (approval of a contemporary philosophy in Islam which has preserved the meaning of intellectual intuition and owes a debt to Avicenna). The pages which follow are an attempt to see more clearly (1) what is being condemned, and the reasons for singling out Averroës, and (2) what is being approved, and the reasons for giving Avicenna special mention.

AVERROËS

There are two ways of approaching Averroës' thought on intellect. One is through the famous doctrines associated with his name: unity of the intellect; possible intellect; the "connection" of the human intellect with the separate intellect. A pursuit of any one of these themes would necessarily deepen one's appreciation of human cognitive activity. But there is another way open to the student of the history of philosophy suggested by the Commentator's well-known encomia on Aristotle.[6] Aristotle touches on the meaning of intellect in the *Posterior Analytics*, the *Metaphysics*, and the *Nichomachean Ethics*, and since we have commentaries of Averroës on all these works, we shall examine them first.

(a) *Posterior Analytics*, I

Kant was not the first one to talk about the foundations of human reason; Plato wondered about it as he viewed the intellectual chaos of the Sophists, and Aristotle gave the gnawing question a typically technical treatment in the *Posterior Analytics*. "All instruction given or received by way of argument proceeds from pre-existent knowledge" are the first words of that work (reminiscent of other famous first words like the "All men by nature desire to know" of the *Metaphysics*). His pursuit of the meaning of "pre-existent" makes it clear that we are now observing a thinker taking stock of thought, and we have a hint of the two profoundly different (although not unrelated) levels on which human thought can function. Because of the impossibility of an infinite series, "Our own doctrine [says Aristotle] is that not all knowledge is demonstrative: on the contrary, knowledge of the immediate premisses is independent of demonstration."[7] He adds: ". . . Besides scientific knowledge, there is its originative source which enables us to recognize the definitions."[8] The impact of these terms upon Averroës will appear in the following section.

(b) *Posterior Analytics*, II

Here the significant words of Aristotle are:

> . . . There will be no scientific knowledge of the primary premisses, and since besides intuition nothing can be truer than scientific knowledge, it will be intuition which apprehends the primary premisses. . . . Intuition will be the originative source of scientific knowledge. And the originative source of science grasps the original basic premiss. . . .[9]

Consistently with the position taken in the first book, thought is viewed here as moving on two levels, but the mode of reference is not the same in these two cases. In the case of the expression "scientific knowledge," the emphasis is on the content before the knower, or on that which is present to the knower, or simply on that which is known. (It is not impossible, of course, to think of knowledge also as a kind of activity.) In the case of "intuition" ($\nu o\tilde{\nu}\varsigma$), on the other hand, the emphasis is clearly on the activity, although, once again, the other meaning is not ruled out.

In his commentary Averroës first enumerates the elements he has before him:

> First, there are three elements involved: intellect, science, and the principle of science. Secondly, intellect is more accurate than science. Thirdly, principles are better known than the science which is produced by them. Finally, in the words of Aristotle, "there is no way in which science can deal with principles." In other words, principles cannot be known through principles, as though the order to be followed in learning them is the order of the science which is produced by them.[10]

An account of a science, then, involves a presentation of certain conclusions and a presentation (literally, a showing or a display) of the way these conclusions are derived from principles, the order followed being all-important. Averroës underlines the fact that the principles from which the whole array stems cannot themselves be the product of such orderly presentation. The brief syllogism which he offers will emphasize the simplicity of his position and the underlying issue which was to have such important effects in the history of Islamic thought and which was to reappear in so many different garbs in the history of Western philosophy.

This is my syllogism [says Averroës]:
  That which reveals principles must be more manifest than scientific
  knowledge;
  The only two possibilities are
    (a) intellect, and
    (b) principles.
  Principles must be ruled out (because principles cannot be the cause
  of principles).
  Therefore, intellect is the cause of principles.[11]

Averroës' task here is simplified by his conviction that what he is looking for is in the cognitive order, that is, some kind of knowledge. The crucial nature of this calm conviction is brought out a few lines later in words which he takes from Aristotle: "If there is no true genus besides scientific knowledge, intellect is the principle of principles."[12]

It is precisely the contention that this is the domain of truth and knowledge and cognitive activity which has been denied or overlooked or disdained in the history of philosophy in so many widely differing positions (James' "passional nature," Schopenhauer's world-will, etc.). This is the point reached by so many thinkers who have had recourse to expressions like "faith," "assumption," "hunch," "common sense," and "feeling." What concerns us here, however, is Averroës' characterization of the phenomenon as he derived it from Greek philosophy and as he transmitted it to twelfth- and thirteenth-century Europe. His translators used the word *intellectus*; it was characterized as *verax* and *verus*; it involved *comprehensio* and *apprehensio*; its exercise was expressed by *notificat* and its result by *notiora*. For Averroës the knowledge of ultimates was the knowledge of principles, and this was the realm of intellect.

(c) *Metaphysics* and *Nichomachean Ethics*

Identifying these principles, and even classifying them (definitions, laws of thought, laws of being, relationships among them, etc.), is not a simple task, but Averroës makes it clear that he has accepted and emphasized an important intellectual activity which is not the same as reason. For example, when Aristotle inquires in the *Metaphysics* whether the same science should be concerned with substance and with first principles, Averroës frames his question as follows:

Aristotle asks whether it is up to the philosopher to investigate the first universal propositions which are the principles of every demonstration.[13]

And he comments on Aristotle's affirmative answer:

These principles are common to all the kinds of being which are considered by speculative sciences. Moreover, whatever is common to all genera belongs to being as being, and, as such, it is to be investigated by the one who studies unqualified being, i.e., the philosopher.[14]

When, a little later, Aristotle denies the possibility of demonstrating everything, Averroës gives the following explanation:

... If this principle [the principle of contradiction] which is the most evident of all could be demonstrated, it would follow that everything is capable of demonstration. And if there is a demonstration for the principles of demonstration, and every demonstration rests on principles, then there is a demonstration for every demonstration. This is an infinite regression and means that there is no demonstration at all.[15]

Finally, Averroës takes advantage of an Aristotelian summary in the *Nichomachean Ethics* to make explicit his appreciation of intellectual insight. He first quotes Aristotle and then explains:

"When it comes to our ability to have truth and never to be deceived concerning objects which are or are not capable of change, there are then four possibilities: scientific knowledge, wisdom, practical judgment, and intellectual insight, and since it cannot be any one of the first three, we conclude that we know principles through intellectual insight."

Aristotle says: "Neither is the grasp of principles scientific knowledge." For scientific knowledge comes from truths one already possesses—the grasp of what is universal and necessary from things which are absolutely necessary for any demonstration, i.e., first principles. We can have scientific knowledge of everything except principles, but there is no such knowledge of principles. By this I mean that the latter are not known through anything other than themselves; indeed, it is through themselves that they are known. . . .

He then says: "When it comes to infallible knowledge in necessary matters, there are three possibilities: scientific knowledge, wisdom, and intellectual insight. But since it is through the last-named that we have knowledge of first principles, i.e., primary intellectual propositions, then practical wisdom, scientific knowledge, and philosophical wisdom are ruled out."[16]

There is, then, a clear appreciation on the part of Averroës of the meaning of intellect, a knowing-power which is not the same as reason or science, and which deals with first principles of thought and being. If the Commentator is to be condemned as rationalistic, it cannot be because he was ignorant of this distinction; other possible reasons for Nasr's criticism will be examined in a concluding section. We turn now to the positive side of Nasr's observation, his approval of Avicenna's position.

AVICENNA

The consideration of Avicenna takes us back a century-and-a-half in time, and, as far as place is concerned, across the entire extent of the Islamic world (from 1126 - 1198 to 980 - 1037; from Cordova in Spain to Bukhara in what is now Turkmen S. S. R., northeast of Iran)—differences in time and place which entail corresponding cultural, historical, and philosophical modifications. Whereas Averroës is first and foremost the *Commentator Aristotelis* and is dead in the world of Islam, Avicenna lives on through the richness and variety of his doctrines and writings. Perhaps he is best known for his Peripatetic writings in which is found a distinctive presentation of Neoplatonic Aristotelianism which was to influence not only Islamic philosophy and theology but also their Christian counterparts. The attack of Algazel upon the "philosophers" did not put an end to the influence of Avicenna's Peripatetic writings.[17]

But these are only part of his work. Nasr credits the Shi'ite world and the thought of Suhrawardi, Ibn-Arabi, and Mulla Sadra with the preservation of aspects of Avicenna's thought which make him a living force in Islam.[18] If there is a blind spot in the eye of Western philosophy, perhaps some reference to Avicennan insights in esoteric and Peripatetic writings will help to identify it.

Theosophy, mysticism, philosophy—all three have found inspiration in this amazing writer, and all three incorporate a doctrine of intellect and point a way to God; but identifying the strands is not easy. As far as number and types of writing are concerned, Nasr has a fourfold classification: (1) philosophical, (2) religious, (3) cosmological and physical, and (4) symbolical and metaphysical.[19] The very names of these divisions naturally raise many questions, but the fact that Nasr separates the last group from the other three might lead to a better grasp of what intellect and reason meant to Avicenna. The symbolical and mystical writings are accessible only to a chosen minority, and the distinction which separates them from the first three classifications is a radical one.

If we envisage the message of these esoteric writings as a manifestation of the first great truth of Islam ("There is no God but Allah"), we might come closer to the way Nasr presents their content. The confrontation of man and God in true wisdom results in the dwindling of the being and knowledge of man before the divine. Here is the basic realization which can be called metaphysical intuition or gnosis (where faith and science are reconciled), but this realization can be obscured and hidden in the wrappings and coverings of reason (which sets faith and science at odds).[20] It would seem from the emphasis with which the distinction is proposed (between intellect and reason; recall that Nasr has referred to intellect as gnosis, metaphysical doctrine, and understanding) that the basic insight has not merely been hidden, but has ceased to exist. And this is, perhaps, the fundamental question to which we are being led, the question of abstraction.

If this is the case, L. Gardet's researches can be very helpful to us. After noticing the difference between the mystical doctrine of Avicenna and his thought as a whole, Gardet proposes to show that they are inseparable, the justification for this position lying in the denial of abstraction in the strict sense in Avicenna's noetic.[21] Gardet, as the title of his book indicates, is interested in Avicenna's philosophy of knowledge as a means of appreciating his mystical doctrine. And Corbin agrees with this starting point because the study of human knowledge must be projected against a vast screen of hierarchical intelligences, and thus becomes the foundation of an angelology, cosmology, and anthropology.[22]

Without attempting anything like a marshaling of texts to estabish an interpretation of Avicenna's position, we might find it useful to re-examine some of his famous statements in the light of our present inquiry. Twice in his De anima there is mention of the "floating" or "suspended" man, an illustration which was to appear frequently in medieval Christian writers. Avicenna writes:

> ... If a man were suddenly created with his limbs extended in space in such a way that he could not see them or touch them, and they could not

touch each other, and he could not hear anything, he would not know that any of them existed, but he would know that he existed. . . . And truly, these parts of the body are no different from garments; it is because they have clung to us for so long that we regard them as ourselves or parts of ourselves. For when we represent to ourselves our souls, we do not have before us souls which are naked but rather clothed with bodies. The reason for this is the length of time involved in this association. We have become used to taking off and putting on clothing which is certainly not the case with arms and legs. Hence the conviction that they are ours is much stronger than in the case of clothing.[23]

Such an uncompromising dualism is of course an open door to idealism, but it is also a commentary on any use of the notion of abstraction by Avicenna and, similarly, an indication of the meaning of intellect for him. Although he does use the language of abstraction, there are indications (as above) that the intelligible content received by the intellect is something fully constituted in its intelligible purity and independent of material and individualizing influences. Reason would appear to be superfluous to Avicenna if by reason we mean the point of insertion of intelligibility into a bewildering material world of change. Reason utilizes the mortise-and-tenon aspect of concepts to fit them together or identify discrepancies, and that is precisely why it must be subservient to the empirical. A theory of abstraction is an attempt to locate both reason and intellect in the world of *human* experience, rather than in a world of spirits. If intellectual insights are not the insights of a *man*, then there is no metaphysics (exactly where Kant left us)—no study of being as being. But it is quite possible to pursue the study of spiritual being and call it metaphysics. This possibility should be borne in mind when Nasr extols intellectual insight and also names Avicenna as one of his inspirations— a point to which we shall return.

In the following paragraphs, however, the meaning of intellectual insight is pursued, and more explicitly. Avicenna distinguishes two kinds of knowledge and says:

One kind is simple [*simplex*] and the other involves steps [*cogitabilis*]. The latter is not complete until a certain structure has been established, although in the former there is no succession of forms. This former kind of knowledge is one; from it forms proceed wherever forms are received;

it produces the step-by-step knowledge and is its principle. This is the unqualified intellectual power of the soul and similar to the separate intelligences. Discursive activity does not belong to the soul except insofar as it is a soul, and if it did not have such activity, it would not have knowledge of itself.

How this is possible, i.e., how the rational soul can have a source within the soul, whose knowledge goes beyond the wisdom of the soul, is indeed a question and one to be investigated in your own soul.

It should also be carefully noted that there is no plurality or order of forms in the pure intellect, since it is the principle of every form which proceeds from it to the soul.[24]

Once again we have a reference to the fundamental distinction between intellect and reason, and some of the terms in which it is presented and the foundation on which it rests are of particular interest. On the side of reason we have (1) the word *cogitabilis*, stressing the process of thinking rather than the intuitive element, (2) the notion of succession in *generari forma post formam*, (3) the role of structure in *ordinare*, (4) the attribution of whatever it has to the pure intellect, and (5) the phrase "insofar as it is a soul."

On the side of intellect (*intellectus purus*) we have (1) an insistence on simplicity, (2) denial of succession, (3) comparison with separate intelligences, (4) its prerogative as the source of reason, and (5) the admission of a knowledge which "goes beyond" the wisdom of the soul. These characteristics and those enumerated in the previous paragraph manifest themselves differently in the Peripatetic and esoteric writings of Avicenna, but their common origin can be perceived.

The impact of this distinction is perhaps seen most clearly in Avicenna's Peripatetic "psychology," his account of the meaning of man. Using the Aristotelian terminology of matter and form, Avicenna nonetheless gives us a radically dualistic picture of man, as we have seen. The soul has "two faces," one looking upward to the world of intelligences and the other downward for the "care" of the body.[25] All the characteristics of what we have called reason belong to the soul insofar as it is involved in the succession, structure, and variety of a sensible world; simplicity and permanence are on the side of a higher intellectual power—on the side of the angels.

But it is in his metaphysics and theology (the highest part of metaphysics, for Avicenna) that intellectual insight and its significance become most obvious.[26] The absolutely basic views of reality are derived from the notions of "being" and "necessary." As absolutely basic, they cannot be arrived at through any other concepts, and it is by a kind of meditation on them rather than by any kind of argument that Avicenna reaches his First, or God. Manifest similarities with Plotinian thought or Iranian angelology aside for the moment, our emphasis at this point is on the way a central theme, the difference between two kinds of knowledge, supports a fundamental position on the meaning and origin of reality, and does so in an Aristotelian context. Whether or not one agrees with Avicenna on this point (establishing the existence of God), the objection should not be that it is a poor "argument" or that it violates rules of reason. If it is to be rejected, it will be because it is fanciful or an illusion.

As we turn from Peripatetic writings to the esoteric, the emphasis shifts from the intuition of necessity in being to one of vision or presence. In the words of Corbin:

> The procedure that is here fundamental and necessary for thought is what we should broadly characterize as an *interiorization*. Choosing the exemplary case of *ta'wil*, which as it were suspends the letter of a sacred text in order to bring into view a *spiritual meaning* assimilable to experienced consciousness, we have termed the effort of freeing a thought from the "wrappings" of the letter "exegesis of the soul." It is an exegesis which the soul itself performs upon itself, which enables it, instead of *subordinating itself* to an external foreign world, to *integrate* that world with itself. Instead of succumbing to the philosophies and experiences of the past, or instead of initiating a struggle, as if in confronting some external obstacle, the soul must learn to surmount them, to give them an abode in itself, to free itself from them in the act of thus freeing *them*.
>
> Certainly this interiorization requires a transmutation of the soul; it supposes a mode and an organ of perception wholly different from those of the ordinary knowledge that receives and undergoes all data ready-made, because it takes them as data necessarily given without asking *who* is the "donor" of them.[27]

The distance from reason is clearly growing here, but even in the realm of intellectual insight, new affirmations seem to be appearing. Where the Peripatetic Avicenna dealt with the necessary and the possible and various kinds of causes, the visionary Avicenna is embarked on a program of asserting and describing a hidden spiritual meaning in the world of ordinary consciousness. In neither case is there an attempt to establish or prove that there is, respectively, objective causality or spiritual meaning, but this initial insight is no longer intellectual in a univocal sense. Avicenna seems to have brought us to the threshold of a possible flight from reality instead of a more profound grasp of reality. As Corbin says:

> . . . This reflection no longer encounters any readymade data; it projects itself toward a vision that is configurable only in a symbol. The Avicennan symbolism, its flowering and its use, as the recitals show them to us, open the difficult road leading to that pure Presence; in this sense, this symbolics can be *Avicenna's lesson* for us.[28]

The discussion could now very well continue on the level of an analysis of symbol, which is beyond the scope of this brief enquiry, but, even there, some light on the distinction between various kinds of symbols could very well come from their varying proximity to intellectual insight. And if the latter is found to have continuity with the work of reason, we shall be confronted with some form of analogy. A corresponding question would concern the permanence or presence in both Avicennas of the analysis of kinds of knowledge referred to above. Is something hidden and veiled under Aristotelian terminology, or has that something disappeared? Should some scope be allowed for emphasis when we find Corbin referring to "a mode and an organ of perception wholly different from those of the ordinary knowledge"?

It is certainly not a matter of denying a sensible world; Corbin says:

> In speaking of this full and autonomous reality [presented by the intermediate world of the symbolic imagination], we could equally well speak of the *objectivity* of the world of symbols, simply on the condition of not understanding the word in the sense in which the *object* is posed as exterior to natural consciousness of the sensible and physical world.[29]

Again:

> They are not mere projections performed at the "subjective" pleasure of the mind; they reveal to the mind a region no less "objective" than the sensible world.[30]

The point at issue is whether the relationship between the "two worlds" is sufficiently developed, and this only in an effort to see how continuous in all the writings of Avicenna is a central awareness of an insight which is intellectual. These references underline the importance of the question and the possibility that the continuity is not maintained.

In other words, *intellectus* has two meanings for Avicenna, one to be found in his Peripatetic writings, the other in his esoteric writings, and although both may be rooted in a single appreciation of abstraction and intellectual awareness, the esoteric *intellectus* seems to emphasize symbolic vision so strongly that it loses its contact, and is at variance, with Peripatetic insight. It is the latter esoteric meaning which receives Nasr's approbation.

CONCLUSION

Should we say, then, with Nasr that the milestones of Western philosophy mark a tragic route and that much of the blame is to be laid at the door of Averroës? There was in Western Europe a surrender first to rationalism and then to empiricism and positivism, leaving it ultimately atheistic and materialistic. But rationalism immediately brings to mind at least two meanings, and both of them are associated with the name of Averroës.

First, rationalism can mean the supremacy of reason *and* intellect over any revelation or the message of any prophetic religion. Human reason, no matter how it is defined, becomes the criterion for accepting any such message. In the case of conflict, the so-called revealed account is to be rejected. Thinking men, however, who have subscribed to a prophetic religion, are in a position to interpret the message of their religion in such a way that it does not conflict with the dictates of reason, and this latter position on "interpretation" can be pushed to such an extreme, theoretically at least, that the interpretation is equivalent to a denial of the revelation: "What is true in philosophy is false in theology; double truth." This position has indeed, albeit unjustly, been attributed to Averroës. What is true is that this position was condemned at Paris in 1277 along with other positions which the Commentator did hold, and it is also true that the latter distinguishes three classes of believers, only one of whom is capable of philosophical understanding of ultimate (Koranic) truths.[31] Moreover, in at least one crucial instance (the question of personal immortality) it is almost impossible to see how his philosophical position is not a denial of Islamic faith.[32] Hence, the "accursed Averroës" of Duns Scotus (and also the later separation of philosophy and theology in Europe).

But there is another possible sense in which an exaggerated devotion to reason might be imputed to Averroës: did he exalt the rights of reason at the expense of intellect (or intuition, or intellectual insight)? Certainly, as a staunch Aristotelian, and in the light of texts like those quoted above, he has accepted first principles in the order of thought and reality which he places beyond the realm of demonstration and which he attributes to intellect. If, then, he is to be censured for failing to appreciate the role of intellect, there are two possible sources for this charge: either he has not made it clear enough that his reasoning rests on foundations which are not themselves the work of reason (thereby opening the door to the charge of dogmatism—an attempt to develop metaphysics from conceptual analysis), or he has not used intellect to get to the source of *being* (content with finding a cause of change and motion in a universe which existed from all eternity).

As far as the first possibility is concerned, European philosophy did go in the direction of metaphysical dogmatism and in doing so set the stage for the Humean criticism of causality and the phenomenal world of Kant. To say that Averroës was unaware of the difference between intellect and reason is false, but that is not the same as saying that he did not develop the role of intellect, especially the function of judgment, in the foundations of metaphysics.

The second possibility is probably closer to the source of Nasr's complaint. A dedicated Aristotelian, even one familiar with the God of Islam—boundless freedom—was unable to raise the question of the cause of the being of the universe. It will be recalled that it is on this score that Averroës criticizes Avicenna—for allowing a religious notion to distort authentic Aristotelianism.[33] Nasr has indeed pointed to a time and context in which philosophy was ready for profoundly new orientations on two fronts: the relation of philosophy to theology, and the meaning of metaphysics. That Averroës was not destined to become the hero of this revolution is admitted by all.

The positive part of Nasr's observation is the praise of intellectual insight, and this is associated with the name of Avicenna, but a very carefully qualified Avicenna. It is only as the proponent of the "Oriental Philosophy" that Avicenna receives the full approval of Nasr, and we have seen that it is not clear whether the intellectual intuition which is part of Oriental Philosophy is continuous with the intuition of Avicenna's Peripatetic writings. Nasr seems to emphasize discontinuity, and presents a brief excerpt from a very interesting but little-known work of Avicenna's in which his Peripatetic writings are renounced as suited only for the multitude, and reference is made to one of his works in which he will go beyond them and treat of a radical deepening of the meaning of intuition.[34]

These possibilities about the meaning of intellect in Western philosophy (and Averroës) vis-à-vis its meaning in Islamic philosophy (and Avicenna) are intimately connected with ways of finding or not finding God, and this is what gives the question we have been examining its importance. The catastrophe which, in the eyes of Nasr, has engulfed Western philosophy is the loss of God, and for centuries European philosophy has been trying to come to terms with that loss. After all, God is purely a matter of faith (which is unintelligible) or emotion, or God is just another way of looking at reality, or theology must be reduced to philosophy, or the whole thing is a matter of symbolism or semantics, etc. This brief inquiry about the perceptive remark of Nasr has attempted to show that the encounter with God, self, and reality includes an element which can be characterized as intellectual, and that this element is nuanced in two ways which are profoundly different: Nasr's way, and another way which might indeed have been lost in the West, but survives in any realistic metaphysics which is rooted in judgment. Neither way, moreover, can be seen in its completeness without some consideration of a neighboring problem (and this is one of the conspicuous omissions of this inquiry): the relationship of intellectual insight to the problem of faith in a prophetic religion.

NOTES

1. Seyyed Hossein Nasr, *Ideals and Realities of Islam* (London: Allen and Unwin, 1966), p. 136.

2. Henry Corbin, *Histoire de la philosophie islamique* (Paris: Gallimard, 1964), I, 8, 13-15; Nasr, *op. cit.*, p. 56, and *An Introduction to Islamic Cosmological Doctrines* (Cambridge: Harvard University Press, 1964), pp. 6-7.

3. *Cosmological Doctrines*, p. 185.

4. Corbin, *op. cit.*, pp. 7-9; Nasr, *Ideals*, pp. 136-37, *Cosmological Doctrines*, pp. 184-85.

5. See Fazlur Rahman, *Islam* (New York: Holt, Rinehart & Winston, 1966), pp. 123-24.

6. For example, speaking of the *intellectus materialis*, Averroës says: "This is such a difficult point that if we cannot find out what Aristotle held it will be very difficult to reach any solution at all, or, rather, impossible unless we can find the equal of Aristotle." *Averrois Cordubensis commentarium magnum in Aristotelis De anima libros*, ed. F. Stuart Crawford (Cambridge: Mediaeval Academy of America, 1935), Book III, #14, p. 433. Translations of the Latin of Averroës and Avicenna are the writer's.

7. *Posterior Analytics*, I, 3 (72B 18-20), trans. G. R. G. Mure (London: Oxford University Press, 1928).

8. *Ibid.*, 72B 23-25.

9. *Ibid.*, II, 19 (100B 10-17).

10. "Postquam autem enuntiavit quod hic sint tres res: intellectus, et principium scientiae, et scientia; et notificavit quod intellectus sit firmioris finis quam scientia; et quod principia etiam sint notiora quam scientia eveniens ex principiis, dixit: 'Scientia vero non est aditus quo cadat in illa.' I.e., principia impossibile est quod sciantur per principia—adeo quod illorum ordo in comprehensione sit ordo scientiae evenientis ab eis." *Aristotelis opera cum Averrois commentariis* (Venice: Giunta, 1562-1574 [Frankfurt: Minerva, 1962]), I, part 2a, *Analytica posteriora*, II, 19, fol. 567ᵛF.

11. "Syllogismus autem componitur sic: Quod notificat principia oportet quod sit notius quam scientia et quando nulla res est huiusmodi nisi intellectus et principia, principia autem impossibile est quod sint principiorum causa, sicque relinquitur quod intellectus sit causa principiorum." *Ibid.*, 568ʳB.

12. *Ibid.*, 568ʳC.

13. "Vult perscrutari etiam utrum ista scientia habeat considerari de primis propositionibus universalibus quae sunt principia omnis demonstrationis." *Ibid.*, VIII, *Metaphysics*, Summa II, cap. I, fol. 72ᵛG.

14. "Ista enim principia sunt communia omnibus generibus entium de quibus considerant artes speculativae, et quod est commune omnibus generibus entis est accidentium entis secundum quod est ens, et quod est tale debet considerari ab eo qui considerat de ente simpliciter, sc. philosopho." *Ibid.*

15. "... Si hoc principium quod est manifestissimum omnium principiorum fuerit demonstratum, necesse est ut omnia universaliter habeant demonstrationem. Et si principia demonstrationis habeant demonstrationem, et omnis demonstratio fiat ex principiis, necesse est ut omnis demonstratio habeat demonstrationem et ut procedat hoc in infinitum et sic nulla demonstratio erit." *Ibid.*, fol. 75ᵛɪ-ᴋ.

16. "Si igitur ea quibus verum et numquam falsum dicimus circa ea quae vel possunt vel non possunt aliter evenire sunt scientia et sapientia et prudentia et intellectus; ex tribus autem horum esse nihil potest, tria dico prudentiam, sapientiam, et scientiam, restat intellectum esse principiorum.

"Dixit: Neque apprehensio principiorum scientia est. Nam scientia est ex habitibus veridicis et est apprehensio rerum universalium necessariarum ex rebus quae sunt de necessitate prima demonstrationis. Intendo propositiones primas et hoc quoniam omnis quod est praeter principia scientia est. Intendo quod non scientia est ex parte alterius a se. Immo sciuntur quidem per seipsa....

"Dixit et ea per quae possibile est ut veraces sumus neque mentiamur in rebus necessariis tria sunt, scientia, sapientia, intellectus. Cum autem intellectus principiorum primorum sit, intendo propositiones intellectas primas, tunc non est prudentia, neque scientia neque sapientia." *Ibid.*, ɪɪɪ, *Nichomachean Ethics*, vɪ, 6, 85ʳᴇ - 85ᵛɢ.

17. See Corbin, *op. cit.*, p. 259.

18. See *Cosmological Doctrines*, pp. 183; 276-81.

19. *Ibid.*, pp. 177-96.

20. *Cosmological Doctrines*, p. 214.

21. L. Gardet, *La connaissance mystique chez Ibn Sina et ses présupposes philosophiques* (Cairo: Institut français d'archéologie orientale, 1952).

22. *Op. cit.*, p. 239.

23. "... si subito crearetur homo, expansis eius manibus et pedibus, quae ipse nec videret nec contingeret nec ipsa se contingerent nec audiret sonum, nesciret quidem esse aliquid membrorum suorum et tamen sciret se esse, et quia unum aliquid est, quamvis non sciret illa omnia. ... Haec autem membra non sunt vere nisi sicut vestes; quae, quia diu est quod adhaeserunt nobis, putavimus nos esse illa aut quod sunt sicut partes nostri; cum enim imaginamur nostras animas, non imaginamur eas nudas, sed imaginamur eas indutas corporibus, cuius rei causa est diuturnitas adhaerentiae; consuevimus autem exuere vestes et proiicere, quod omnino non consuevimus in membris: unde opinio quod membra sunt partes nostri, firmior est in nobis quam opinio quod vestes sint partes nostri." *Avicenna Latinus. Liber de anima* ɪv-v, ed. S. Van Riet (Leiden: Brill, 1968), v, 7, 162-63.

24. "Unus autem istorum modorum est scientia cogitabilis, cuius ultima perfectio non completur nisi cum ordo eius componitur. Alius autem est scientia simplex, in qua non solet generari forma post formam, sed est una ex qua proveniunt formae in receptibili earum, et haec est scientia efficiens id quod vocamus scientiam cogitabilem et est principium eius. Et ipsa est virtus animae intellectiva absoluta, quae est similis intelligentiis agentibus; ordinare

autem non habet anima nisi ex hoc quod est anima, quod si non haberet, non haberet scientiam animalem.

"Anima autem rationalis quomodo habeat principium ex anima quod principium habet scientiam praeter sapientiam animae, hoc est considerandum, hoc autem debes intelligere ex tua anima.

"Debes etiam scire quod in nostro puro intellectu non est multitudo ullo modo nec ordo formarum; ipse enim est principium omnis formae emanantis ab eo in animam." *Ibid.*, pp. 142-43.

25. See, e.g., *ibid.*, pp. 99; 101.

26. See E. Gilson, *History of Christian Philosophy in the Middle Ages* (New York: Random House, 1955), pp. 206-16.

27. *Avicenna and the Visionary Recital* (New York: Pantheon, 1960), p. 258. We are grateful to the Bollingen Foundation for permission to quote from M. Corbin's work. Emphasis is M. Corbin's.

28. *Ibid.*, pp. 258-59. Emphasis is M. Corbin's.

29. *Ibid.*, p. 259. Emphasis is M. Corbin's.

30. *Ibid.*

31. See P. Mandonnet, *Siger de Brabant et l'averroïsme latin de XIIIᵉ siècle* (Fribourg, 1899), p. 175.

32. See S. Van den Bergh, *Averroës' Tahafut al-Tahafut* (London: Luzac, 1954), 2 vols.

33. See Gilson, *op. cit.*, p. 210.

34. *Cosmological Doctrines*, pp. 186-87.

3

A New Look at the Immutability of God

W. Norris Clarke, s.j.

ANYONE WHO HAS EVEN A SUPERFICIAL ACQUAINTANCE with the field of philosophical theology today is aware that one of the most crucial areas of debate concerns the immutability of God and the reality of His relation to the world. The traditional Scholastic position (henceforth for greater precision we shall call it the Thomistic position) on the immutability of God and the absence of any real relation on His part toward the world has been radically challenged from two sources which at present we frequently find coalescing into one. These two sources are: (1) process philosophy, in terms of the speculative exigencies of its own metaphysics of reality, and (2) existential religious consciousness, with its strong emphasis on the truly personal relation which must exist between a religiously available personal God and finite persons He has created.

If the only challenge came from the first source, it might be relegated to the domain of just another technical dispute in the realm of purely speculative philosophy. But the challenge coming from existential religious consciousness seeking an intellectual understanding of itself adds a new and greater urgency to the question. For any sound philosophical theory must do justice to the basic phenomena of human experience which it is its task to illuminate.

Now, if we are to take seriously the religious dimension of human experience—and we are taking for granted here that this is the case, especially for a Christian philosopher—then it is clear that one of the central tenets of man's religious belief in God (at least in Judaeo-Christian religion) is that He is one who enters into deep personal relations of love with His creatures. And an authentic interpersonal relation of love necessarily involves not merely purely creative or one-way love, but genuine mutuality and reciprocity of love, including not only the giving of love but the joyful acceptance of it and response to it. This means that our God is a God who really cares, is really concerned with our lives and happiness, who enters into truly reciprocal personal relations with us, who responds to our prayers—to whom, in a word, our contingent world and its history somehow make a genuine difference. In short, the God of Judaeo-Christian religion must be a "religiously available" God on the personal level, as Whiteheadians put it.

There is no doubt that any adequate philosophical or theological concept of God must be such as to render intelligible such a personal relation between God and ourselves. Yet traditional natural theology insists that God is unconditionally immutable and has no real relation to the world, i.e., no relation which is a dimension of His own real being, affecting His own real being, but only a "relation of reason" (*relatio rationis*), as it is technically called by St. Thomas—a relation which is not real in God objectively but is only attributed to Him by extrinsic denomination because of the way minds have to think about Him as cause. Now, this traditional doctrine of the God of philosophy seems to many to be in clear conflict with the exigencies of the God of personal religion. And since theory must always yield to life, they have rejected the above philosophical notion of God as unqualifiedly immutable and having no real relation to the world. In order to do justice to what they believe are the implications of religious belief and experience, many have substituted the theoretical framework of process philosophy. According to this philosophy, the "primordial nature" of God is immutable and infinite, but the "consequent nature" of God, as related to the ongoing world process by knowledge and love, is truly involved in this temporal process itself, affected by it in His life of knowledge and love, hence really related to it and truly changing and growing with it, as He knows it and responds to it. Hence God is both mutable and really related to the world in His consequent nature—a view of God apparently in direct contradiction to the traditional Thomistic one.[1]

This process conception of God first arose among Protestant Christian thinkers, under the inspiration of Whitehead, but is now spreading among Catholic thinkers as well. As a result, we are witnessing a widespread rejection, among Judaeo-Christian religious thinkers of all persuasions, of "the immutable, unrelated, impassive, non-dialoguing, religiously unavailable God" of Thomistic metaphysics in favor of the involved, really related, changing God-in-process of process philosophy.[2]

The problem is clearly a crucial one for anyone concerned with thinking through his religious belief in some coherent intellectual framework. What I should like to do in this essay is to explore the resources of the Thomistic metaphysical system to see how far it is capable of making a place for a God who can enter into truly personal relations with His creatures. In the past Thomistic metaphysicians seem to have been content for the most part to assert and defend the absolute immutability of God and to relegate all change and diversity to the side of the creature. But they have not gone on to explain how He can enter into a truly interpersonal dialogue with created persons, how His loving of them and their response to Him in the particular contingent ways which are proper to a free exchange between persons can truly make a difference to Him, how He is not the completely impassive, indifferent metaphysical iceberg, or at least one-way unreceptive Giver, to whom my loving or not loving, my salvation or damnation, make no difference whatever, as Hartshorne and other process philosophers have accused Him of being. It does seem to me that they have a legitimate grievance against the way Thomists have handled, or failed to handle, this problem.

On the other hand, it seems to me that it is quite possible to draw upon the latent resources of the system, in particular by developing the traditional distinction between the orders of real and intentional being, hitherto very little exploited with respect to God, and by adapting the notion of immutability to fit the perfection appropriate to personal being, so that the loving dialogue of God with His creatures becomes truly possible and intelligible, though always clothed in mystery on His part. This seems to me a wiser strategy than simply to jettison the traditional doctrine lock, stock, and barrel before testing out its resources to the full, and substituting a totally new metaphysical framework of process philosophy which, as I see it, introduces a host of new difficulties which might well leave us worse off philosophically than we were before.[3] In a word, let us try evolution first rather than an over-hasty revolution.

I should like to present this paper, therefore, as an essay in creative Thomistic metaphysics, an effort to adapt what still seems to me an incomparably rich and profound metaphysical system to the newly felt and now better understood exigencies of the domain of interpersonal being. (For reasons of space, this will have to be almost entirely a speculative presentation, with no attempt at detailed grounding in the texts of St. Thomas or discussion with his commentators.) But since every creative development and adaptation of one philosopher's thought by another always involves the risk of introducing such profound and sometimes unnoticed seismic tremors into the original system so that its own author might well repudiate it, I must take full responsibility upon myself for this "Thomistic adaptation" and not blame it upon St. Thomas, even though I believe it to be authentically and coherently Thomistic in its inspiration. Let me also acknowledge from the start that I owe a great debt in what follows to the inspiration, though not always the conclusions, of other Thomistically inspired contemporary Christian thinkers—such as Karl Rahner and others[4]—who in recent years have been trying to grapple in their own way with various aspects of this complex and difficult problem.

THE IMMUTABILITY OF GOD'S REAL BEING

In working out any treatise on the attributes of God, the central notion which must remain constant and command all the rest, setting limits to their meaning and application and ordering their mutual relations, is that of absolute or infinite perfection or, if you like, the fullness of perfection. Thus the affirmation that God is absolutely perfect functions as a kind of formal constant down through the history of philosophical conceptions of God, whereas philosophical and cultural evaluations of precisely what constitutes perfection often vary down the ages or across cultures, with corresponding variations in the set of other attributes which are affirmed of God in order to spell out the central exigency of perfection. Hence it is only because, and precisely insofar as, immutability is seen as a necessary corollary of this fullness of perfection that it should be affirmed of God, and not vice versa. Immutability is not an absolute self-justifying value in its own right to which the notion of perfection itself must be made to conform. This key point must be kept in focus throughout the discussion which follows.[5]

Why does St. Thomas affirm the immutability of God? Because mutability, as he understands it in the Aristotelian metaphysics of change, necessarily involves imperfection. In order to grasp the point of this conclusion, it is imperative to remember that the whole context of the Aristotelian doctrine of change as a passage from potency to act and requiring an extrinsic cause—which is St. Thomas' own context, too—is that of real change, or change in the intrinsic real being of a thing. To change in this context is to acquire (or lose) some new mode of intrinsic real being not possessed before. Hence it implies an increase (or decrease) in the ontological perfection of the being undergoing change, a passage from imperfection to greater perfection. It is for this reason that if the subject of change does not already possess, at least in some equivalent way, the new perfection it acquires, it must receive this from some extrinsic source, which is called the efficient cause of the change. For nothing can give to itself what it does not already have in some equivalent way.[6] It must be remembered, too, that in St. Thomas' theory of real relations every real relation must be founded in something in the intrinsic real or absolute being of that which is related. Hence every change or new-ness in the real relations of a being must be founded on something new in its intrinsic real being (unless the relations are in the purely static dimension of quantity or similitude—relations which St. Thomas, mistakenly to my mind, calls real—where only one term need vary).[7]

Now, if we interpret change in this strict Aristotelian sense, then for God to be mutable would mean that He could pass to some new higher mode or level of perfection of His own intrinsic real being which He did not possess before; He would become more perfect in His intrinsic being than He was before. But it is not at all clear how such a growth in God's intrinsic perfection makes any sense, or is needed for any religious or personalist purposes. For if one is to hold to any traditional concept of God at all, one must affirm that God is already and from all eternity positively infinite in the fullness of His perfection. Would we want God first to be a non-loving type of person, then to grow or improve to become a loving type? Surely what we look for in Him is that He be loving, disposed to love by His very nature, that He be the eternally steadfast, faithful, indefectible Lover, unchangeable, rather than inconstant and mutable, in the fullness of His loving goodness.

What we do indeed expect of Him is that the *expression* of this love for us should be constantly growing and developing, unfolding throughout our lives to anticipate and respond to our own contingent history of unfolding—and highly variable—love-relations with Him. We expect, therefore, that the field of His loving *consciousness* should be contingently other because of His personal relations to us. This is quite true, and we shall see how this must and can be taken care of by determinate contingent modifications of the field of intentional or cognitive being within Him (or, more accurately, by determinate contingent *differentiation* of His intentional consciousness, since, as we shall see, we have no grounds for attributing real temporal succession to this consciousness).

But that the intentional content of His loving consciousness should be contingently other because of the unfolding expression of His unchanging personal love for us does not entail that His own intrinsic real being, the level of His own intrinsic perfection, in any way undergoes real change to acquire some new higher mode of perfection not possessed before. Even in the order of knowledge and love He already knows and loves the highest possible fullness of being and goodness, His own self. Any further knowledge of a finite being will not be a passage to a higher fullness of knowing, but only an inner determination, or limitation of its focus, to some new limited mode of participation of His own infinite perfection. It will be a numerically new item of knowledge, but not a passage to a higher or richer level of knowledge than that attained in knowing Himself. Similarly, in loving some new created person in an unfolding sequence of ways, He is loving a numerically new object of love, but one which is only a limited participation and overflow of His own already totally loved infinite Goodness. No created object of God's knowledge and love adds any new *higher* dimension to the eternal fullness of being and goodness which He already knows and loves in Himself. It adds only a new determinate sharing of this eternal plenitude, determinately known and loved, in a never-ending process of new *expression* of His eternally infinite plenitude of goodness and love, but without the current's ever rising higher, so to speak, than its original source. In one word, to add a new finite content of knowledge and love to an already infinite plenitude of knowledge and love is not to pass from potency to act in the order of real being, to acquire a new higher mode of intrinsic perfection of being not possessed before. To add the finite to the infinite can only be in the mode of a sharing, an overflow, an expression of the plenitude which is already infinite. There is genuine novelty, to be sure, both in the real being God communicates to creatures and in the intentional content of His consciousness determinately knowing and willing them. But this is not change in His own intrinsic being or perfection.

Much of the insistence on the mutability of God as implied in His freely creating and loving these determinate creatures in time, rather than others equally possible, arises, it seems to me, from an anthropomorphic projection onto God of the mode of consciousness proper to us as finite consciousnesses incarnate in a body and thereby inexorably immersed in the flow of temporal succession. It is quite true that we, as finite, must unfold our knowledge in a succession of limited and incomplete acts, and that as incarnate or enfleshed spirit we have to receive the objects of our knowledge and love from without through action on our body which modifies our own intrinsic real being; in addition, every act of knowing or loving which we make is accompanied by and expressed through some intrinsic real change and motion in our bodies, if only in the constant firing of neurons in our brain cells.

But suppose we project knowing, loving, and efficacious causing (whether creation or some partial communication of new being makes no difference here) onto the level of a purely spiritual, infinite cause, where causing becomes simply efficacious spiritual willing. When a purely spiritual cause efficaciously wills (or loves) something or someone, there is clearly a focusing of the intentional consciousness of the willing agent on the object-term of its willing. This means

that its field of intentional consciousness is modified, or, more accurately, is determinately other in its intentional content than it would
be if it did not so will. But this determinate differentiation is in the
order of *intentional being* or objective focus, the being of the *other*
as held within consciousness. (We shall examine explicitly in a moment
the difference between the orders of real and intentional being for
St. Thomas.)

What about the intrinsic real being of the agent? In a purely spiritual willer there are no wheels to go round, no brain cells to fire, no
physical motion to bring it close to its effect, since it is present wherever
it wills to act. In a word, we can locate no grounds for internal motion
or intrinsic change; there is only a pure motionless intentional ecstasy
of the agent's conscious will focused on the intentionally represented
objective term of its knowing-love. The only change is in the field
of intentional consciousness, not in the "physical" or natural intrinsic being or perfection of the spiritual agent. This is precisely
what it means for A to will X: it means to-will-X, not to change
or move around inside A's own absolute being. This is precisely what the realm of interpersonal relations is all about in
its pure essence, abstracting from the accidentally accompanying
motions in us as finite and corporeal agents: it is concerned with
the way in which the mutually interrelated persons focus on each
other in their intentional consciousness, reaching out to each other
not physically but spiritually, in the immanent ecstasy of mutual
inherence in each other's consciousness by knowing-love. Of course,
this modification of intentional consciousness is important, "real"
in this sense; it is precisely what determines the quality of our
interpersonal relations, how we know and love. But this still does
not permit us to attribute any further modifications or motion to the
intrinsic real "natural being" of the agent, in the strict Thomistic
sense of the terms. To love rather than not to love indeed makes a
real difference in the intrinsic perfection of a person. But God is by
essence always and totally loving, with infinite intensity and fullness,
His own infinite goodness, both in itself and in all its participations.
The only difference in such a love lies thus in the intentional focus
applying it to this or that finite recipient. Hence the differentiation
in the objective content of intentional consciousness does not *ipso
facto* allow us to infer any change in the intrinsic or absolute real being

of the willer. We must resolutely resist here the spontaneous tendency to project our own mode of incarnate willing onto a pure spirit and to picture all willing as such as some kind of physical "moving around" inside. The will as such has no "muscles" to flex—even in us.

Here is the place to recall the classic metaphysical position of both Aristotle and St. Thomas—still as valid and profound as ever, it seems to me—that efficient causality "takes place," or is ontologically "located," in the effect, not in the agent as such: *actio est in passo*.[8] For to cause is precisely to make *another* be (in whole or in part), to enrich *another*. It affirms nothing at all about enriching (or impoverishing) the agent. Change, on the other hand, is the exact opposite: it is enriching *oneself*, acquiring something new for *oneself*, and it says nothing at all about any enrichment of another. Hence the affirmation of a causal action, taken strictly and solely as such, gives no grounds for affirming any new intrinsic being in the agent. There is only one new reality resulting from a causal situation: this is in the subject or receiver of the action. And this one identical new reality simultaneously grounds three equally true and objective affirmations or attributions: (1) that there is real novelty, new real being, in the recipient Y, (2) that this is brought about by agent X, that X is the cause-of-Y, and (3) that there must be a determinate focusing of X on Y in the intentional order, the order of final causality, in X itself. No more can be affirmed without some added data outside the causal relation itself. And the presence of the final cause (the term-to-be-effected) in the dynamic intentionality of the agent is a presence in the intentional order only, and not in that of real being (otherwise the term would already be really present, and there would be no need to produce it at all). All this is traditional Thomistic metaphysical analysis, except that point (3) is too frequently omitted or left implicit in simplified expositions or in the heat of debate, thus giving initially plausible ground for the objections of process thinkers.

One more point. Real relation, in the strict Aristotelian-Thomistic meaning of the term, always requires some foundation in the intrinsic real being of the related subject; hence a new real relation requires some new intrinsic change in the real or absolute being of the *relatum*. It follows that purely and simply from the attribution of causality to a being, with no further data added from the special mode of operation of the agent, one has no right to attribute any real relation in the agent toward its effect, though of course one can and must attribute a relation in the intentional order—a point consistently forgotten, it seems to me, in most disputes on this matter between Thomists and others. Thus St. Thomas maintains that creation as such, by a purely spiritual and infinite Cause, does not posit any real relation in God as cause, in His strong and technical sense of "real being."[9]

It follows from all this that the attribution of authentic loving and efficacious willing to God gives no grounds for affirming real change or mutability in God in the strict and strong sense of the term for St. Thomas—or for anyone, in fact, who holds the distinction between the orders of intentional and real being. But clearly if one says only this and no more, he has not said enough, and we would still remain in the dark about the way in which God can be said to be truly related to us in interpersonal relations of mutual love. Hence we must now turn our attention to the companion piece to the above doctrine of the real immutability of God, the otherness in the divine intentional consciousness which I am convinced we must affirm and which seems to me also authentically Thomistic in principle, though all too often it has been left totally in the shadow or even denied. I consider the explicit drawing-out of the implications of this distinction with respect to God the principal contribution of this essay.

CONTINGENT OTHERNESS AND PROCESS
IN THE DIVINE CONSCIOUSNESS

Up to now we have tried to show why we have no good grounds for asserting real mutability in God, mutability of His own intrinsic real being and perfection. But the reader will not fail to have noticed that we have been able to do this only by referring constantly to another and complementary order of being in God, that of "intentional being," to which we ascribed the contingent differentiation we excluded from His intrinsic real being. We must now turn our attention explicitly to this order of being and its relation to that of real being.

St. Thomas distinguishes between (1) the being or existence of a thing in its own right, with its own intrinsic act of existence or "natural being," by which the thing exists with its own nature in itself and not merely as an object of thought in a mind (its *esse naturale, esse in re,* or *in rerum natura*) and (2) the mode of being which it has as an object of knowledge (or love) existing or present in the consciousness of a knower (or lover), which he calls its "intentional being," or being as the object of a consciousness "intending" it, or focusing its attention toward it, either as an object of contemplative knowledge or of actual willing of it as a real other (*esse intentionale, esse cognitum, esse volitum*).[10]

It is absolutely essential to distinguish these two orders of being in a realist epistemology and metaphysics, and for the following reasons. (1) If it is not distinguished, then we will have to say that when I—or any knower—know a raging fire outside of me, there is also a real raging fire existing in my consciousness, since the fire as known must be somehow truly present within my consciousness. This is patently absurd. (2) If the object known were in my consciousness in its own real being, then my knowledge would not be of the real fire outside of me at all but of a second real fire within my consciousness. But this would defeat the whole purpose of the act of knowledge in the first place, which is precisely not to create a second real world in duplication of the first, but to know one and the same identical real world already existing. In a word, knowledge is *of* a real other as present in the knower in the mode of a self-effacing cognitive duplicate or intentional representation of the real other. This cognitive presence of one real being in another is called "intentional being" because its whole being points or refers as a cognitive sign to the real object it stands for and makes present to the consciousness of the knower. This intentional mode of being, distinct from, but intrinsically related to, a thing's real being, is required for any act of knowledge where what is known is other in its real being than the knower itself; hence it holds even in the case of God Himself, as knowing and loving a real world other than Himself.[11]

Now, the only being of an object of knowledge, existing as such in a knowing consciousness, is, as St. Thomas puts it, its *being-known: esse eius consistit in ipso intelligi* (its to-be is its to-be-thought-about).[12] It has no real being of its own, but exists entirely within the consciousness of the knower, with an "existence" or presence given and maintained entirely by the real act of knowing in the knower, and only as long as the knower actually thinks about it. Hence its intentional mode of being is entirely according to the mode of being of the knower: if the knower is completely spiritual in its own being, then the mode of being of the object as known will also be completely spiritual, even though it may be *of* or *about* the most solidly material thing imaginable. And since the order of intentional being within a knower is intelligibly distinct from—although, of course, always inseparable from and dependent on—the order of its real being, it follows that multiplicity, materiality, or motion in the intentional objects of consciousness do not in any way of themselves divide up, materialize, or introduce change into the real being of the knower. (It should be noted, of course, that the distinction between the real being of a mind thinking and the intentional being of the contents of its thinking cannot be, for St. Thomas, a *real* distinction, since that would require that *both* terms be real. It is a *sui generis* "relation of reason" or mental relation.) Thus a spiritual knower can know a material object without its own real being or its real act of knowing being material; it can know many objects without necessarily introducing multiplicity into its own real being or into the real act by which it knows them; it can know things in motion without its own being or its own act of knowing being in motion. If, however, it has to receive the content of its knowledge from without by action of the object itself on it, then the real being of the knower is also going to be altered as the necessary accompaniment of its new content of knowledge.

There are also two sources from which intentional being arises: from the objects toward the knower, and from the knower pointing outward toward its objects. The first occurs when the real object acts upon the knower from without, communicating an intentional extension of its own form to become an intentional presence of itself within the knower, molding the consciousness of the knower to its own form to make itself known there. The second occurs when the knower actively forms the objects of its thought within its own consciousness and uses them as self-determined intentional forms of its thinking and guides for its action.

Let us now apply the above ontology of intentional being to God. What follows has been developed only very sketchily by St. Thomas and little more by Thomists after him.[13] The main distinction of orders of being and its application to all knowers is explicit enough. But the further implications with respect to God, strangely enough, never seem to have been pursued. Following St. Thomas, Thomists have mostly contented themselves with saying that, since God cannot receive knowledge by being acted on by creatures from the outside but only by knowing Himself as actively causing all creatures, His own essence as acting must be the "species" or cognitive medium by which He knows all things. Creatures do not actively project their intentional being into His consciousness by acting on it from without. Thus only the second mode of origin of intentionality is present in God: from His creative intellect-will constituting the intentional objects or terms of His active sharing of His own goodness with creatures. That this position raises problems about how God can know our free actions without totally determining them Himself and how He can "receive" our love in return is clear. We shall consider these later. Let us proceed first to draw out the implications of the *fact*—which all must admit—of the intentional presence of all creatures in the divine consciousness as determinate objects of His knowledge and love.

1. God's intentional "field of consciousness," whose content is the order of intentional being, of intentional objects of His knowledge and love, necessarily contains the whole multiplicity of all creatures in their unique individuality and distinctness; otherwise He would not be their intelligent and loving Creator and could not exercise providence over them. All admit this.

2. It follows that because of His free decision to create this possible world rather than that, to respond lovingly to this person in this way rather than that, God's field of intentional consciousness must be determinately and contingently *other* than it would and could have been had He decided in some other way. For free decisions are by definition contingent, could have been otherwise, and we should not have the least reluctance to affirm that in its creaturely *intentional objects* or terms the divine consciousness is contingently and determinately differentiated. Nor does this in the least militate against the necessity and immutability of His intrinsic real being. (Remember that a spiritual willing as such is a pure motionless act of willing *this* rather than *that*.) Our God, therefore, the only God there is, is precisely the one who in His intentional loving consciousness chooses

us and not some others. It should be clear, therefore, that we must admit at least this much about God: that His consciousness, in its intentional content, is *distinctly, determinately,* and *contingently differentiated* or *other* with respect to creatures because He has freely chosen this world, than it would and could have been had He chosen a different world or none at all. (Whether or not this determinate otherness in His consciousness is "from eternity" without change at all, or involves Him in some kind of temporal succession, is a further question which must be treated in its own right.) Let us first see what implications are contained in what we have achieved already.

GOD IS TRULY RELATED TO HIS CREATURES BY AN INTENTIONAL RELATION OF PERSONAL CONSCIOUSNESS

Let us presume for the moment that the above intentional differentiation in the divine consciousness does not involve temporal succession in God, but is eternally present in Him, since it proceeds from and is grounded in His own real being and real act of knowing, which exist in a timeless moment "outside" or independent of, and yet contemporaneous in every point with, all our temporal succession. Even granting this, without any concession to temporal process in God, it follows that God is truly related through His intentional consciousness to us whom He has freely created and freely loves. For His consciousness is truly other, determinately and contingently differentiated, precisely because of us, because of His free decision to create us, and all His subsequent knowledge and expressions of love of us are consequent upon these decisions and our own free response to them.

Thus we do make a difference to Him, a very important difference in the domain of personal relations. But this, in St. Thomas' metaphysical framework, is still a relation in the intentional order, grounded in the differentiation of intentional terms in the divine consciousness, and not in any otherness of His real being. Hence it cannot be properly called a "real relation" in his strict terminology. But it should definitely be called a relation of intentional consciousness, by which He is truly related to us. Accordingly, it is truly a personal relation. For where else does the quintessence of interpersonal relations as such reside save in the order of knowing and loving, of *conscious* relationship, which, for St. Thomas, is precisely the order of intentional being, of consciousness as differentiated by its intentional terms? Hence it seems to me perfectly legitimate and in fact necessary to say that God is truly related to His creatures by a relation of personal consciousness (understood as the equivalent of the technical term "intentional" which so many non-Thomistic thinkers are unfamiliar with).

Here I should like to register my own criticism of the Thomist tradition in the way it has handled this problem of the real relation of God to the world. From St. Thomas on, Thomists have been content for the most part with insisting on the absence of any real relation (in St. Thomas' strict meaning of the term) in God toward the world, and with explaining and defending the reasons for this position. But this done, they have simply stopped there, and have not gone on to say anything further about what other kind of relation can be truly predicated of God, beyond predication by extrinsic denomination because of our way of thinking about Him as cause; nor have they indicated how He can be said to be truly involved in a personal dialogue with us, in a mutual love relationship which is the ground of our religious devotion. In failing to draw the implications of intentional relationship in God, which is no less significant and important for not being "real" in the strict sense, it seems to me that they have not lived up to their full responsibility as philosophers of God sensitive to the exigencies of religious belief and experience. Hence it is with great satisfaction that I note that another philosopher speaking from within the Thomistic perspective has already come forward with the same suggestion as the one I have made. In fact I have borrowed his exact—and to my mind very felicitous—terminology in expressing my own independently-arrived-at conclusion: there is in God "a relation of personal consciousness" to the world (*relatio conscientiae personalis*).[14]

It seems to me that once one has admitted such authentic personal relation in God to us, so that He is truly other, different, in His consciousness, because of His relations with us, the essential demand of religious consciousness is satisfied. What we really want to know, what really matters to us, is: do we make a difference to God, is He truly related to us in the personal dimension of knowledge and love? Whether this relation is described as real or intentional is a technical speculative problem which can be left to specialists to argue over.

And I see no compelling reason why the religious person should insist on going further and affirming some further "real change, real difference," in the intrinsic real being or perfection of God. "Truly related" seems to me to verify enough what the ordinary person means by "really related."

Of course, the process philosopher may here quite relevantly object that it is a peculiar, paradoxical, and unsatisfying terminology for the modern mind to call something as important as this personal relation of consciousness not "real." To the contemporary mind, oriented to value rather than to being, what is important should be termed "real," and what is most important, "most real." This is a legitimate criticism. One can simply step back from the whole conceptual framework and find it not wrong—for it does the job to be done in its own way—but unsatisfactory, aesthetically inadequate, if you wish. One certainly has the right to set up a new conceptual framework to handle the same problem. But in so doing, he must be careful to take care of all the key aspects of the situation handled by the old framework. For instance: should "the important" always be convertible with "the real"? Suppose that I am thinking about building a space ship or entering a Carthusian monastery. Surely how I think and decide about these possible goals of action is of great importance for my life. Yet clearly neither of the two goals is yet real, even when I decide on one before executing it.

Or suppose again that I decide that a difference in one's intentional consciousness is so important for personal life that intentional being should be called "real." Fine! But then one is going to have to invent a new distinction inside of real being to take care of the indispensable Thomistic insight that the being of something as known and loved, as in the consciousness of the knower-lover, is not identical with its real natural being as it exists in its own right, nor is it a second real being of the same ontological density. One is going to have to distinguish real being into (1) real intentional being, and (2) real natural being, or something of the sort. Otherwise we shall be thrown back again into the old unsolved problems of exaggerated realism which have plagued the Platonic tradition from its inception. And I must confess that I do not find process philosophers nearly sensitive enough, for my metaphysical taste, to the distinction between the real and the intentional order, or to the exigencies of pure spiritual knowing and loving which we must all postulate, even though we cannot directly experience it, when we are talking about God. Perhaps the root lies in the lack of an authentic analogy of being in Whitehead, though hints are certainly there to be developed.[15]

There is also the difficulty, I might add, that to speak of "real intentional being" brings the new disadvantage with it of being an expression considerably at variance with ordinary language use. In ordinary language, something is called "real" precisely to set it off from what is merely "ideal" or thought about, though I admit that the term has many fuzzy edges. Perhaps part of the trouble comes from the fact that "really" in ordinary language has gradually developed a weaker sense where it means simply "truly," as in the question: "Does this theorem in logic (or mathematics) really follow from these premisses?" "Really" here surely does not imply that logical or mathematical entities or propositions are real beings. Perhaps all that people finally mean when they ask whether God is "really related" to them is whether He is truly related to them. And the answer in terms of my own exposition above would be a resounding "Yes."[16]

TEMPORAL SUCCESSION IN GOD

Our efforts to meet the challenge of process philosophy are by no means over with the above conclusion that God can be said to be truly related to us by a relation of personal consciousness, because His intentional consciousness is contingently different in view of us. A process philosopher might perhaps concede that by the distinction of the real from the intentional order a Thomist can take care in his own way of the demand that the world make a difference to God. But the process philosopher insists on considerably more. He also wishes to claim that a God who knows, acts in, and responds to a world unfolding as a process in time must Himself be involved in process, hence in temporal succession. God is thus a God who is Himself in process, that is, changing, mutable. In a word, even if he were to concede that the contingent otherness in the divine consciousness were only in the order of intentional and not real being, a process philosopher would still maintain that this entails *temporal process* in the divine consciousness, at least in the order of intentional being. As some have put it, if God is a personal being who responds to created persons, then He cannot be a timeless being.[17] He can be an eternal being, but one whose eternity is that of an eternal duration, extending over all time and beyond, with temporal succession in it matching ours, and not the eternity of a timeless moment, outside of all duration and temporal succession. The latter is the classical Thomistic concept of the divine eternity (traditional also in most classical Christian thinkers from Boethius, through Anselm, down to the present).

We must now come to grips with this difficult problem of the time-lessness or in-time-ness of God. Let us proceed step by step, following always the rule that unless one must affirm something of God one cannot do so. What must we affirm of Him with regard to temporal suc-cession? First, what the problem is *not*: it is not that the real effective expression of the divine causality and God's real response to us (the novelty in the order of real being) take place in time. Of course they do, and Thomists have always asserted this. For this effective action and response, following the classic axiom that causal action takes place *within* the recipient (*actio est in passo*), as *from* or *due to* the agent, occur precisely down in us, not back in God. This is precisely where it should be, where we would *want* it to be, immanent *in us*, communi-cated *to us*, not consisting of some moving-around of inner wheels in God or change in His own intrinsic real being remaining in Him. A response should be precisely *in* the one to whom the response is being given. So the real being of His action on and response to us occurs down in our temporal process. Causality is the ec-stasy of the agent present by its power *in* its effect. The failure to understand this key metaphysical point in the nature of causality in-validates a large amount of what seems to me simply uncritical "com-mon sense" criticism of the divine-immutability position, as though it were obvious that to do something, to produce any change, in time necessarily puts change and time in the doer.[18]

Our problem, then, is concerned exclusively with the content of the divine intentional consciousness, which is truly in God and which is the point of origin of the real changes produced in us. What must we affirm of it?

(1) We must first affirm that for every knowable item in our world of process there is a corresponding cognitive content in the divine

intentional consciousness, since He knows determinately in all its detail all that is. (Note that this does not yet allow us to infer a distinct real act of knowing corresponding to every distinct item known, since there is no difficulty in principle in one spiritual act's knowing many things in one act of vision, if it is powerful enough to do so. And the divine act is infinite. We simply have no vantage point to do a "phenomenology" of the divine mode of knowing as it is in itself.)

(2) Since these created items known have as part of their intrinsic intelligibility their sequence in time, the content of the divine consciousness must contain or represent this internal time-sequence of the items as related to each other; in other words, it must be a cognitive representation of the time process, perfectly isomorphic in this cognitive content to the time process it represents. In this sense, therefore, one can speak of a "cognitive or intentional sequence" in God, or sequence within the *objective content* of the divine cognition.

(3) Does this introduce real process, and hence "real" time, into the divine consciousness itself? It must be recalled here that for St. Thomas, following Aristotle, time is present only as the cognitive measure of some real change or process of succession in the order of real being. "Time is the measure of motion"—i.e., real motion. Where there is no real motion there can be no time in the proper sense of the term, only understood sequence of cognitive contents. This cognitive sequence can be *correlated* with a real time-sequence by extrinsic intentional reference to the latter, but is itself of a different order (intentional and not real being) and hence incommensurable with the latter and unable to be timed by any time standard, since time is always the measure of real motion. In a word, it is impossible to time a pure cognitive sequence unless there is some real succession underlying it in the knower. Thus for there to be authentic time in God there would have to be some real change or succession underlying the cognitive sequence in His intentional consciousness and allowing us to spread out these contents in an *extended continuum* of succession and distinguish them as moments before and after in a process of real change.

But in the divine consciousness there is not the slightest real change or real motion going on *between* the successive items known, even though these do feed up to Him earlier and later, from really distinct moments down in the process from which they originate. But they coalesce in His eternal moment outside of all and present to all moments. Let us call moments A and B two distinct moments in our temporal process, and A' and B' the corresponding "moments" in the divine cognitive field. We can distinguish A and B temporally because of the real motion going on between them. But how are we to distinguish A' and B' in God? How long is it between them? Since there is no motion going on in the real being of God (including the real being of His consciousness), there is absolutely no way to distinguish, by examining this inner being of God in Himself, whether a second has elapsed, or a million years, or any determinate length of time, or none—*between* or *within* the items of the intelligible sequence of His world-directed consciousness. All the moments in Him telescope into the single real moment of His motionless eternal presence, contemporaneous with all the moments of our or any other created time-sequences. For if there is no time between any two moments, they coalesce into the equivalent of simultaneity.

One can, of course, *correlate* this understood sequence of cognitive contents in God with the real temporal sequence to which they correspond and from which they come. They correspond item for item. One can also, if one wishes, measure the duration of the divine existence and cognition by an *extrinsic* standard or point of reference, namely, the motion going on outside of Him in our world. Thus one can say that God has existed as long as the world has existed, or that His knowledge of World War II took four years to complete, etc. We can "time" Him by our clocks, if we wish. But this is in terms of pure extrinsic denomination, somewhat like the projection of a point onto a line in projective geometry. It posits no real time-sequence, because it posits no real succession, in Him, only an understood sequence between the objects of His consciousness in the order of intentional being, each referring to a really distinct point in our real temporal process. And these two orders of real and intentional being are simply incommensurable with each other in any time framework, since there is no change in real being in one of the terms of comparison and therefore nothing to be measured by any time standard. However, I am perfectly willing to admit that just as we have allowed an intelligible sequence in the order of intentional being in God, so too we can allow an intelligible or "intentional time" in the divine consciousness corresponding to this sequence. This intentional time would be analogous to our real time in the same way that intentional being is analogous to real being.

The position I am maintaining, therefore, is that there is a correlate in the intentional order in God of the real temporal succession in the world, but that this pure cognitive sequence cannot be called "temporal succession" in any proper meaning of the term, since there is no real change in God underlying it and spreading out its "moments" into an extended continuum. Now, if a process philosopher wishes to object that for him any kind of succession, whether in the intentional or the real order, is a time process, then of course he is at liberty to say that God is in time, or that there is process in God. But he must still respect the radical difference between the two kinds of process and time, one of objects as known, the other of intrinsic real being, and not immediately conclude *ipso facto* from the first to the second.

I see no serious difficulty for a Thomist to admit such a "process" or sequence in the intentional order in God with its correlate of "intentional time." For just as the traditionally admitted multiplicity of intentional being in God does not in the least prejudice the simplicity of His real being, and just as the contingent otherness of the divine intentional consciousness with respect to freely willed creatures does not prejudice the necessity of His own intrinsic real being, so it follows that there is no reason why process or succession in the purely intentional order—understood sequence of objects as known—should prejudice the immutability and timelessness of God in His real being.

Perhaps the real difficulty which is disturbing those who insist on process and time in God is that they wish His knowledge and love of the world to be only *contemporary* with what is going on in the world and not prior to it in some predetermined eternity where all would somehow be pre-known and pre-loved independently of the actual course of created history (with the consequent endangering of true contingency and freedom), and actual history would make no difference to God, since He had pre-decided the whole thing on His own anyway.

This to my mind is a real misunderstanding of the theory of the divine knowledge and love as eternal. First of all, the notion of any "foreknowledge," properly speaking, in God must be rejected. He does not know anything, let alone a free action, "before" it happens (understanding "before" as before to Him). It may be before to us, from our limited vantage point as fixed at one point in the process, although I am not sure how much sense that makes either. But God knows all real things, past, present, and future, St. Thomas says, in their actual presence as going on, in their *now*, by His "eternal presentiality" to the whole time process from the motionless moment of His real being outside of the process, though working immanently within it.[19] Hence He knows our free actions as *contemporary with them*, not before they exist in actuality. And being an infinitely perfect purely spiritual knower-willer, He can "improvise" His providence instantly, from His timeless moment outside our time, to match each unfolding phase of the world as it takes place, without any need of knowing "ahead of time" what is going to happen, as though He would somehow have to have enough time to plan things out well. To impose on God a process of first deliberation then later decision would be a pure anthropomorphic projection of our own body-bound consciousness into Him.

For this reason it seems to me unwise, because it is easily misleading, to say that God knows our free future acts "from all eternity," as though from some eternal duration stretching out far back before creation. For where there is no real process (in fact, before creation there is not even any "intentional time"), there is no meaning to "before" and "after" and no standard for measuring it. Hence it would seem wiser to say that He knows my free actions and all of history not *from* all eternity but *in* His eternal, i.e., timelessly present, ever-contemporaneous moment.

At this point, however, we are faced with two different modes or conceptual models of the divine eternity, between which one must choose. Many, including myself, think that both are compatible with the minimum requirements of an authentic Christian notion of God, though the second is not compatible with the classical Scholastic tradition represented by Boethius and St. Thomas. The first or classical model is that of an absolutely durationless eternity, durationless even in the intentional order, where the whole of history is seen *tota simul*, in a single simultaneous vision where all points of the temporal process are equally simultaneous to God as outside the whole temporal order, with no privileged ongoing "now" in His knowledge matching the ongoing "now" of history itself. As Lonergan puts it, the whole of history is seen as a single strictly concrete actualized world order. This is certainly St. Thomas' view, and there is much to recommend it, although the "how" remains a total mystery. There is no decisive way of ruling it out, though I myself am beginning to lean toward the view of many contemporary Christian thinkers that there is an implicit incoherence hidden somewhere within it.

The other model of the divine eternity is a durational one—durational, that is, only in the intentional contents of the divine consciousness as directed toward the world of creation. In this model the divine field of intentional consciousness is constantly expanding to match the ongoing evolution of temporal history, in exact contemporaneity with the latter's ongoing "now." This does not entail, of course, any expansion or change in the qualitative level of the intrinsic real perfection of God. For the latter is eternally infinite in plenitude, and all the new finite determinations of the field of His intentional consciousness are but limited participations in His own unlimited plenitude, never rising to a higher level than their original source, hence involving no real change in the Aristotelian sense. In this view, the ongoing now of actual history is normative for all thinkers who know it as it is, including God, and cannot be relativized into a simultaneous whole as an actual present. Such totalization can only be done when the history is all a finished past. Since the being of our evolving world is a not yet finished being in process, it cannot be known as finished without distorting the kind of being it is.

Such process and expansion in the intentional field of consciousness of God with regard to the world would not, however, constitute an imperfection in His knowledge. For it cannot be an imperfection not to know what is not in itself knowable—i.e., the future, the not yet real, at least in its free or not yet determined aspects. Perfect knowledge of an evolving reality would by nature have to evolve with its object. And since the intentional content of this expanding consciousness would always be only more finite participations of God's own infinite plenitude, the perfection of the content would never rise higher than the ever present primary object of the divine knowledge, His own infinite intrinsic perfection.

This model of the divine infinity is certainly not a Thomistic one. Whether or not it is a more adequate model than the classical Thomistic one is an excellent subject for debate. I myself am now leaning more and more toward it and inclining to agree with the implicit suggestion by Hilary Armstrong, in his recent study of Plotinus' unsuccessful attempt to handle the same problem, when in the last line he raises the question "whether non-durational eternity is a concept which can be usefully employed in any philosophical or theological context."[20] But the only point I would really like to make here is that whether one is forced to adopt the durational concept of eternity or not, it is *possible* to adopt it without compromising the divine perfection of knowing and the immutability of God's intrinsic real being. By restricting the Thomistic metaphysics of immutability in God to the Aristotelian dimension of change in the intrinsic real perfection of a being, we have opened up the possibility of a whole new dimension of intentional process and time in God which leaves intact, while transcending, the entire Aristotelian dimension of real change and immutability.

CONCLUSION

All that we have done thus far really comes down to reinterpreting the immutability in God to fit the perfection proper to the dimension of personal—and therefore interpersonal—being, hence proper to God as truly, though analogously, personal. I grant that this is not the unqualified immutability in all domains which seems to have been the ideal of the classical Greek mind, conceived at least implicitly on the model of being as object rather than subject, and resulting in the self-absorbed, unrelated self-contemplation of the Aristotelian Prime Mover or the Neoplatonic One (the latter above all otherness even in its knowledge, since this would imply real duality). Such a notion of immutability simply does not fit our new sensitivity to the meaning of being as interpersonal, with its exigency of mutual relatedness and reciprocity—a notion which itself is perhaps largely the result of the "good news" of the revelation of the Judaeo-Christian God of love. The notion of immutability must always be controlled, as we said earlier, by the central normative notion of perfection.

Let us say, then, in conclusion, that the immutability which must be affirmed of God is the unchanging, indefectible steadfastness of an infinite plenitude of goodness and loving benevolence, but a benevolence which also *expresses* itself in a process, a progressive unfolding, of mutual interpersonal relationships, spread out in real temporal succession at our receiving end and matched by a distinct differentiation of intentional consciousness in God for each real external expression in us, in terms of which He is truly related to us by an intentional relation of personal consciousness. With less immutability we would not have a truly infinite God; with more, we would not have a truly personal God. And I cannot see the slightest imperfection introduced into God by the "intentional process" we have postulated in Him—even from the point of view of Thomistic metaphysics and epistemology. Hence I conclude that it is perfectly legitimate, from the metaphysical point of view, quite adequately metaphysically grounded, even in a Thomistically inspired metaphysics, for the religious consciousness to speak in the warmest personalist terms of God's truly caring, mutual relation of love with us.

POSTSCRIPT: HOW CAN GOD "RECEIVE" FROM US IN THE ORDER OF KNOWLEDGE?

Throughout this paper we have been taking for grated the *fact* that God knows our free actions, our free responses to Him, which of course implies that He leaves their freedom intact, that He Himself does not one-sidedly determine them. All accept this fact—at least those in the Catholic philosophical tradition, including, naturally, St. Thomas himself. But just *how* it is possible for God thus to know our free actions without either determining them or being acted on, and hence changed, by us constitutes a celebrated and very difficult classical problem, with various thinkers in the tradition presenting diverse and never very satisfactory solutions. St. Thomas, perhaps wiser than most, is very laconic on the subject, contenting himself with affirming that God knows all the actions of creatures by "moving them" to their actions, those which act by determination of nature to act by natural necessity, those which act freely to act freely.[21] The precise *how* he leaves a mystery.

We could also do the same thing. But process philosophers insist—and with good reason, it seems to me—that if God knows our free actions without determining them, He must be learning from us, receiving knowledge from us. They then argue that this necessarily implies that He is changed by us, acted on by us in time. Hence

I feel obliged to say something on this point: is God's knowledge of our free actions *determined by us*, and if so, how?

My answer is in brief outline as follows:

(*a*) It seems to me that one must resolutely affirm that God's knowledge of our free actions is determined by us in some significant sense. For the essence of a free act as *mine* is that it is self-determined by me, that I am responsible for the determination, not God, though He can positively cooperate with my action in carrying out the pursuit of the good once chosen.

(*b*) The whole question now comes down to *how*. The classical Dominican Thomist school rejects my above affirmation on the grounds that if creatures etermine God in any way, then He will be causally dependent on them, contingent, etc., which is impossible for an infinite self-sufficient being. I do not accept this dilemma. The kernel of my solution is that there are *two ways* in which one's knowledge can be determined by another. In the first way the object known acts causally on the knower as on a passive recipient. This way is, of course, excluded in the case of God.

In the other way a superior agent freely offers its indeterminate abundance of power to a lower agent, allowing the latter to channel, or determine—which means here to delimit (partially negate)—the flow of the former's power along lines determined by the lesser agent, to help him execute his own limited operation. In this case the determination contributed by the lower agent does not add any new being to the power of the higher agent. It "adds on" only a partial negation or delimitation of the higher plenitude, hence does not introduce any change in, or addition to, the real being of the higher agent. In this situation the higher agent knows what the lower is doing, not by being positively acted on to receive new real being from the lower, but precisely by knowing *its own action*, by knowing just how its own power is allowed to flow through the lower agent, along the channel which the lower agent determines. So God can know my free action by knowing just how I allow His freely offered power, always gently drawing me through the good, to flow through me. He knows my choice by knowing His own active power working within me, as thus determined or channeled determinately here and now by me. Hence He knows by acting, not by being acted on, but

I supply the inner determination or limit of this power at work—
which I repeat is not a new positive being at all but only a limiting
down of an indeterminate plenitude. Clearly I am not limiting the
real being of God or the inner plenitude of His power as in Him,
but only the exercise of it in me.

A crude image might be of help here. Suppose a strong man
pushing gently against two doors (not forcing them), which are being
held by another man on the other side, while the latter deliberates
which door he wishes to open. When the latter has made his decision
he lets one of the doors go and the power of the one pushing immediately follows through to push it open. The pusher knows what decision the second man has freely made, not by being acted on by
the latter, but by knowing where his own power is allowed to flow
through. Only the negative determination or channeling of the offered
power is provided by the decider. And to determine in this context
is not to act upon—a point consistently overlooked, it seems to me,
by those who refuse to allow that God's knowledge can in any way
be determined by creatures.

I see no reason why the above-described conjunction of power and
determination cannot be found analogously in the conjunction of the
divine power with our free self-determination. God then truly
"receives" the determination of His knowledge of our free actions
from us, but without in the least being a passive recipient of a new
mode of real being in Himself, impressed upon Him by any positive
causal action of ours.

(c) The perceptive reader will surely have noticed that implied in the
above theory is the assumption that the actual self-determination
which is the heart of the human free choice is entirely caused by us
and not by God, is not the "work" of God. This seems at first glance
quite contrary to the traditional position: there is nothing we can do
which God does not do with us. But this is precisely the key to the
problem: the crucial moment in free decision is *not a doing at all*.
It is precisely the moment of *negation* or *exclusion* of all possible avenues
of choice save one, the saying "No" to all but one. For, given choices
A, B, C, we cannot choose C unless we first negate A and B. This
negation is not a positive *act* at all, producing anything new; hence
it cannot be shown that it requires any causal cooperation of God.

It is completely in "our power" thus to negate, i.e., to exclude from the focus of our intentional consciousness, all but one good. Then as soon as we have closed the door to all but one good—our responsibility alone—the active pursuing of this remaining good becomes a positive act and God's power immediately follows through to cooperate with us in this positive side of the coin of free decision, as in all positive actions of creatures. God only says "Yes" with us in our free choices; we alone say the "No" which is the necessary prelude to our combined "Yes."

Since the above hypotheses all seem to me to make reasonably good sense, I have sufficient grounds for affirming that it is not impossible (unintelligible)—though I cannot, of course, claim positive insight into how this is done—for God to "receive" His knowledge of my free actions from me, to let it be determined by me, since this determination does not add on any new mode of positive being but only a delimitation (i.e., partial negation) or channeling of the way in which I allow His active cooperating power to flow through my will. Hence I neither need to, nor have the right to, affirm any *real change* (hence real temporal succession) in God, change in His own inner real being, in order to affirm that He is truly receptive to me in His knowledge.

NOTES

1. See such standard works as Charles Hartshorne, *Divine Relativity* (New Haven: Yale University Press, 1964); John Cobb, *A Christian Natural Theology Based on the Thought of Whitehead* (Philadelphia: Westminster, 1965); E. H. Peters, *The Creative Advance: An Introduction to Process Philosophy as a Context for Christian Faith* (St. Louis: Bethany, 1966); the fine collection *Process Philosophy and Christian Thought*, edd. D. Brown, R. James, and G. Reeves (Indianapolis: Bobbs-Merrill, 1971); and the careful study of Alix Parmentier, *La philosophie de Whitehead et le problème de Dieu* (Paris: Beauchesne, 1969).

2. See, for example, in addition to note 1, J. W. Felt, s.j., "Invitation to a Philosophic Revolution," *The New Scholasticism*, 45 (1971), 87-109; J. C. Robertson, "Does God Change?" *Ecumenist*, 9 (1971), 61: "For a large number of both Catholic and Protestant theologians, of the younger ones at least who are trying to disengage the Gospel from the classical world-view and to re-

express it in terms of the modern one, the processive idea figures in their interpretation of Christian doctrine in a large way."

3. See R. C. Neville, "The Impossibility of Whitehead's God for Christian Theology," *Proceedings of the American Catholic Philosophical Association*, 44 (1970), 130-40.

4. I am thinking in particular of the creative synthesis of Whitehead and St. Thomas which the late Walter Stokes, s.j., was in the midst of working out: "Is God Really Related to the World?" *Proceedings of the American Catholic Philosophical Association*, 39 (1965), 145-51; "Whitehead's Challenge to Theistic Realism," *The New Scholasticism*, 38 (1964), 1-21; "God for Today and Tomorrow," *ibid.*, 43 (1969), 351-78. I also call my readers' attention to the accompanying historical article of Gerald McCool, s.j. (Chapter 7, "The Philosophical Theology of Rahner and Lonergan").

5. See Frederick Sontag, *Divine Perfection: Possible Ideas of God* (New York: Harper, 1962).

6. See *Sum. theol.*, I, q. 2, a. 3; q. 9, and parallel passages.

7. See *Sum. theol.*, I, q. 13, a. 7; *Contra gentes*, II, 12; *De potentia*, q. 7, a. 10; and the first article by Stokes cited in note 4.

8. See F. Meehan, *Efficient Causality in Aristotle and St. Thomas* (Washington, D.C.: Catholic University of America Press, 1940); W. N. Clarke, s.j., "Causality and Time," *Experience, Existence and the Good*, ed. I. C. Lieb (Carbondale: Southern Illinois University Press, 1961), pp. 143-57.

9. For a careful study of the whole question of the meaning and importance for St. Thomas of naming God "cause" by extrinsic attribution, and the absence of change or real relation in the cause as such, see the unpublished doctoral dissertation by Thomas Loughran, "Efficient Causality and Extrinsic Attribution in the Philosophy of St. Thomas" (Fordham University, 1969).

10. See, for example, *De spiritualibus creaturis*, a. 1, ad lim.; *De veritate*, q. 22, a. 10; q. 2, a. 2; *Contra gentes*, IV, 11; I, 55; *Sum. theol.*, I, q. 14, a. 1; q. 15; *In II De anima*, lect. 24, nn. 552-53; and the studies of A. Hayen, *L'intentionnel selon S. Thomas* (2d ed.; Paris: Desclée de Brouwer, 1954); L. M. Régis, *Epistemology* (New York: Macmillan, 1959), Chap. VI, with the abundant texts cited there.

11. *Contra gentes*, I, 55: "A knowing power does not know anything in act unless an intention is present."

12. See, among others, *Contra gentes*, IV, 11.

13. See S. Breton, *Conscience et intentionalité* (Paris: Vitte, 1957), for a comparison of St. Thomas, Brentano, and Husserl.

14. A. J. Kelly, c.ss.r., "God: How Near a Relation?" *Thomist*, 34 (1970), 191-229. See also the articles by Walter Stokes cited in note 4.

15. See H. R. Reinelt, "A Whiteheadian Doctrine of Analogy," *Modern Schoolman*, 48 (1970-1971), 327-42.

16. I feel that I must meet here the penetrating objection raised by my colleague Joseph Donceel, s.j., to the effect that an increase in knowledge through intentional being is certainly an increase of real perfection in us,

otherwise growth in knowledge would be no growth in real perfection for us
—which is clearly false and contrary to St. Thomas himself. I admit that such
growth in knowledge in us is a growth in real perfection, a change to a higher
level of perfection, precisely because it gives us knowledge of real beings we
did not know before and which are not a limited participation in our own
pre-existing perfection, but are quite independent of us in the source of their
being. Were we, however, to know something we had totally thought up
and totally produced in all its being from our own pre-existing plenitude, then
knowledge of such a being would not add to our perfection, though it would
add a new determination to our field of intentional consciousness. This is the
case with God.

17. See Nelson Pike, *God and Timelessness* (New York: Schocken, 1970).
In this carefully argued book the author allows that the concept of a timeless
God as *cause* can be meaningful and correct, but not the concept of God as
both personal and timeless.

18. See W. N. Clarke, "Causality and Time" (note 6). From this point of
view I also find the article of Felt (note 2) metaphysically defective in its
criticism of St. Thomas, namely in its apparent assumption that the act of
creation precisely as act of causality necessarily implies change in the cause.

19. See *Sum. theol.*, I, q. 14, a. 13.

20. A. H. Armstrong, "Eternity, Life and Movement in Plotinus' Accounts
of *Nous*," *Le Néoplatonisme*, Colloques Internationaux, Royaumont 1969
(Paris: Centre National de la Recherche Scientifique, 1971), pp. 67-76 at 76.
In a subsequent letter of the author to me, he furthered clarified his suggestion—namely, that it may be necessary to use both models, durational
and non-durational eternity, in dialectical complementarity, in order to speak
properly about God.

21. *Contra gentes*, III, 88-90; *Sum. theol.*, I, q. 105, a. 4; *De potentia*, q. 3,
a. 7 et ad 12-14m.

4

The Cartesian *Cogito* and the Death of God

ALEXANDER VON SCHOENBORN

THE TITLE OF THIS BOOK IS A CAPSULE FORMULA for one of the primary concerns constitutive of the Western tradition. Yet, for well over a hundred years now, the claim has been made that in spite of this multiform concern—perhaps indeed because of it—God is dead. The question of the death of God has received increasing attention lately, especially in its religious, theological, and pastoral aspects.

It is not my intention in this paper to bring this question to thematic focus or to investigate any one of its formulations and resolutions. What I wish to do is both more modest than and preliminary to such efforts. I wish to reflect on a particular transformation within our tradition which is of crucial importance to the question of the death of God: the initiation of the modern age. Taking metaphysics as the profoundest conceptual articulation of that tradition, I wish to focus on the metaphysical dimension of this transformation and to do so in its widest setting which, in classical language, is that of the transcendentals.

This aim intertwines with a second one. For it has been urged by Whitehead and others that major conceptual revisions take the form of trying to put new wine into old bottles. In other words, such changes tend to occur in the language and the views of what is left behind. In the particular case of Descartes—whose first metaphysical principle, *cogito, ergo sum*, I take to be the initiation and grounding of the modern epoch—his able commentator L. J. Beck argues that Descartes was forced to pour the new wine of the *cogito* into an old bottle, the substance language of the Scholastics.[1]

Hence my second aim is to grasp the specific modernity of Descartes' work as judged by the subsequent tradition, that is, to free the *cogito* from the substantialist framework of the preceding tradition within and in terms of which Descartes sought to articulate and communicate his claims. The realization of this second aim will result in the thesis that Descartes' use of the substantialist framework deceived him into thinking that he could continue classical God-talk without realizing the difficulties for such talk engendered by his principle.

The two aims dictate a complex path for this paper. I shall begin with a very partial outline of the Scholastic matrix by recalling the ontological "deduction" of the transcendentals as undertaken by Aquinas in *De veritate*. I shall then specify a partial list of at least five metaphysical functions assigned to God in and by that matrix as outlined. With this as background, I will then turn to Descartes' principle, analyze its meaning, and attempt thereby to show that the five specified functions of God should fall away. In Descartes' own view, they do not. The reason, already suggested, is that the demands of the *cogito* remain couched in the language of substance. To buttress this account, I will then attempt to show negatively how the *cogito* forces Descartes into incoherence whenever he uses the concept "substance" and, conversely, to suggest that the *cogito*, once unfolded in Kant's synthetic unity of apperception, does negate the five functions of God as discussed by appropriating them unto itself.

The point of this journey should now be apparent. For if it can be shown that the functions allotted to God in the metaphysical matrix of an earlier phase of our tradition came increasingly to be appropriated by transcendental subjectivity and that this historical transformation occurred in and was made possible by Descartes' fundamental principle, then we will have seen at least one way in which one might philosophically speak of the death of God.

Having now specified the point of this journey, let me make a remark about its form. Both the systematic framework behind this paper and the interpretation of Descartes in this paper lean heavily on the work done by Martin Heidegger. It must suffice that I note that, more than anyone else with the possible exception of Hegel, Heidegger has scrutinized and sought to appropriate the philosophical tradition and thus serves as a suitable guide in the present endeavor.[2]

Let me now begin cashing the promissory notes which I made above by briefly recalling the "deduction" of the transcendentals from *ens* or being as undertaken by Aquinas. The term *ens* here refers not to *entitas*, to pure beingness and meaning structure, but to the concrete existent as so structured; substances always are the primary realities. Now the ontological deduction of the transcendentals takes the form of a derivation from *ens* of its *modi expressi*, i.e., modes of being exhibiting an intelligible aspect not expressed by the term "being" itself. Aquinas distinguishes between special modes, which are the particular modalities and perfections of being which a given *ens* exhibits, and general modes, which are consequent upon every being in general. These latter modes are the transcendentals. Such a general mode can be taken in two ways: first, as that which follows upon every being taken in and by itself, and second, as that which follows upon every being in relation to something else. Taken in the first way, the mode expresses something in the being either affirmatively or negatively. What is affirmatively expressed is *res* or essence; what is negatively expressed is lack of division, or unity. Taken in the second way, a general mode must again be considered in twofold fashion, according to the differentiation of one thing from another, which is expressed by the term "something," and according to the conformity of a being to another. This conformity can, as the good, be that between being and rational appetite, or, as the true, that between being and intellect.[3]

Let us now consider some of the metaphysical functions of God within the general framework thus very partially outlined. First, God is perfect being. To the extent, then, that the ontological deduction is from *ens*, it is, implicitly at least, from God. God is both source and proper locus and, as unique substance and *ens perfectissimum*, the being pre-eminently expressed through the transcendentals. Second, since it is being-true, construed as being-known, which becomes the primary theme of modern philosophy, let us take a closer look at the conformity between being and intellect constitutive of the true. This conformity is a dual one. The human speculative intellect makes true empirical judgments to the extent that it conforms itself to things. It is the thing which here serves as norm and measure. But a thing itself is, and thus is transcendentally true, insofar as it derives from and conforms to God's own creative vision. As Aquinas, therefore, goes on to suggest in the next article of the same question (*De veritate*, q. 1, a. 2), a thing is true insofar as it is measured and ordered by the divine intellect. In short, God is source of both order and measure. Third, the transcendental is an ontological *a priori* for any true cognition, and it is completely independent of the factual existence of a human intellect and solely dependent on the creative thought of God. Fourth, God is somehow and rather mysteriously involved efficaciously in that virtual knowledge or human pre-grasp of the transcendentals which is in part constitutive of the *lumen naturale*. For my purposes it is sufficient to note that this natural light which is the precondition of all human knowledge is not simply a function of the human self, but at its source broadens into a mysterious participation in and dependence on God. Fifth, it is possible to know God to the extent of being able to predicate transcendentals in an analogy of proportionality of being.

As I have already indicated, we will rediscover these functions in transcendental subjectivity. But to do so, we must now undertake an interpretation of the Cartesian *cogito*. I shall first try to understand Descartes' principle with the aid of Heidegger and then proceed to a résumé in terms more explicitly Cartesian.

For Descartes, the term *cogitatio* designates what is thought and the thinking of what is thought, and also, as we shall see, the overarching whole within which this polarity occurs. Let me begin with the correlatives. As is well known, Descartes in arriving at his famous principle makes the point that, in seeking to think all things false, it is essential for the "I" so thinking to be something.[4] Whatever the status of a particular *cogitatum*—be it hallucinatory, real, imagined, remembered, or whatever—the *cogitatum* implies, qua *cogitatum*, an *ego cogito*.[5]

Heidegger explicates this to mean that *ego cogito* is equivalent to *cogito me cogitare*.[6] To say that I represent something to myself is thus to say that I also represent myself, the representor, to myself. The question, of course, is how this "also" is to be understood. Heidegger answers for Descartes that in an immediate seeing, in a remembering or anticipating, that which in each case is represented is so present to me, so stands in front of me (*re-presentatio*), over against me (*ob-jectum*), that, without becoming myself the object of a new and further representation, I am nevertheless present to myself.[7] How? In the representation of an object (that is, in the grasping of something as an object, as standing over against and before), that against which and before which the object is posited and stands (namely, the representor, the ego) must already be pro- and pre-posed by and for itself.[8] Thus the ego as representor belongs essentially to the *cogitatio* and this not subsequently but rather as ground of the possibility of the representation. Positional consciousness of objects presupposes self-consciousness. It is only as self-consciousness that thing-consciousness is possible. Thus for Descartes the reflexivity of consciousness provides the basis for any cognition whatever. Moreover, it should be clear that what has been noted, up to this point, about the structure of a *cogitatio* applies not only to thinking in the narrow sense. Other modes of human comportment—Descartes mentions willing, imagining, and feeling—also exhibit the structure just considered and are rightly classed as *cogitationes*.[9]

In the light of this partial analysis of *cogitatio*, let me now turn to the *cogito, ergo sum*. In this principle, Descartes uncovers the self's existential affirmation of itself as *cogitans*. Spinoza's rendition of the *cogito* as *sum res cogitans* is appropriate, provided that we recall that this *res cogitans* is always a *res cogitata* as well. Heidegger thus takes the *sum* in Descartes' principle to mean that my, the ego's, being is essentially characterized as the process of the *cogitatio*.[10]

We saw above that self-consciousness serves as the ground of the possibility of thing-consciousness. Consequently, not only is my being determined as and in the *cogitatio*, but my presence to myself *qua* ego, *qua* the necessary and hence indubitable co-representation, is the measure of the presence of anything re-presented. This measure of presence thus determines the being of things as the objectivity of objects. And to the extent that something approximates the indubitable, i.e., certain or clear and distinct, character of that "first knowledge," it is perceived as true.[11]

From this vantage point, it becomes clear why, in the context in which the *cogito, ergo sum* is uttered, *cogitare* is synonymous with *dubitare*, with doubting.[12] For the *cogitare* is essentially a specific doubting. To be grasped as an object, a thing must be taken to account as intrinsically dubitable so as to see by this test how it "measures up" to the necessarily present indubitable, the *ego cogito*, and where and how it is to be ranked and ordered within the context of objectivity.[13] To the extent that the object passes this test and is thus adequately secured, it is grasped with certainty, i.e., it is known in its *ordo*. Correlatively, each *cogitatio* is essentially—Descartes himself uses *mea cogitatio* and *action de mon esprit* interchangeably[14]—an *agere*, a fitting into the *ordo* of objectivity as *co-agitare*.

Let me now attempt a brief application of the above in terms more explicitly Cartesian. Descartes' major work is entitled *Meditations on First Philosophy*. "First Philosophy," he notes, is a synonym for metaphysics.[15] He is interested, then, in that within which and in terms of which the real discloses itself as real. The regions of the real studied by the special sciences are regions within and of this realm of disclosedness. If then one will "trust only what is completely known and incapable of being doubted,"[16] it becomes necessary to elucidate and ground "the foundations of metaphysics."[17] In this effort, one ought not to select any one special science.[18] One must study objectivity as such, and its investigation is called by Descartes "universal mathematics"[19] or "pure mathematics."[20] Things are real, i.e., "recognized as external objects," to the extent that they are disclosed within "the object of pure mathematics."[21] Needless to say, pure mathematics is not to be confused with the special mathematical sciences.[22] The inner structures of objectivity are the interconnected "simple natures" which in their totality constitute for Descartes, according to Beck, the whole of reality and the whole of knowledge.[23] But pure mathematics is not simply the study of objectivity as such. Since this objectivity is grounded in the subjectivity of the self as *cogitatio*, it is necessary to seek out the primary rudiments of human reason. It is only when we "mark that which is most absolute"[24] in this sphere that subjectivity itself is secured. This is achieved by recourse to the one entity disclosed within the *cogitatio* as the necessary correlate of any entity represented. It is only when the transcending self encounters itself as ego, as necessarily posited by itself, and on the basis of that identity can say "I," that we finally mark that which is most absolute. At the same time, we have the norm of certainty for pure mathematics as the science of order and measure. The *cogito, ergo sum* is thus the first principle in the order of philosophizing. It is such not because Descartes discovered self-consciousness—that occurred several eons earlier—but because this relation to the representor assumes the role of the essential measure of the being, and thus of the being-certain, and thus of the truth, of what is.

On the basis of this interpretation of Descartes' *cogito*, let me now return to the transcendentals and to the five metaphysical functions of God which I specified earlier. Descartes nowhere talks about transcendentals as such and consequently attempts no "deduction." He does, however, list substance, duration, order, and number as those structures which "range through all the classes of real things,"[25] structures, in other words, which the medievals would have called transcendentals. Now, any attempt to derive these from being *qua* being in a manner analogous to Aquinas would fail.[26] These Cartesian transcendental structures are, however, derivable from the *cogito*. For we saw that, no matter what the flow and variety of representations, what is in each instance already present is the *ego cogitans* as that toward which and over against which an entity is posited as object. The ego in its being underlies and grounds the process of the *cogitatio* and as such is subject. "Subject" is the traditional synonym for "substance." Hence substance in the sense of substantiality (subjectivity) is derivable.[27] Again, the subject endures as always already "in" the representation. This constant presence requires that objectivity be characterized in terms of "duration." Indeed, this characterization could have been in terms of "extension" except for Descartes' mistaken identification of the latter with space. Further, since the objectivity posited in the *cogito* must be graspable with certainty and since certainty requires clarity and distinctness, what is presupposed is a structured or ordered objectivity. The "object of pure mathematics" is thus characterized in terms of "order." But the order of which one can most readily "give an accounting" is the numerical order. Thus "number" must be a transcendental, making mathematics in the ordinary sense the pre-eminent μέθοδος of the study of reality.

Let me now turn to the five functions I previously specified as belonging to God in the metaphysical matrix of Scholasticism. It should be clear that all these functions fall away with the establishing of the *cogito* as the first metaphysical principle. The most general reason for this is that it becomes impossible to use the classical conception of God meaningfully within a matrix in which God would have to be an object, and thus both finite and dependent for His being on a transcendental human subjectivity, or else be identical with man, or be merely a function of reason as a regulative ideal.

More positively, the functions in question become functions of the *cogito*. First, the being pre-eminently expressed through the "transcendentals" is the *ego cogitans*. Second, it is the *cogito, ergo sum* which is the source of both order and measure in regard to being-true. Third, the transcendental is an ontological *a priori* and it is completely independent of the creative thought of God and solely dependent on the factual existence of a human intellect. Fourth, the natural light which is the precondition of all human knowledge is simply the ontological constitution of the human self. Fifth, the *cogito*'s projection of objectivity may allow for a doctrine of Analogies of Experience, but it does not allow for a doctrine of proper proportionality. For these reasons, then, the functions assigned to God fall away.

Now, Descartes himself not only does not draw the conclusions we just did from the *cogito* but, on the contrary, maintains expressly each of the five functions (although, of course, in a form different from that of Aquinas). First, all reality derives from God. And Descartes also maintains that God as unique substance and *ens perfectissimum* is pre-eminently expressed through the transcendentals of Aquinas. Second, Descartes considers God the ultimate measure and guarantor of truth. Third, he maintains, in the doctrine of simple natures, an ontological *a priori* for any true human cognition which is solely dependent on God's will and not on the factual occurrence of a human knower. Fourth, God is even more strongly implicated in the exercise of the "natural light" of reason; and fifth, we are able to know God, not through the analogy of being but because of the divine imprint left in the soul.

How is the divergence between this stand and our interpretation of the *cogito*'s implications to be explained? A partial reason for this is Descartes' identification of the philosophical problem of finitude with its theological counterpart. Being finite is construed as being

created.[28] This allows Descartes to move immediately to the presupposed creator or infinite being.[29] But the main reason, I believe,
is that Descartes had to articulate his vision in the language of substance
which the tradition made available to him. If there is any merit to
this latter suggestion, then my next and final step will have two phases.
Negatively, this step will show that the new Archimedean point of
the *cogito* ultimately forces Descartes into incoherence when speaking
about or in terms of substance. Positively, I will indicate again, in
somewhat freer fashion, that when the *cogito* is finally articulated in
terms demanded by and suited to it, the five designated functions of
God fall away and thus justify us in viewing the Cartesian shaping
of our tradition as implicated in the death or at least a dying of God.

One of Descartes' several definitions of substance is in terms of something existing in such a way as to need nothing else in order to exist.[30]
Descartes recognizes that in the light of this definition God alone is
a substance. But this substance is also a being perfect in every way.
Now if the creator is an *ens perfectissimum*, then the *ens creatum* must,
qua *ens*, also be characterized as substance. Noting, however, the
infinite gulf between creator and created, Descartes echoes the Schoolmen in maintaining that substance cannot be predicated univocally
of both. The Scholastics had tried to bridge the gap by a doctrine of
analogical predication. But here the *cogito*, with its new circumscrip-
tion of truth, again comes into play. A doctrine of analogy cannot be
acceptable since, as necessarily harboring an ambiguity, it violates
the *cogito*'s demand for certainty, i.e., clarity and distinctness. What
then? Descartes leaves the matter an ontological puzzle.[31] But
if this be the case, may we not ask how Descartes can possibly speak
meaningfully about both infinite and finite substance?

Thus far, I have considered infinite substance in its relation to finite
created substance. Let me now focus on created substance. Here
again Descartes' dependence on past interpretations of substance—a
dependence intensified by his employment of the language of the
Schoolmen to fulfill his burning desire to be understood by those
speaking that language—manifests itself at variance with the demands
of the *cogito*.

I noted above that the self-positing of the *cogito* is intrinsically a
positing of the context within which a thing must appear to be
grasped as real. Our investigation of that context showed it to be

objectivity as such. Since for Descartes objectivity is grounded in subjectivity, we note here neither trace nor need of any radical bifurcation of the world. But Descartes is unable to see this implication since his analysis is cast in the framework of substance and attribute language. The objectivity of the object is interpreted as an "attribute" or property of the object—for example, thought and extension.[32] The ontological is "reified": being becomes a real predicate. The world is then split into thinking substance and extended substance. This, in turn, leads to a further definition of substance. For what is needed is a principle to unify the various attributes into an object. Descartes consequently takes it to be an "axiom" that, since "nothing is possessed of no attributes," the perception of any attribute requires the existence of a substance to which it may be attributed.[33] This conception of substance, Descartes suggests in the same text, may be attributed univocally to soul and to body. But since thought is totally different from extension[34] and since each is the one principal property of substance which constitutes its nature,[35] one may still wonder just what the univocal meaning of substance here might be.

Returning now to the positive side of my claim, let me conclude by simply pointing to the *cogito* as it unfolds in the guise of Kant's synthetic unity of apperception. For everyone will, I think, agree that Kant's "I think" appropriated the first four of the five metaphysical functions of God, while the fifth—God as term of human knowing—became illusory. Granted, God still survived as a postulate of rationality. But be it as transcendental ideal or as postulate of practical reason, God hung by the slender thread of the thing-in-itself, a thread cut by German idealism, by Neokantianism, by positivism, and by Husserlian and Heideggerian phenomenology. With that, transcendental subjectivity became and has remained the absolute. Nietzsche's proclamation of the death of God may have been cultural prophecy: philosophically, it was but a post-mortem.

NOTES

1. L. J. Beck, *The Metaphysics of Descartes* (London: Oxford University Press, 1965), p. 110, and *passim*.
2. Because of the almost proverbial "violence" of Heidegger's historical interpretations, it seems advisable to make two comments. First, since the focus of this paper is simply on the modernity of Descartes, there is no need to justify Heidegger's interpretation in terms of Cartesian scholarship. As a matter of fact, however—and this is my second comment—I believe that his interpretation can be justified, at least as it bears upon Descartes' dictum that the *cogito, ergo sum* is the first principle in the order of philosophizing. The following indication must suffice. In an excellent article, Hiram P. Caton argues, by way of a careful analysis of the *Discourse*, that there are in fact two foundational orders to be found in Descartes: a methodological order, resting on reason and extension (mathematics), and a metaphysical order, resting on reason and God. He goes on to indicate why he considers the former the genuine one and the latter order an interpolation dictated by Enlightenment prudence ("On the Interpretation of the Meditations," *Man and World*, 3 [1970], 224-43). Now, it seems to me that such equally erudite defenders of the second foundational order as L. J. Beck, in the work already cited, or E. Salmon, in her "Mathematical Roots of Cartesian Metaphysics" (*The New Scholasticism*, 39 [1965], 158-69), would be unable to contest successfully Caton's view because they share his fundamental premiss: the substantive priority of Cartesian method. Heidegger does not share that premiss, thus opening vistas more consonant with that Cartesian dictum with which I began this comment.
3. Thomas Aquinas, *De veritate*, q. 1, a. 1. See *Truth*, trans. Robert W. Mulligan, s.j. (Chicago: Regnery, 1952), I, 5-6.
4. René Descartes, *Discourse on Method* in *The Philosophical Works of Descartes*, trans. Elizabeth S. Haldane and G. R. T. Ross (New York: Dover, 1955), I, 101.
5. Reference might here be made to the contemporary reformulation of that principle by E. Husserl.
6. Martin Heidegger, *Vorträge und Aufsätze* (Pfullingen: Neske, 1954), p. 74.
7. Martin Heidegger, *Nietzsche* (Pfullingen: Neske, 1961), II, 153.
8. *Ibid.*, p. 160.
9. Descartes, *The Principles of Philosophy* in *Works*, I, 222.
10. Heidegger, *Nietzsche*, II, 161.
11. Descartes, *Meditations on First Philosophy* in *Works*, I, 158.
12. Descartes, *The Search After Truth* in *Works*, I, 324. This point also holds for the pertinent passages in the *Meditations* and the *Principles*.
13. Heidegger, *Vorträge*, p. 152.
14. Descartes, *Meditations*, I, 159n1.

15. Descartes, *Principles*, I, 212.
16. Descartes, *Rules for the Direction of the Mind* in *Works*, I, 3.
17. Descartes, *Principles*, I, 212.
18. Descartes, *Rules*, I, 2.
19. *Ibid.*, p. 13.
20. *Ibid.*, p. 17.
21. Descartes, *Meditations*, I, 191.
22. Descartes, *Rules*, I, 11, 57.
23. L. J. Beck, *The Method of Descartes* (Oxford: Clarendon Press, 1952), pp. 71-73.
24. Descartes, *Rules*, I, 16.
25. Descartes, *Principles*, I, 238.
26. Such an attempt would fail because of the fundamental confusions inherent in Descartes' concept of substance and in his handling of the problem of being. For a good account of these confusions, see Martin Heidegger, *Being and Time*, trans. John Macquarrie and Edward Robinson (London: SCM Press, 1962), pp. 125-27.
27. This move, however, requires dropping the further Cartesian doctrine that duration, number, and order are "modes" of substance. See Descartes, *Principles*, I, 241. If "substance" means subjectivity—and that seems to be Descartes' view for the most part—then the doctrine of "modes" is a confusion.
28. Descartes, *Meditations*, I, 177.
29. It would be highly instructive to compare and contrast this construct of finitude with those of Kant, Hegel, and Heidegger.
30. Descartes, *Principles*, I, 239.
31. *Ibid.*, pp. 239-40.
32. Descartes, *Notes Directed Against a Certain Programme* in *Works*, I, 435.
33. Descartes, *Principles*, I, 240.
34. Descartes, *Third Set of Objections with Author's Reply* in *Works*, II, 64.
35. Descartes, *Principles*, I, 240.

5

Hegel's Critique
of Kant's Theology

Quentin Lauer, S.J.

OF ALL THOSE WHO HAVE UNDERTAKEN to criticize Kant's philosophy
—and their number is legion—none, it would seem, has been more
consistently caustic than Hegel. This, despite the fact that Hegel
never ceased to acknowledge the greatness of Kant or the debt which
he himself owed to Kant. It has, of course, been pointed out more
than once that Hegel, particularly in his younger years, based his
interpretation of Kant's philosophy on what it had become after
being transformed by Fichte.[1] Although there is undoubtedly some
truth in this contention—Hegel himself speaks of Fichte as the one
who presents Kant's principles in abstract form[2]—Hegel's criticism is
still at its most devastating when he addresses it directly to Kant's
own words. It is clear that he at least thinks that he is criticizing
Kant, not merely Fichte.

The criticism ranges from minor complaints regarding Kant's use
of language to major attacks against what is fundamental to the entire
Kantian philosophical endeavor. Hegel refers to Kant's terminology
as "barbaric"[3] and to his method as "psychological" and "empirical"
rather than "philosophical."[4] He sees the whole of Kant's philosophy
as a "complete philosophy of the understanding, which dispenses

with reason," a good "Introduction to Philosophy."[5] Kant's philosophy of nature is "thoroughly unsatisfactory,"[6] and his paean to the infinity of time and space at the end of the *Critique of Practical Reason* simply sings the praises of endless "boredom."[7] More significantly, Hegel pokes fun at Kant for demanding that knowledge be validated by a knowledge of the faculty of knowing—like learning how to swim before going into the water![8] Kant, Hegel tells us, "describes reason very well, but does so in an empirical manner from which thought is absent and which deprives itself again of its own truth."[9] "No human being is so mad as is this philosophy," which clings to empty concepts,[10] "sifting empty straw through the empty . . . straw of ordinary logic."[11] There is no part of Kant's philosophy which escapes Hegel's criticism: his *Critique of Pure Reason* fails to come to terms with genuine reason; his moral philosophy is purely formal and empty; his philosophy of religion is purely subjective, has no object at all.

THE CHARACTER OF HEGEL'S CRITICISM

One wonders at the end of all this what, if anything, is left of Kant's philosophy as Hegel sees it. To answer this question we must seek to understand what Hegel himself means by criticism of a philosophy. As we learn from his most extensive critique of Kant, in the Introduction to the section on "subjectivity" in the *Science of Logic*,[12] it is not the function of criticism to refute what another philosopher has said—above all not by the application of principles foreign to that philosopher's own thinking. Rather it is to show that this very thinking demands that the philosopher go further than he did, or that his thinking demands to be developed beyond the point where he left it. Thus, in regard to Spinoza, Hegel attempts to show that what Spinoza said about substance demands in reality the kind of development which it finds in Hegel's own thinking, resulting in a substance which is subject, active, self-determining, free.[13] By the same token, although Kant has made a tremendous contribution to the progress of philosophy by his insistence on the autonomy of reason, "for whose authority nothing external is an authority—no authority can be valid except through thought,"[14] Hegel will insist that what Kant has said about reason will not be consistent with itself if it does not get beyond the point of finitude where Kant left it. There is a sense, then, in which everything which Hegel has to say in criticism of Kant comes together in one point. The "Copernican Revolution" which had freed philosophy from the futility of a "dogmatic" metaphysics by making reason genuinely autonomous and, thus, dependent for its truth on nothing external to itself, had not been sufficiently revolutionary. Kant had persuaded reason to look into itself and not outside itself for all that it was capable of knowing, and then had so reduced this capability of knowing that it had to stop short of being objective, of coming to terms with the absolute, short of which knowing is not truly knowing at all. We can say, then, that Hegel's principal criticism of Kant is theological, in the sense that he finds fault with Kant's thought for not being adequately theological, for not going so far as Hegel's own thought would in coming to grips in thought with God Himself. Kant's thought is inadequately philosophical because it is inadequately theological; it stops short of the one object which would make it truly philosophical.

With the publication by Hermann Nohl of *Hegels theologische Jugendschriften*[15] it became clear that Hegel's preoccupation with matters theological, which manifests itself so clearly in the *Phenomenology of Spirit*, in the *Science of Logic*, in the *Lectures on the Philosophy of Religion*, and in the *Lectures on the History of Philosophy*, was a preoccupation which dated back to his earliest years. When we read what Hegel had to say in these early manuscripts (presumably he had good reasons for not publishing them) we are immediately struck by two characteristics they manifest: (1) they are strongly influenced by Kant, particularly by his *Religion innerhalb der Grenzen der blossen Vernunft*, with its insistence on the moral foundations of religion; and (2) they already testify to a growing dissatisfaction on the part of Hegel with Kant's approach to the religious problematic. What Hegel was looking for was a religion which would make rational sense, as opposed to a merely "positive" religion based on authority, but he was also looking for a religion whose object—God—would make rational sense and would not be simply the object of a non-rational intuition or a non-rational faith. Hegel's dissatisfaction with the Kantian - Fichtean emphasis on religion as a subjective response, as opposed to theology as a rational investigation of religion's object, comes out more pointedly in two other early writings which he did publish, the *Differenz des Fichteschen und Schellingschen Systems der Philosophie*, published in 1801, and *Glauben und Wissen*, published in 1802. In the first of these Hegel seeks to come to grips with a problem which had plagued both theologians and philosophers from the earliest times: how can human reason, which is a finite capacity, be a capacity for the infinite, i.e., God? Spinoza had solved this problem to his own satisfaction but not to Hegel's; Kant and Fichte had simply shelved the problem by turning God into a moral absolute, infinite in one sense, perhaps, but not a real object for reason. Hegel's solution —although it is not terribly clear at this stage in his career—is that reason is a capacity for the infinite precisely because it itself is not finite, i.e., because in genuinely speculative thinking it passes beyond the finite to the infinite, by recognizing that even the finite object is really known only in a knowing which is infinite.[16]

In *Glauben und Wissen*, Hegel voices the fear that reason (philosophy) in vindicating its autonomy from faith (religion) may have cut itself off from the rich content which faith supplies.[17] This, he contends, is what "has happened in the philosophies of Kant, Jacobi, and Fichte."[18] The suprasensible has become the suprarational, and the only approach to God left is through faith.[19] This sort of philosophy cannot get beyond reason's reflection on itself,[20] and thus becomes a mere critique of the capacity to know the finite.[21] What it comes down to is that rational knowledge is denied, since its only object is the capacity to know, not reality.[22] It is true that Kant has given us the "beginning of an idea of reason,"[23] but what he did not see was that there is no distinction between what reason truly thinks and what is truly real;[24] Kant's reason is forbidden to affirm the reality of what it knows.

As Hegel develops his own independent philosophy, it may seem strange to us that the main target in his polemic against Kant should become more and more Kant's philosophy of religion. We shall be able to understand this, however, if we realize that one of the most significant aims in Hegel's own thinking is to overcome the romantic religious intuitionism of a Jacobi or a Schleiermacher. Hegel is convinced that Kant has made a great contribution to the accomplishment of this aim by recognizing the uniqueness of that response which we call religious and which is at the same time rational. In doing this, however, Hegel felt, Kant has so concentrated on the subjective religious response as to deprive the God to whom religion was responding of all objectivity—as though the subjective response were something reason could fathom, since as a subjective response it is finite, whereas the God to whom religion responds, being infinite, is beyond the capacity of reason to grasp. Kant's reason, so to speak, is conscious of its incapacity to grasp any reality outside (or above) itself; Hegel's reason is "conscious of being all reality"[25] and, thus, is conscious that there is no reality outside (or above) itself for it to grasp. This will have to mean ultimately a dialectical identification of finite and infinite reason, and precisely this identification Hegel will dare to make: "There is but one reason. There is no second, super-human reason. Reason is the divine in man."[26]

THE STORY OF REASON

This last, however, is the story of Hegel's *Phenomenology of Spirit*, which from this point of view can be looked upon as the Hegelian counterpart of—and answer to—Kant's *Critique of Pure Reason*. The whole point of the *Phenomenology* is to show that philosophical thinking need not—and indeed cannot—be preceded by an investigation of man's capacity to do philosophical thinking. Rather, to begin at the beginning with the mere fact of human consciousness—which Kant, and even Hume before him, will grant as "given"—is already to engage in philosophical thinking. It is not going to be an easy matter, as Hegel tells us in the Preface to the *Phenomenology*, but if we are faithful in following the process of human consciousness, it will lead us from the minimal awareness of mere sensation to the total fullness of "absolute knowing." Along the way it will be revealed that mere objective consciousness, culminating as it does in the abstract conceptualizations of understanding, will not be true to itself if it does not pass beyond itself to self-consciousness, involving a realization that ultimately whatever object consciousness has will be itself. But even this consciousness is incomplete if it does not come to recognize that, despite the fact that there is no source outside itself for its grasp of reality, no reality is closed to it. This recognition comes to it when consciousness becomes reason, which finds all reality

in itself. If the reason here spoken of, however, were merely individual, subjective reason, the identification of reason and reality would
be simply nonsense; reason must universalize itself, not by abstract
generalization but by identifying itself with the totality of reason,
which in the concrete is spirit. It is spirit, then, which is not only an
infinite grasp of reality but also a grasp of infinite reality, which it
renders present to itself by expressing itself, first in the form of sensible
images, *art*, then in the form of internal representations, *religion*,
and finally in the form of thought, *philosophy*—the only form which
is adequate to the infinite reality which is its content.[27]

In this hasty and, therefore, inadequate rundown of the *Phenomenology* we can see how far Hegel has moved in 1807 from the Kant
who influenced him so strongly in his youth. The explicit criticism
of Kant in the *Phenomenology* is not extensive, but the reason (spirit)
Hegel speaks of here is a far cry from the reason of either the *Critique of
Pure Reason* or the *Critique of Practical Reason*. Nor should it be too difficult to see from this why the major thrust of Hegel's criticism of Kant
is focused on the latter's philosophy of religion. From the beginning, as
we have seen, Hegel had recognized with Kant that religion must in
some sense be the work of reason. But, as he matures, as Emil Fackenheim has pointed out, Hegel takes more and more into account the
historical religious realities which Kant had not.[28] It is not merely religious reason (or rational religion) with which Hegel is concerned; it is
the God of religion—of concrete religion, and particularly of Christianity—who must be shown to be the same God that philosophy thinks.
A God in whom faith believes but whom thought does not think is
an unknown God, adequate to neither religion nor philosophy.[29]
Hegel had developed Kantian reason to the point where its function
was no longer that of determining regulative principles for the use
of understanding, but where it was genuinely *capax Dei*, an infinite
capacity for an infinite object. In so doing Hegel compels philosophical thought to come to grips with the God he sees revealed in Jesus
Christ.[30] Thus, in Fackenheim's words:

> The Hegelian philosophy radicalizes not only the Kantian autonomous reason.
> It radicalizes, as well, the Kantian and post-Kantian search for an existential
> matrix of philosophical thought. And in this process it is driven into a unique
> philosophical confrontation with historical Christianity.[31]

INFINITE REASON

This brings us back to the Hegelian notion of a criticism which is not the refutation of a philosophical position but the drawing out of the implications which that philosophical position left undeveloped. It was the "confrontation with historical Christianity" which permitted Hegel to see the non-rationality of a merely finite reason which could come to terms only with a finite religious response to God and not with the infinite God to whom religion responds. From the *Logic* on, Hegel's criticism becomes at once more pointed and more explicitly directed against Kant. If Kantian reason can examine understanding and determine regulative principles for its use, then reason must transcend understanding. By the same token, however, if reason can examine reason it must also transcend reason, which is to say it must transcend the merely finite reason which transcends mere understanding.

> Even so, Hegel radicalizes the Kantian reason. This latter remains finite and human; for it is empty self-activity except when united with a sensuousness which, by itself, is blind. In contrast, the Hegelian *Logic* has "raised" rationality to infinity.[32]

In the Preface to the first edition of the *Logic* Hegel agrees with Kant that it is impossible for the human mind not to be metaphysical. The conclusion he draws from this, however, is neither that the human mind is bound to deceive itself nor that it must confine its metaphysical investigations to those principles within itself which can be known without any appeal to experience. Rather, the conclusion is that a genuine science of metaphysics must be possible and that what reason finds to be absolutely necessary must necessarily be. Thus, if in investigating being reason ultimately discovers that being must be infinite, then being is infinite. The whole of the *Logic*, then, becomes an extended proof that being is infinite—or that infinite being is— and, correlative to this, that the reason which knows infinite being is itself infinite. This does not mean that any individual thing which is is infinite or that any individual human reason is infinite; but it does mean that only if infinite being is can finite being make sense at all, only if reason is infinite can finite reason make sense. That the term "infinite" is negative in form is clear enough; the point is, however, that the negation of the finite is the determination whereby the finite is what it is—it negates what is negative in the finite.[33] This sort of infinity could, of course, be quite empty, as it is in Kant's "category of the infinite,"[34] and empty it will continue to be so long as we remain, with Kant, on the level of understanding, which keeps infinite and finite apart, finding no means of going from one to the other.[35] The only infinite this sort of thinking permits is a kind of infinite progress—in time or space—a calculus which always approaches an affirmative infinite, but never arrives.[36]

What Hegel is looking for is an infinite which makes sense, and he agrees that Kantian reason will never attain to it—only in a union of the finite and the infinite will it make sense,[37] and this union will never be achieved if the point of departure is simply the finite which is to be overcome by passing beyond it.[38] What is needed, then, is not a passage from the finite to the infinite but a recognition that in the finite itself there is an infinite dimension, without which the finite does not make sense as finite.[39] Hegel states the same thought pithily in his earlier *Jenenser Logik*: "This alone is the true nature of the finite, to be infinite, to supersede itself in its being."[40] The finite is real enough, and it is really finite—no human being who experiences himself could say otherwise—but it is real only as a "moment" of the infinite.[41] Admittedly, of this, understanding, as the faculty of abstract conceptualization, can make no sense,[42] but this is no reason to reject the dialectical unity of finite and infinite; it is reason to go beyond the abstractness of understanding to the concreteness of reason.[43] What Kant had done, according to Hegel, was to see a contradiction in this (cf. the "antinomies of pure reason") and then, out of unwarranted "tenderness" in regard to reality, to blame the contradiction on the finitude of reason.[44]

INFINITY OF CONCEPT

In the second volume of the *Logic*, in the introduction to what he calls "subjective logic," Hegel returns to the polemic against Kant. Recognizing that all he has said in the first two books of the *Logic* regarding "Being" and "Essence" is not customarily considered to be logic, Hegel now turns to an analysis of the subjective function of thinking.[45] His task is to show that nothing he has said previously, particularly about the infinity of being, will make sense unless he makes clear that all he has said about "objective reality" is contained in the "concept," the function of subjective reason. What he will attempt to do will be to show that if logic has truth as its goal, it cannot stop short of an affirmation of infinite being, which is God.[46] It is a difficult task, and it is intended to meet Kant head-on. Kant will grant, particularly in his analysis of the traditional proofs for the existence of God, that human reason is inevitably led to think of an "unconditioned," "infinite" being. What he will not admit is that the necessity of thinking that way is any justification for affirming the being of the infinite. What Kant, in effect, is saying is that any attempt to *prove* that God exists is ultimately reducible to the "ontological argument," which involves an illegitimate leap from the order of concept to the order of being. What Hegel will attempt to show is that the passage from concept to being is neither illegitimate nor a "leap," precisely because the truth of being is to be in the concept.[47]

Thus, the movement which Hegel describes in the *Logic* is not one from concept to being, but rather from being to concept as that in which being realizes itself fully as being—as being all that being truly is, i.e., infinite being. In the "Doctrine of Being" (Book I) being is simply posited, and its objective determinations are manifested. In the "Doctrine of Essence" (Book II) what being essentially is is shown to be contained only in reflection. In the "Doctrine of Concept" (Book III) Hegel will attempt to show that "Being" and "Essence" are dialectical "moments" in the becoming of concept, which is thus their "foundation and truth," "as the identity into which they have been resolved and retained."[48] The multiplicity of relationships which being manifests, and apart from which being simply is not known, have been shown to be relationships of causality and interaction, the determinations of "substance." Now it will be shown that "the dialectical *movement* of *substance* traced through causality and interaction is, therefore, the immediate *genesis* of the *concept*, whereby its *coming-to-be* is presented."[49] Just as being, then, had been shown to make sense only in the process of becoming, and essence had been shown to make sense only in the process of reflection, so both will be shown to make sense only in the process of thinking which is the activity of subject—not merely of substance[50]—and this activity is not determined by anything outside subject; it is self-determining, i.e., free.[51] What is being said here is that the determinations of reality are to be found nowhere but in the activity which is concept, and that substantial reality manifests itself as what it really is rational in concept, i.e., it necessarily is what it is truly thought to be.[52]

Hegel recognizes, of course, that the concept has had hard sledding in his day;[53] it has been identified with the empty activity of the individual I,[54] and has thus been characterized as what such a subject *does* or *has*.[55] Kant had the merit of seeing through this and of recognizing that the unity which constitutes the essence of the concept is "the *originally-synthetic* unity of *apperception*, as unity of the *I-think*, or of self-consciousness."[56] In conceiving an object, Kant saw, the subject makes the object its own in such a way that to know the object is to know its own concept, its own self.[57] Kant's problem, however, was that he recognized only a purely formal concept, a sort of intellectual form unifying a manifold of sense and universalizing it[58] but of itself empty of content, containing no reality.[59] It is obvious that from this point of view "no amount of effort can hammer reality" out of the concept.[60] What Kant has failed to see, thinks Hegel, is that the concept is not something which the subject forms for itself; rather, as self-developing the concept "gives itself its own reality."[61] Granted that without intuition there will be no concept, intuition is not to be separated from concept as a condition of the latter; it is part of the continuous process which is the coming-to-be of the concept.[62] Without the manifold of intuition the concept-process will not get started, it is true, but this does not mean that the concept is so enduringly conditioned by sense that it never gets beyond it. "Synthesis" should not mean the mere putting-together of disparate elements; it is the concept's superseding of the merely intuitive character of its content.[63] What Kant has done, then, is to substitute the formal character of the concepts of understanding for the concrete character of concepts of reason.[64] Even though Kant sees the object of thought as the unification of the manifold of intuition in the unity of self-consciousness—hence the objectivity of thought in the identity of concept and reality—he still sees this identity as merely phenomenal, because the content of the concept never ceases to be merely the manifold of intuition.[65] The point which Hegel will make here is that the concept is no more separated from reality than is sense intuition, that it is, therefore, justified in its self-determination as real:

> On this point it has been recalled that this manifold, to the extent that it belongs to intuition in opposition to the concept, has been superseded precisely in the concept, and the object through the concept has been brought back to its non-contingent essentiality. This latter enters the appearance, and for this very reason the appearance is not simply essenceless but it is a manifestation of essence. The thoroughly liberated manifestation of the same, however, is the concept.[66]

The concept is not dependent on reality outside itself, and it is no less real for all that. Thus, the whole point of the third book of the *Logic* is to show "how it [the concept] constructs in itself and from itself the reality which has disappeared in it."[67] This reality which the concept produces is true reality.[68]

To get back to Kant, Hegel feels that he has simply missed the boat in failing to see the concept as concrete (in which thought and reality "grow together"—*concrescunt*):

> *Deducing* [*die Herleitung*] the real out of it [the concept]—if one wants to call it deducing—consists first of all essentially in this: the concept in its formal abstraction shows itself to be incomplete, and through the dialectic grounded in itself passes over to reality in such a way that it produces this reality from itself and that it does not fall back again to an already given reality over against itself and take refuge in something which had shown itself to be the inessential in the appearance, because, having looked around for something better, it found nothing of the sort.[69]

As Hegel sees it, then, the rational knowledge of which Kant speaks is simply not rational, precisely because to exclude reality from it is to exclude rationality.[70] It is not enough that reason should be autonomous in its formal function of unifying the concepts of understanding, which depend for their content on the manifold of sense; reason must be autonomous in regard to the content which it justifiably gives to itself. What is more, says Hegel, in his notion of "the *a priori* synthesis of the concept" Kant has a principle which should have enabled him to bridge the gap between thought and reality, "but sensible matter, the manifold of intuition, was for him too powerful to permit him to get away from it to a consideration of the concept and the categories *in and for themselves* and to a speculative philosophizing."[71] Thus, Kant, because he sees the categories as merely subjective forms of self-consciousness, explains them as finite determinations incapable of containing true reality.[72]

GOD AS OBJECT OF REASON

In all this, of course, one might see only a direct critique of Kant's epistemology or of his failure to find room for a genuine metaphysics, not a critique of his theological (or anti-theological) argumentation. If we recall, however, that even Kant refers to God as the *ens realissimum*, the reality of all realities, it is not difficult to see that the most significant "reality" he withdraws from man's rational grasp is God.[73] What is more, after the *Logic*, Hegel's critique, particularly in the third volume of the *History of Philosophy*, where it becomes most caustic, will concentrate on Kant's inability to see any rational validity in proofs for the existence of God. Kant had said quite clearly with regard to himself: "I had to suspend [*aufheben*] *knowledge* in order to make room for *faith*."[74] Hegel is convinced, not only that this separation of knowledge and faith is illegitimate, but also that the God in whom religious consciousness *believes* is identical with the God whom philosophical consciousness *knows*. Much of his Introduction to the *Lectures on the History of Philosophy* is devoted to an exposition of this identity of content in religion and philosophy.[75] Although there is nothing in this Introduction which Hegel has not said before, here it becomes abundantly clear that, in the words of Wilhelm Dilthey, Hegel's "theological work as a whole can be adequately summed up as a confrontation with [*Auseinandersetzung mit*] Kant's *Religion Within the Bounds of Reason Alone*."[76] Like Kant, Hegel had as his goal a religion which would make rational sense,[77] but he would not pay the price of impoverishing that rational sense by confining it to finite reason. The reason of which he speaks is but the abstract expression of Spirit; "Spirit and reason are the same. We do, it is true, represent reason to ourselves abstractly; but active, knowing reason is spirit."[78] Spirit, however, is truly spirit only when it knows God (the summit of reality), and in knowing God it is infinitized.[79] Thus, any talk about not *knowing* God sets an unwarranted limit to spirit.[80]

When, then, in the third volume of the *Lectures on the History of Philosophy*, Hegel comes to treat of Kant's philosophy he focuses on the limited character of the reason Kant presents, on its inadequacy precisely as reason, if it cannot ascend to a genuine knowledge of God by breaking the bonds of individual subjectivity.[81] Thus, having put an end to the "dogmatism" of a causal metaphysics Kantian philosophy falls back into a "subjective dogmatism," which cannot get beyond the finite determinations of understanding.[82] Hegel interprets understanding here, in Kant's own words, as "the faculty of thinking the object of sensible intuition."[83] A reason which does not get beyond understanding, says Hegel, is no reason at all; it is no more than "individual self-consciousness,"[84] and even though Kant sees reason as the faculty of the unconditioned, the infinite, he is unwilling to let the infinite be a real *content* of reason.[85] Spirit, however, is not to be identified with a simple subjective reason; it is the totality of concrete reason.

It is not surprising, then, that at this point Hegel turns to a critique of Kant's treatment of "proofs" of the existence of God,[86] something which he will do in much more detail later in his *Lectures on the Proofs for the Existence of God*. Kant agrees that God is an "ideal" corresponding to the Wolffian definition of "the most real Being." The question, however, is whether reason can justifiably ascribe reality to this ideal. This Kant denies. The basis of this denial is the contention that any attempt to ascribe reality to this ideal (to "prove" it) will involve an illegitimate passage from concept to reality, since existence is not a conceptual content at all and cannot, therefore, be derived from the concept.[87] This, as Hegel sees it, is but another way of saying that the concept is finite and must remain so.[88] It is here that Hegel becomes sarcastic regarding Kant's example of the "hundred possible Thalers." That no amount of *thinking* is going to make them real he agrees; if one wants to have them one must stop thinking and get to work! The trouble is, says Hegel, that Kant has confused "representing" (*vorstellen*) and "thinking" (*denken*). Real thinking does not merely represent its object—as represented, the object is precisely not real—it grasps (*begreifen*) it in its reality, and "concept" (*Begriff*) is this grasping.[89] It is not, then, a question of ascribing a non-conceptual content to the concept; the real *is* the content of the concept. "Thinking, concept is necessarily this; not to remain subjective but rather [*bass*] to supersede this subjective and to show itself as objective."[90] What Kant has done is to reduce reason to being "no more than the formal unity for the methodical systematization of understanding's cognition."[91] When subject and object, thought and reality, are separated in this way they cannot be brought together again.[92]

"PROVING" GOD'S EXISTENCE

If all we had were Hegel's critique of Kant from the *Lectures on the History of Philosophy* we should know that Hegel disagrees with Kant and that he disagrees with him for not doing what, as he told us in the Introduction, it is philosophy's task to do. We should not know what is to be done or why Kant can be criticized for not having done it. Since the main thrust of this critique is directed against Kant's philosophy of religion—or lack thereof, i.e., the failure of genuine reason to function religiously—we might expect to see it crop up again in Hegel's *Lectures on the Philosophy of Religion*. Surprisingly enough, in these *Lectures* he leaves Kant very much alone. He does, however, return to the attack in his independent *Lectures on the Proofs for the Existence of God*[93] and in a separate lecture, usually included with these *Lectures*,[94] "On Kant's Critique of the Cosmological Proof."

In introducing this course of lectures Hegel makes a remark which is particularly interesting in the context of what we are examining in this paper. Since he is also lecturing on logic, he says, he has chosen to give another series of lectures on a topic "related [to logic] and constituting a sort of supplement to the latter, not from the point of view of content but from that of form, since the topic is simply a specialized form of the fundamental determinations of logic."[95] Clearly, then, Hegel still (in 1829) looks upon the question of God's existence as integral to the logical problematic. An investigation of knowing cannot sidestep the issue of what knowing knows, and in Hegel's view knowing knows nothing if it does not know God. Faith and reason, then, are not separate operations, in the sense that faith could deliver an object which reason could not; they are united in such a way that neither can be without the other—even though pure (independent) thought is a development out of the dependent stage of belief.[96] It is by separating the two that contemporaries think they can investigate rationally the subjective function of religion, while leaving God, who is religion's object, entirely outside rational investigation—a philosophy of religion is permitted but not a theology. The result is that "we hear much, endlessly much—or rather, little, endlessly repeated—spoken of religion, the less we hear of God. This perennial explication regarding religion, . . . combined with an insignificant or even suppressed explication regarding God, is a unique manifestation of the intellectual culture of the time."[97] Equivalently this is saying, Hegel remarks, that divine revelation does not reveal God, since God is not a content with which the mind can cope.[98] In this context it is interesting to note that throughout these *Lectures* Hegel speaks of "the ascent of thinking spirit to God," i.e., when philosophy thinks what religion represents. Since it is known that Hegel was familiar with St. Anselm, one is tempted to ask whether he is applying to *philosophy* Anselm's famed definition of *prayer*: *ascensio mentis in Deum.*

In any event, we are back with the problem with which we are already familiar, the finitude of human spirit over against the infinity of God. If we are not to say that the human spirit cannot grasp God at all, and this Hegel will not permit, are we to make this grasp possible by finitizing the infinite or by infinitizing the finite?[99] If nothing else, putting the question this way makes "Religion" as a dialectical moment in the movement of the *Phenomenology of Spirit* more intelligible. Because the infinite object has been presented to man in religion, the human spirit must rise to infinity if it is to be adequate to its object—it cannot simply leave that object unthought. What stands in the way of admitting that human thinking can know God is, first of all, the assumption that the passage from finite thinking to an infinite object is a "leap";[100] secondly, the presupposition that the finitude of human spirit is "absolute," i.e., contained within itself,[101] sufficient to itself as finite; and thirdly, a refusal to see that the activity of the infinite in the finite does not cease to be an activity of the finite.[102] What needs to be grasped is that the relation of God to man, unlike the relation of objects in the world to subjects in the world, is the relation of spirit to spirit.

That man knows of God is, on the basis of the essential community [of God and man in spirit] a communal knowing—i.e., man knows of God

only to the extent that in man God knows of himself; this knowing is
God's consciousness of himself, and at the same time it is God's knowledge
of man, and this knowledge of man by God is man's knowledge of God.[103]

Strong words, to be sure, and they have led some to conclude that
in knowing God either man is no longer man or he no longer really
knows, since it is God who is doing the knowing.[104] It would seem
preferable to see in what Hegel is saying an echo of what Meister
Eckart and other mystics said when they spoke of a union with God
which "divinizes" man. Hegel's philosophical knowing, certainly,
is more analogous to the *ascensio mentis in Deum* of the mystics than
it is to the critical thinking of Kant. Is it too much to say that philosophical thinking itself can see more than its finite self in its thinking
of God? Kant, it is true, will see a contradiction in this unity of the
finite and infinite, and, as he does always when the mind gets into
contradiction, he will see the contradiction in reason, not in reality.
Hegel, too, sees contradiction, as he does wherever he sees life, but
he feels that both reality and reason are equal to the contradiction,
especially if that is the only way that life (here life of the spirit) avoids
stagnation. In his lecture "On Kant's Critique of the Cosmological
Proof" he tells us:

> In fact, however, reason can decidedly put up with contradiction—and,
> of course, also resolve it—and things at least know also how to put up
> with it, or rather they are simply existing contradiction, whether it be that
> Kantian schema of the thing-in-itself or empirical things—and only to the
> extent that they are rational do they also at the same time resolve the
> contradiction in themselves.[105]

The unity of finite and infinite does not present an irresolvable contradiction; it is a condition for the very being of being. If we look back
at the overall movement of the *Logic* we find that it begins with a
being which is infinitely empty—and therefore in no way different
from nothing—and ends with a being which is infinitely full,
and that the path from the one to the other has been marked by
a progressive negation of the limitations of abstraction. In a
very important sense it is the same being which is infinitely empty
and infinitely full, the same being which is finite and infinite. Hegel's
point is that if we begin at all, we must continue, and the movement
from the finite is a continuous movement. The finite makes sense not

in itself but in being integral to the movement toward the infinite. The question, then, is not so much whether reason can know that the infinite really is; rather it is whether reason must know that being is infinite.[106] Being must be known as both finite and infinite, or not known at all. "Being is to be characterized not only as finite but also as infinite."[107] It is for this reason that Heidegger characterizes Hegel's metaphysics as essentially "ontotheological"; the being without which no being makes sense is the highest being, or God.[108] To return to Hegel's own words: he is convinced that the mistake which has been made is to look upon the finite as the originally affirmative which is negated in the infinite. Rather the infinite is affirmative; it is negated in the finite, and reaffirmed in the negation of limitation. "The essential point in this mediation however is that the being of the finite is not the affirmative, but rather that it is the self-superseding of the finite whereby the infinite is posited and mediated."[109] There has been no leap from the finite to the infinite; the very positing of the finite as real entails the positing of the infinite as real. Moreover, the spirit which posits both finite and infinite is itself both finite and infinite; its movement and the movement of being are not to be separated.[110] Kant was certainly not wrong in criticizing the form in which proofs for the existence of God had been presented; what he failed to do, however, was to see the profounder foundation upon which they rested.[111] The exposition of this profounder foundation, Hegel is convinced, is his own *Logic*. There we are told there is no being which does not imply the infinity of being, no thought which does not imply the infinity of thought; and the infinite, God, is the perfect identity of thought and being.[112]

NOTES

1. Walter Bröcker, in Preface to Ingtraud Görland, *Die Kantkritik des jungen Hegels* (Frankfurt: Klostermann, 1966), p. v.
2. *Wissenschaft der Logik*, ed. Georg Lasson (Leipzig: Meiner, 1932), I, 230.
3. *Vorlesungen über die Geschichte der Philosophie*, ed. Hermann Glockner (Stuttgart: Frommann, 1928), III, 558.
4. *Ibid.*, p. 559.
5. *Ibid.*, p. 610.

6. *Ibid.*, p. 587.

7. *Logik*, I, 226-27.

8. *Geschichte*, III, 555. Cf. *Phänomenologie des Geistes*, ed. Johannes Hoffmeister (6th ed.; Hamburg: Meiner, 1952), Einleitung.

9. *Ibid.*, p. 554.

10. *Ibid.*, p. 585.

11. *Ibid.*, pp. 585-86.

12. *Logik*, II, 213-34.

13. See *ibid.*, pp. 216-18.

14. *Geschichte*, III, 552.

15. (Frankfurt: Minerva, 1966).

16. "Differenz des Fichteschen und Schellingschen Systems der Philosophie," *Aufsätze aus dem kritischen Journal der Philosophie*, ed. Hermann Glockner (3rd ed.; Stuttgart: Frommann, 1958) I, 58-59.

17. *Glauben und Wissen*, ed. George Lasson (Hamburg: Himmelheber, 1962), p. 1.

18. *Ibid.*, p. 2.

19. *Ibid.*

20. *Ibid.*, pp. 10-11.

21. *Ibid.*, p. 14.

22. *Ibid.*, p. 23.

23. *Ibid.*, p. 25.

24. *Ibid.*, pp. 37-38.

25. *Phänomenologie*, p. 176.

26. *Einleitung in die Geschichte der Philosophie* (3rd ed.; Hamburg: Meiner, 1959), p. 123. There is an English translation of the *Einleitung* in the present writer's *Hegel's Idea of Philosophy* (New York: Fordham University Press, 1971).

27. This argumentation can be found developed in greater detail in an article by the present writer, "The Phenomenon of Reason," in Carl G. Hempel, et al., *The Isenberg Memorial Lecture Series 1965-66* (East Lansing: Michigan State University Press, 1969), pp. 163-92.

28. Emil Fackenheim, *The Religious Dimension in Hegel's Thought* (Bloomington: Indiana University Press, 1967), p. 53.

29. Cf. Hegel's criticism of the Enlightenment, *Phänomenologie*, pp. 187-91.

30. See Fackenheim, *op. cit.*, p. 231.

31. *Ibid.*, p. 228 (italics in the original).

32. *Ibid.*, p. 226.

33. *Logik*, I, 127.

34. *Ibid.*, p. 128.

35. *Ibid.*

36. See *ibid.*, p. 131.

37. *Ibid.*, p. 132.

38. *Ibid.*, p. 136.

39. *Ibid.*, pp. 144-45.

40. *Jenenser Logik Metaphysik und Naturphilosophie*, ed. Georg Lasson (Hamburg: Meiner, 1967), p. 31.

41. *Logik*, I, 139.

42. *Ibid.*, pp. 137-38.

43. *Ibid.*, pp. 139-40.

44. *Ibid.*, p. 136.

45. *Logik*, II, 211.

46. *Ibid.*, p. 212.

47. For a detailed explanation and documentation of this statement, see the present writer's article "Hegel on Proofs for God's Existence," *Kantstudien*, 55 (1964), 443-65.

48. *Logik*, II, 213.

49. *Ibid.*, p. 214.

50. *Ibid.*, pp. 216-18.

51. *Ibid.*, p. 214.

52. See *ibid.*, p. 216.

53. *Ibid.*, p. 220.

54. *Ibid.*, pp. 220-21.

55. *Ibid.*

56. *Ibid.*, p. 221.

57. *Ibid.*, p. 222.

58. *Ibid.*, p. 224.

59. *Ibid.*, p. 225.

60. *Ibid.*, p. 223.

61. *Ibid.*, p. 225.

62. *Ibid.*, p. 226. The whole of the *Phänomenologie* is a detailed description of this development.

63. *Ibid.*, p. 227.

64. *Ibid.*, pp. 227-28.

65. *Ibid.*, pp. 228-29.

66. *Ibid.*, p. 229. To say that the concept is "thoroughly liberated" is to say that in conceiving (*begreifen*) reason is determined by no alien source.

67. *Ibid.*

68. *Ibid.*, p. 230.

69. *Ibid.*

70. *Ibid.*, pp. 231-32.

71. *Ibid.*, p. 233.

72. *Ibid.*, p. 234.

73. *Logik*, I, 99; II, 61.

74. *Kritik der reinen Vernunft*, Preface, B xxx.

75. See Quentin Lauer, s.j., "Hegel on the Identity of Content in Religion and Philosophy," *Hegel and the Philosophy of Religion*, ed. Darrell Christensen (The Hague: Nijhoff, 1970), pp. 261-78.

76. *Werke*, IV, 61, quoted by H. S. Harris, "The Young Hegel and the Postulates of Practical Reason," *Hegel and the Philosophy of Religion*, p. 61.

77. Lauer, "Hegel on the Identity of Content," p. 262.
78. *Einleitung in die Geschichte der Philosophie*, p. 175.
79. *Ibid.*, p. 178.
80. *Ibid.*, p. 179.
81. *Vorlesungen über die Geschichte der Philosophie*, III, 554.
82. *Ibid.*
83. *Ibid.*, p. 565 (the reference is to *Kritik der reinen Vernunft*, A 51).
84. *Ibid.*, p. 571.
85. *Ibid.*, p. 574.
86. See *ibid.*, pp. 575; 578-79.
87. *Ibid.*, pp. 583-84.
88. *Ibid.*, p. 584.
89. *Ibid.*, p. 585.
90. *Ibid.*
91. *Ibid.*, p. 586.
92. *Ibid.*, p. 587.
93. *Vorlesungen über die Beweise vom Dasein Gottes*, ed. Georg Lasson (Hamburg: Himmelheber, 1966). In a publisher's note to this latest edition, it is remarked that, although earlier editions published these lectures as an appendix to the *Lectures on the Philosophy of Religion*, more recent scholarship has shown that they not only constituted an independent series of lectures (delivered in 1829) but also treated the topic in a manner quite independent of that of the *Lectures on the Philosophy of Religion*. Fackenheim (*op. cit.*, note 31 to p. 175) refers to these *Lectures* as "vitally important and much-neglected."
94. For a reason which the editor can throw no light on, this lecture, which is clearly independent, was in the earlier editions an "insert" between lectures ten and eleven. It is no longer possible to date it.
95. *Vorlesungen über die Beweise*, p. 1 (First Lecture).
96. *Ibid.*, pp. 8-9.
97. *Ibid.*, p. 46 (Fifth Lecture).
98. *Ibid.*, p. 48.
99. See *ibid.*, p. 110 (Fourteenth Lecture).
100. *Ibid.*, pp. 111-12.
101. *Ibid.*, pp. 112-13.
102. *Ibid.*, p. 113.
103. *Ibid.*, p. 117.
104. See the article by Joseph Donceel, s.j., in the present volume (Chapter 8, "Can We Still Make a Case in Reason for the Existence of God?").
105. *Vorlesungen über die Beweise*, p. 148.
106. *Ibid.*, pp. 149-51.
107. *Ibid.*, p. 152.
108. See Martin Heidegger, *Identity and Difference*, trans. Joan Stambaugh (New York: Harper & Row, 1969), pp. 59, 70-71.

109. *Vorlesungen über die Beweise*, p. 152.
110. See *ibid.*, pp. 153-54.
111. *Ibid.*, p. 154.
112. *Jenenser Logik*, p. 159. It may seem strange that throughout this paper no reference has been made to the *Enzyklopädie der philosophischen Wissenschaften*. Although it is true that the *Enzyklopädie* is a rich source for the kind of thinking we have been describing here, containing abundant passages which would be very much to the point, we have omitted references to it since it is primarily a summary of Hegel's abiding conviction of the truth of what he has said elsewhere.

6

Metaphysics as Mystery:
From Kant to Marcel

KENNETH T. GALLAGHER

KANT'S REJECTION OF THE POSSIBILITY of metaphysical knowledge is based upon his distinction between phenomena and noumena, and his restriction of knowledge to the phenomenal realm. Along with all other pretensions of metaphysics, the claim to have a philosophical knowledge of the existence and nature of God is thereby eliminated. Although Kant goes to considerable length to show in particular the impossibility of all "proofs" for God's existence, the outcome is foreseeable as soon as his basic position is grasped. Since God is not a phenomenal object, and since only phenomenal objects can be, properly speaking, known, then no genuine knowledge of God is possible.

Any rebuttal of this position in behalf of the metaphysician—and such is what the present paper will attempt—must obviously consider further the ground upon which Kant's view rests. Why does Kant restrict knowledge to phenomena? From the very first paragraph of the *Critique of Pure Reason*, his orientation is clear. He sets up an immediate correlation among three terms: knowledge, experience, object. All knowledge begins with experience—such is his fundamental concession to the camp of the realists. Yet, contrary to what many might believe, this invocation of experience cannot be decisive since it is in no way self-explanatory what "experience" signifies. It is actually Kant's way of conceiving experience which is crucial for his conclusions. Experience is said to be the name for that "knowledge of objects" which the understanding effects upon the basis of the raw material of sense impressions.[1]

What, however, is an object? Although the first paragraph by no means gives Kant's full mind on this, it does manifest some indispensable initial assumptions. The conception of an object is the conception of a unity correlative to the manifold of sense data which form one side of what Kant calls "experience." An object is a thing which "affects our senses," in the language of common sense (and in Kant's own language in this first paragraph). From the start he is willing to grant the understanding a role in constituting what he means by an object since an object is not the manifold of sensation as such, but the unity apprehended through the understanding, which "combines" this manifold and so "works up" the representation of an object. From the beginning, then, we are prepared for the famous later aphorism, "intuition without concepts is blind." Perception alone does not give objects—and hence, of course, perception alone does not constitute experience, nor, correspondingly, does it amount to knowledge.

At this stage of the *Critique*, Kant is still speaking the realistic language of common sense, and he is in fact taking his stand within what Husserl later called the "natural world-view." To "know" is to be aware of "objects" which affect me and so give rise to "experience." By an assumption which is so basic that it does not even get stated, these objects are understood to be independent of the subject which is aware of them. Not only is an object a unity corresponding to the affection of my senses, but it goes without saying that it is something public and available for every senser. If it were not, if it had no status independent of my sensoria, then we would be speaking of something subjective, not objective. To be assured that knowledge is actually being achieved, then, is to be assured that my understanding's grasp of the unity affecting my senses is not private or peculiar to me, but duplicates what would be the understanding of any knower in encounter with these sense data.

Yet how do I know that my act of consciousness actually bears on such a supra-individual object? When is such an object indubitably present to consciousness? Kant's well-known reply is that it is present to any consciousness in which the factors of universality and necessity are constituents. For to ask how I can know that my synthesis of sensations bears necessarily upon an object is, from the transcendental viewpoint, simply to ask which syntheses of sensations are necessary syntheses. The element of necessity, Kant decides, can never be sought in empirical content, which is always merely factual and contingent, but must be sought in the *a priori* factors of sense and understanding.[2] Whatever is indispensably presupposed on the side of sense and whatever is indispensably presupposed on the side of understanding, if one is to speak about an "object" at all, apply *necessarily* to an object. Space and time, on the one hand, and the twelve categories, on the other, are the constituents which together enter into the necessary synthesis which is involved even in speaking about objects. Knowledge, therefore (always conceived as knowledge of objects), is defined and delimited by this necessary synthesis.

With this move, Kant thinks he has dealt the death-blow to Hume's skepticism, especially to his skeptical critique of the notion of "cause." For, on Kant's premiss, Hume's question cannot really be raised. Hume is asking: how do I know that my idea of cause is really a source of objective knowledge, and not just a psychological and merely subjective habit of thought? But for me even to raise the question of the objective value of any component of knowledge, I must have the subject - object distinction already present to consciousness. The real question is: how do I come to inhabit this distinction, or how is "object-consciousness" possible? The skeptical question collapses because its being raised presupposes that it has already been answered. Whatever is necessarily involved in the distinction between subject and object is already validated in any speech about objects. Since the idea of cause is one of the twelve categories, it already has a hand in constituting all possible reference to an object (including, of course, all questions raised in respect to objectivity). It is nonsense to ask whether the category of cause applies to objects since it is only through the aid of this category that we know what we *mean* by an object.

Although Kant regarded his approach as telling decisively against Humean skepticism, it had an equally devastating effect upon the claims of the metaphysician. The metaphysician claims to speak about what transcends experience, but if Kant is right, all knowledge (or, in contemporary terms, all genuine assertion) is correlative to experience, since it is correlative to objects. An object, however, is not given to the understanding alone. Our consciousness has a finite structure, and therefore inevitably contains a *receptive* aspect: not being *in toto* creative of its object, it must wait upon a given.[3] Through its formal categorial structure it then *thinks* this given in determinate modes of unity, and this synthesis of form and content is what constitutes experience of objects. The whole role of the categories, conversely, is in their unification of this intuitive sense given, and apart from this they are empty—they do not present us with an object. The metaphysician mistakenly attempts to use the categories, specifically the category of cause, to vault beyond experience. He tries to reach God as the "first cause" of the world, forgetting that the notion of cause is exhausted by its role as synthesizer of the sensory manifold. Apart from this role, it cannot lead to knowledge since it cannot of itself present us with an object. A species of empty "thinking" may go on when we soar beyond experience, but this is to be distinguished from genuine "knowledge" which always bears on an "object" and therefore always requires a content which concepts alone do not supply.[4] In using the categories in a transcendent direction, we do not really *know* anything; we may "make as if" to know, but our thought remains poised in vacuity. Philosophical theology vainly attempts to beat its wings in this void.

Such, in brief, is Kant's case against metaphysics. Now, the obvious direction in which an attempt at rebuttal suggests itself, and one which most traditional metaphysicians have taken, is in a contesting of the conclusiveness of his notion of cause. Properly understood, it may be argued, the notion of cause does not permit itself to be dismissed as Kant tried to dismiss it. This contention, in turn, must be understood against the background of an estimation of an even more fundamental failure on Kant's part, the failure to grasp the unconditional value of the concept of *being*. For, whatever merit Kant's distinction between noumenon and phenomenon may otherwise have, it cannot apply to the sort of knowledge which is made possible through our ability to apprehend the datum of being. The meaning given therein is absolute, all-inclusive, and extends to both sides of the phenomenon -

noumenon distinction, even granting that this makes sense up to a point. Through the concept of being, our thought embraces, at one blow, every individual entity, every difference between such entities, all that is past, present, future, or merely possible. Whatever else we may be able to say about such things, we know at least that the notion of being applies to them. This holds, too, for Kant's "noumenon." Let there be something beyond experience altogether, incapable of presentation in the phenomenal world, transcendent in principle to the structure of both our understanding and sense, an unknown "x" forever inaccessible to our consciousness. Still, we know something about such an inaccessible reality—indeed, we have already asserted it; if it *is* at all, it is included within the intelligibility included within the concept of being. This notion represents the immovable center around which all thought turns, at which all relativizing ceases, because it is through it that all relativization is recognized. If there is any meaning, then, which is made possible through the concept of being itself, this meaning we know as unconditional and absolute truth, and no distinction between phenomenon and noumenon could possibly count against it; if the noumenon *is*, then it is held fast in the truth we grasp in grasping being.

Through this last realization, the metaphysician then passes judgment on the inadequacy of Kant's doctrine of cause. For among the knowledge made possible through the concept of being is the principle of causality. Far from the idea of "cause" being consumed in its role in the phenomenal realm, its role as an organizer of phenomena is a consequence of an absolute meaning which not only transcends phenomena, but no doubt makes the recognition of their phenomenal status possible. The authentic metaphysical idea of cause is founded upon the application of the notion of being to the order of change. A changing being proclaims its contingency in existence and hence its dependence. One somewhat simplified way of bringing this out is as follows. A being which changes, whether fundamentally or superficially, is a being which begins-to-be. As beginning-to-be, it is not intelligible in and through itself. In knowing something as beginning-to-be, we know it under a double aspect: it *is*, and it *was not*. Thus in apprehending this thing as beginning, we are already referred beyond it, and are moved to inquire into the ground of its beginning; for its mode of being as *begun* does not explain its *begin-*

ning. This extrinsic ground for a beginning-to-be is what the meta-physician means by a cause. This meaning has nothing directly to do with an antecedent in time or rules for the regular occurrence of events (which are sought in *consequence* of the principle of causality and do not comprise its essence), but is based solely on the apprehension of something which "begins" as "being."

It is not that long a step from here to the metaphysical argument for the existence of God, although no attempt will be made to trace this in detail. The metaphysician soon sees not just individual in-stances, but the whole order of beginning-to-be as not intelligible in itself, as providing not a terminus in which thought can rest, but a reference to a ground beyond such beginnings. He does not, incidentally, necessarily say that this whole order itself began-to-be (that, in familiar terms, the world must have had a beginning), but only that an order in which beginning-to-be is implicated is not intelligible in itself. We may pass over any consideration of the validity of this argument since the concern here is with the basis of the argu-ment, rather than with its precise form. The point to be seen is that the metaphysician considers his line of reasoning safe from Kant's objections since it starts out from a point prior to Kant's.

Kant's reply to the procedure of the metaphysician would not be hard to guess. In his eyes, the notion of being would be first of all suspect as lacking *content*. What is to prevent us from regarding it as an empty form, a thought-category with whose aid we organize our experience most economically, and place it, as it were, at our disposal, but whose entire role is just that—to organize experience? In itself, "being" is just an empty, formal concept, and cannot be said to present any *evidence* of which thought can make privileged use. It may be granted a certain priority among the categories, perhaps as pervading them all, but its *content* must be filled in from the receptive side of consciousness, from sense intuition. Apart from this filling in, the notion of being is incapable of presenting us with an object, so that, even if we were capable of doing the impossible and using a thought-instrument whose whole signification was to synthesize experience to turn us beyond experience, we would find that, thus turned, we were thinking an empty thought. We would in no sense have knowledge since the notion of a ground or First Cause is in-capable either of giving us by itself a thing to be known or of being filled in by intuitive content. It stands, rather, as a straining of thought to do what cannot be done: to present an object of knowledge in terms of thought alone. In Kant's eyes, then, the field of knowledge remains linked to the objective: I can *think* the First Cause, but I cannot *know* it.

How might a metaphysician deal with this Kantian position? It is apparent that he would have to concentrate his attention on showing the very special character of the idea of "being." Kant's case rests on the point that the idea of being does not give us an object and that knowledge, and presumably truth, is restricted to what can be an object for consciousness. (For him, even the self is known only insofar as it is an object in the phenomenal world.) Obviously, however, the idea of being transcends any dichotomy between subject and object, just as it transcends all other dichotomies. Being spans both sides of this dichotomy, for the subject which thinks being is also being. This means not simply that it is the repository for the category "being" (as Kant's transcendental subject is the locus of the twelve categories), but that the very meaning "being" which it thinks applies to itself as thinking it. I, who think being, I, too, *am*. It is true that there is no way to think being as an object. Not only is there no object "being," but there is no object from which this meaning could be drawn. It is also true that through this concept, nothing is added to the knowledge of a phenomenal object just *as* an object: in Kant's terms, being is not a predicate. But this only means that I must miss the intelligibility which is made possible through the meaning "being" if I approach it in the mode of a pure object. It does not mean that being has no intelligible content, only that it does not display this content to the thought which knows objects.

Then for what thought does being display intelligible content? If the meaning of being transcends the subject - object dichotomy, for what self is it available? This can be most easily answered through a contrast with the self which is involved in Kantian knowing. For the notion of "object" is clearly correlated with a certain notion of "subject." Kant's "transcendental" subject, that subject which makes the world of science possible, may be denominated a "logico-sensory subject." It has at its disposal two types of equipment: the formally universal categories of logic and the sensorily universal determinants of space and time. Scientific knowledge of objects is based on the synthesis of these two elements; the possibility of a phenomenal community of knowers rests upon them. The "knower" of the sciences, then, that cognitional self which every member of the phenomenal community is bound to be, is a logico-sensory subject. Can such a subject be the self to which the datum of being is present? Hardly, since the datum of being is present precisely as that which transcends the very subject - object dichotomy which this logico-sensory subject founds. To think the genuine meaning "being" is therefore at the same time to think the non-ultimate character of the logico-sensory subject. It is not the self which founds objectivity which can think that which transcends objectivity. Consequently, to think "being" is also to say "I" in a new way.

Here we abut upon a realization which has formed a cornerstone of the thought of Gabriel Marcel. Being is intelligible, even hyper-intelligible, but it is intelligible only as mystery.[5] This last word tends to irritate some, but all Marcel means by it is that there is meaning beyond the subject - object dichotomy, and that therefore there is truth beyond what can be known by the logico-sensory subject. A mystery is a question raised in respect to a datum which, as datum, includes the questioner. The thought of being includes the very self which thinks this thought—and includes it in its *singularity*. It must be emphasized that Kant's logico-sensory subject is not really a singular self at all; it is a *Denken überhaupt*, an anonymous knower whose anonymity constitutes the anonymity which is the hallmark of the "objectivity" of science.

In this area, the area of a "problem," in Marcel's words, "objectivity" and "impersonality" go hand in hand. The reason for this is not hard to seek. Because to be objective is to be public, it is thought to be incompatible with what is merely private and idiosyncratic. But the empirical subject seems to be stamped as an individual precisely by those differences which set him apart idiosyncratically from other individuals. Hence to seek objectivity is to seek what sheds individuality, what is common and, presumably, impersonal. Who "knows" chemistry, for example? Each self insofar as it is a knower of chemistry is in principle identical with every other knower of chemistry, a representative of a generalized cognitional consciousness. It is easy enough to see why Bertrand Russell, for one, motivated by a similar viewpoint, will use its impersonal character as a defining characteristic of knowledge.[6]

Yet it is also easily overlooked that this purely cognitional subject is in principle incapable of knowing the singular. And the idea of being must also apply to the singular. The self which thinks the authentic idea of being (there is no question here of the simulacrum of use to the logician) is not the transcendental subject, nor the idiosyncratic empirical individual, but the self in its singularity. In fact, this thought may actually *be* one of the ways in which the singularity of the self is revealed—that is, in which it becomes conscious that there is a concrete meaning to "I" apart from what can be assigned to it as an empirical item within the world. If the concrete is understood as that which is unique and unrepeatable, then the idea of being, far from being the most abstract, is the most concrete of all ideas since through it thought meets the unique and unrepeatable. The self which thinks this idea is not a generalized knower, but the existing self in its uniqueness. Yet here we cannot see the unique as something which divides. On the contrary, the concrete singular is our mode of entry into the concrete universal. The existential "I" which thinks the thought "being" belongs, through that thought, to a realm of absolute otherness which unites it concretely with everything which is. Metaphysics is the reflection which is made possible through this thought.

Some fairly pressing questions are inescapably raised by these observations. There is first of all the question of what use this set of considerations can be for any proof for the existence of God. To vindicate the idea of being is not automatically to establish the existence of God, unless one makes an inadmissible identification of the idea of being with God. Yet it is hardly without significance that in the history of Western metaphysics God has been approached through this idea. "Being" is the medium in which the concrete is present for thought. The concept of being *is* a concept, but it is the concept by which thought is unreservedly opened to the concrete. To bring this out is not already to have validated its use in respect to any particular metaphysical argument for the existence of God, including the argument for causality. It may even be said that the dispute between realism and transcendentalism of a certain sort remains open after the evidential character of the idea of being has been established.

Perhaps the argument from causality is only the manner in which the transcendent is approached by a thought which operates with the authentic datum of being from within realist assumptions not necessarily implied in the datum itself. What our present considerations establish, if they are well founded, is simply the context within which the metaphysical issues can be genuinely raised.

It must be admitted, however, that one who takes his stand as an existential subject within this context will be very hard put to deny the existence of God. This is surely what accounts for the perpetual fascination of the ontological argument, and establishes it, one could make bold to say, as the fundamental argument for the existence of God— just as Kant saw. One is doubtless justified in rejecting this argument in the erroneously "objective" fashion in which it is usually offered: as if the idea of being were an *object* of knowledge, a premiss which thought "has" and from which it can ingeniously deduce conclusions. If, to begin with, the idea of being is non-objectifiable, then no thought based on it is a deductive argument. In fact, what inspires the ontological argument is the conviction that no argument for the existence of God is either necessary or possible. The point is that one who genuinely thinks the idea of being cannot deny that God exists. In bringing this out, one does not so much "demonstrate" as "monstrate" or "show forth" what is there from the beginning. Given that philosophy is a meditation on the meaning of being, Karl Jaspers' remark is both defensible and inevitable: in philosophy God is not really an entity whose existence is to be proved, but a presupposition of all its thinking.[7] In a similar manner, Marcel holds that all "proofs" for God's existence are simply transpositions to the order of reflective thought of truths which are already there in a more primordial way.[8]

The process by which thought comes to affirm the ultimate reference of the idea of being is best understood as a coming-to-recognition. No doubt this meaning can only come to recognition in dialectical interplay with the wealth of experience, as the anti-rationalist tradition insists. In this it has much in common with the creative idea of the artist: it is the mainspring and mover of the very work by which it comes to self-consciousness. For that reason, one could speak of Marcel's "blinded intuition" of being[9] as a "creative intuition": a non-objectifiable comprehension which thought attempts to paint on the canvas of language and which serves as the criterion through which the adequacy of that painting is reflectively recognized. Philosophical reflection brings to light the very light by which its search is made possible.[10] We know, but we do not know: this is the paradox. Here it may be said that Marcel rejoins the great tradition in philosophy which comes down from Plato. The ultimate truth is not learned, but "recollected," called-to-mind from the depth of the self. For him, as for Plato, this recollection entails a process of conversion, a calling of the self to itself, to its center. So that thought comes to the absolute and to the self as two sides of a reciprocal process of clarification.

A second difficulty arises in respect to the profit which is gained in reaching a God who is not an object in the ordinary sense. What good to assert God's existence, if we can assert nothing more about Him? And in passing beyond the subject - object dichotomy, do we not pass beyond the bounds of meaningful discourse? Kant might be understood in contemporary terms as saying that since knowledge is registered whole and entire in the subject - object dichotomy, we cannot actually assert anything about what transcends that dichotomy. This is Wittgenstein's position and forms the Kantian moment of his thought. What can be said at all can be said clearly, and this is confined to the factual realm of science. No doubt there is that which transcends the limits of my language, that which he calls the "mystical," but about that we must be decently silent.[11] Karl Jaspers, too, in so many other ways similar to Marcel, agrees with the Kantian outlook that knowledge in the proper sense is confined to the subject - object mode of consciousness, and that therefore no cognitive assertions about God can be literally true.[12] Jaspers' solution was to hold that we may speak of God only in ciphers whose symbolic revelatory worth is historically indisputable, but which do not constitute in any sense literal statements about the being of God.

Although this difficulty is an aggravated one for a theist, it cannot really be regarded as insuperable. It is helpful to remember that the point which it makes has long been known within the philosophical tradition itself and is by no means a contemporary discovery. It was St. Thomas himself who said that we can say *that* God exists, but not *what* He is,[13] and in saying this he was merely echoing a common refrain, perhaps emphasized by the tradition of negative theology, yet in no way peculiar to it. It would be easy to pick at utter random statements out of the Christian theological literature which unambiguously stress the transcendence of God in respect to human language. St. John Damascene, for example, writing in the beginning of the eighth century, begins his treatise on orthodoxy with the statement that God is ineffable and incomprehensible;[14] and he adds, in language foreshadowing St. Thomas': "It is clear that God exists, but what He is in essence and nature is unknown and beyond all understanding."[15] St. Cyril of Jerusalem, in lectures for catechumens given around A.D. 349, says: "We do not declare what God is but we frankly confess that we have no exact knowledge concerning Him."[16] True enough, these are representatives of apophatic theology, but was there ever, or could there be, a Christian theology which was not in part apophatic? These thinkers thought that they had roots sunk deep into the scriptures and were explicating orthodoxy. Had not the apologist-philosopher St. Justin Martyr, writing around A.D. 150, declared (in terms which ought to be of interest to contemporary linguistic analysts) that God is actually unnameable, that no proper name can apply to him?[17] There is no need to multiply evidence of the acknowledgment of the ineffability of the deity, and yet these philosophers do not—strangely—feel that this warrants remaining silent about Him, even while they are aware of the obvious aptness of this counsel. "Someone will say," remarks St. Cyril, "if the Divine Nature is incomprehensible, then why do you discourse about these things?"[18]

Apparently the objection, though superficially compelling, does not carry the day. For if all speech were equally unacceptable in speaking about the transcendent, then all speech would also be equally acceptable, and this is a hard saying. Granted that all language uttered in the phenomenal community has a tendency to fall into the objective in the very utterance and therefore to be inadequate to expressing its reality: all cannot be equally or similarly inadequate. Otherwise, "God is a stone" could not be recognized as any more inadequate than "God is intelligent." Therefore, although we may recognize that Marcel's remark, "When we speak about God, it is not about God that we speak,"[19] is motivated by a conviction that it is as an uncharacterizable Presence, and not as an object of predication, that we are oriented toward the transcendent, this statement in its turn cannot be treated as a piece of objective information.

Unless some doctrine of analogy or its equivalent is brought into play, then, as Paul Ricœur has said, there would be no way to distinguish negative theology from atheism.[20] It is true that we cannot apply predicates to God in the way in which we apply them to objects. "God is omnipotent," for example, is not, in philosophical depth-grammar, identical in form with "The ball is round." The "attributes" which we ascribe to God are much more like multiple ways, illuminating from our side, in which we maintain Him as beyond speech, than they are instruments for reducing Him to speech.

Marcel's way of approaching this is highly suggestive. Since it is the existential subject which thinks "being," it is as the thither side of the unconditional exigences which arise in the existential subject that the transcendent pole of being is revealed. The non-objectifiable transcendent is explicated via an explication of the full range of the non-objectifiable self. For the existential, concrete self is likewise non-objectifiable. It is neither an object in the world nor a subject for whom there are such objects. The "predicates" of this self do not characterize an object called man. They are not so much predicates *of* man at all as ways in which the concrete singular participates in a presence which is beyond him. For the concrete self is not an autonomous thing with characteristics, but a being-by-participation. There is no experience of existing which is not an experience of participation; the original moment of the self is a moment of participation. So that in knowing himself as a non-objectifiable singular, man always knows what is other than himself.

Traditional metaphysics was, no doubt, moved by a similar consideration in fastening upon man's intellect and will as properly applicable to the transcendent, since these are concretely experienced as unconditional exigences for truth and goodness: they are not "merely subjective" predicates of man, but exigential participations in what is infinitely beyond man. Marcel, while not discarding this, has been much more preoccupied with experiences like love, hope, and fidelity, experiences which are obviously intelligible only to the singular existential subject.[21] In these experiences a new dimension of the non-objectifiable emerges: to be a singular is to belong to communion. Communion is both an assurance of the supra-cognitional dimension of the self and an appeal to live and think out of that dimension. Still, while the proper beginning of metaphysics is not

"I think," but "We are," communion is not the end of philosophical reflection.[22] It is the pre-eminent mode through which we are invited to learn and to cling to what it means to be a self-beyond-the-world-of-objects, and thus to be opened to the ultimate presence which summons us beyond objectivity. It is, also, through communion that we learn to address this presence as Thou. Marcel's approach to God has thus been aptly termed an "analogy of presentiality": from the intelligibility of presence, to the hyper-intelligibility of Presence.[23]

Now this emphasis upon singularity gives rise to a third important question. If metaphysical reflection is carried on in function of the singular self, how can metaphysics be a science? It is a long-standing truism that there is no science of the singular; can there be a science made possible through the singular? Matters are particularly difficult if we keep in mind that the unique self is the *free* self. To say that being is present only to the singular is to say that it is present only to freedom. This is, of course, Karl Jaspers' explicit view, for whom *Existenz* and Transcendence are mutually significant terms.[24] Nor does Marcel steer away from it, for he distinctly holds that the meaning of being is given as an appeal, and it is of the essence of an appeal that it can be refused. The affirmation that God exists is an affirmation of my freedom; the metaphysical reflection in which thought justifies this affirmation is a "logic of liberty."[25]

On this basis, it would seem that metaphysics might have to give up all claims to being a science and lapse into a fideism with rhetorical flourishes added. Even more, does not our position simply obliterate the Kantian distinction between knowledge and belief? For if metaphysical reflection, and ultimately the affirmation of the transcendent, is correlative to freedom, it would appear to be a form of faith, rather than knowledge. Kant was willing to grant an important place to this mode of consciousness—see the place of moral consciousness in the second *Critique*—but he would not designate it as knowledge. Indeed, once we talk of a truth which is revealed to freedom, how could we any longer talk of the distinction between knowledge and faith?

There is some temptation to treat this difficulty simply as a wrangle over how generously the honorific term "knowledge" should be dispensed. One might claim that Kant should be understood as having really distinguished between two kinds of knowledge, rather than between knowledge and belief. Let knowledge be understood as an assured mode of openness to the co-presence of an other (rather than in terms of objective validity), and there seems less anomaly in saying that freedom can be the vehicle of knowledge. This is rendered more plausible by the realization that the "freedom" here involved is not construed as a freedom of indifference or even a freedom of choice, but as a freedom of response.[26] This tack is by no means just a verbal sleight-of-hand, and yet there is still something wanting. It amounts really to the view that in respect to ultimate philosophical truth, the distinction between knowledge and faith no longer fully obtains. But why then speak of knowledge here, rather than faith? Perhaps the reason is that there continues to be a strong element of the *universal* at this ultimate point, and that where this is present, one inclines to talk of "knowledge." True, the universal intelligibility which is rendered possible here is revealed to a free certitude, and yet it is revealed as bringing with it a non-arbitrary and binding evidence. Being, while it is revealed to the singular, opens up a whole new process of thought to this singular, a process of implication, insight, and coherence, grounded through the singular, and assured, by that grounding, of an attachment to the concrete and to content.

This thought-process, once incorporated into the life of reason, claims a role in determining what the proper scope of "reason" is. For itself, it differs from the posture of the "believer," since its affirmation and understanding of the transcendent are rooted in the necessitous evidence in the thought of "being," while the believer's need not be. Its title to be treated as knowledge is its ineradicable refusal, in the light of its own fundamental thought, to view as anything but arbitrary and question-begging any definition of knowledge which leaves it aside.

NOTES

1. *Critique of Pure Reason*, trans. Norman Kemp Smith (New York: St. Martin's Press, 1965), B1.

2. *Ibid.*, B3-5.

3. *Ibid.*, A19, 50-52.

4. *Ibid.*, A247-260; B302-315.

5. On the distinction between problem and mystery, see *Being and Having*, trans. Katherine Farrer (Boston: Beacon, 1951), pp. 100ff., 117ff., 126ff.; *The Mystery of Being*, trans. G. S. Fraser (Chicago: Regnery, 1951), 1, 204ff.; and the entire essay "On the Ontological Mystery," *The Philosophy of Existentialism* (New York: Citadel, 1961).

6. Bertrand Russell, *Human Knowledge* (New York: Simon & Schuster, 1948), pp. xi; 52.

7. Karl Jaspers, *The Perennial Scope of Philosophy*, trans. Ralph Manheim (New York: Philosophical Library, 1949), p. 32.

8. *Being and Having*, p. 121.

9. *Metaphysical Journal*, trans. Bernard Wall (Chicago: Regnery, 1952), p. x.

10. *Being and Having*, p. 118.

11. Ludwig Wittgenstein, *Tractatus Logico-Philosophicus*, trans. D. F. Pears and B. F. McGuinness (London: Routledge, 1961). See the preface and 6.44; 6.45; 6.53; 7.

12. Karl Jaspers, *Philosophie* (Berlin: Springer, 1956), 1, 34-36.

13. *Sum. theol.*, 1, q. 1, aa. 11 and 12; q. 13, a. 1.

14. St. John of Damascus, *An Exact Exposiiton of the Orthodox Faith*, in *Writings*, trans. Frederic H. Chase, Jr. (New York: Fathers of the Church, 1958), p. 165.

15. *Ibid.*, p. 170.

16. *Catechesis*, VI, 1, in *The Works of St. Cyril of Jerusalem*, trans. Leo P. McCauley, S.J. and Anthony A. Stephenson (Washington, D.C.: Catholic University of America Press, 1969), 1, 148-49.

17. *Exhortation to the Greeks*, Chap. 21, in *Writings of Saint Justin Martyr*, trans. Thomas B. Falls (New York: Christian Heritage, 1948), p. 398.

18. St. Cyril, *Catechesis*, VI, 5, in *loc. cit.*, p. 150.

19. *Du refus à l'invocation* (Paris: Gallimard, 1940), p. 53.

20 Paul Ricœur, *Gabriel Marcel et Karl Jaspers* (Paris: Éditions du Temps Présent, 1947), p. 288.

21. *Being and Having*, p. 119. See "On the Ontological Mystery" (note 5).

22. *The Mystery of Being*, trans. René Hague (Chicago: Regnery, 1951), II, 9.

23. Pietro Prini, *Gabriel Marcel et la méthodologie de l'invérifiable* (Paris: Desclée de Brouwer, 1953), p. 117.

24. *Reason and Existenz*, trans. William Earle (New York: Noonday Press, 1955), p. 61.

25. *Du refus à l'invocation*, p. 40. See also p. 35.

26. *Being and Having*, pp. 173-74.

7

The Philosophical Theology of
Rahner and Lonergan

GERALD A. McCOOL, S.J.

THE PHILOSOPHICAL THEOLOGY of Transcendental Thomism is
of the type which Whiteheadians describe as classical. God is not
simply the highest exemplification of the actual entities which constitute the universe. Neither is He the dipolar God, the necessary
being of the neoclassical theists, who can surpass Himself through
His free interaction with the universe, although He cannot be sur-
passed by any other entity. On the contrary, God is Pure Act, the
Infinite Prime Mover whose causal influence is required to ground
the movement of the human spirit. Although freely related to the
world and engaged in its history as its creator and conserver, God
is eternal, not temporal. He does not grow, pass from potency
to act, as a consequence of the dynamic interrelationship between
Himself and His created universe. The attributes through which
He is defined are rooted in being rather than process. They are
identical, in fact, with the traditional attributes assigned to the divinity by Aquinas. God is *ipsum intelligere, ipsum esse, summum
bonum*, the exemplar, efficient cause, first agent, and last end of all
that is or could be.[1]

THE STARTING POINT AND METHOD OF
TRANSCENDENTAL THOMISM

Nevertheless the philosophical theology of Transcendental Thomism is not without its novelty. Its starting point and method have
been influenced by Kantian and post-Kantian philosophy. Transcendental Thomism is a movement whose practitioners, despite
significant differences, establish their metaphysics of man, the world,
and God by bringing to light the transcendental conditions of possibility for our human experience of knowing and loving. A distinguishing characteristic of Aquinas' philosophy of cognition is
the importance which he attaches to the metaphysical identity of
knower and known in the act of knowledge. This union in being
of knower and known, founding the relation of truth, is the metaphysical ground of knowledge. Conscious awareness of known
and knower is simply the consequence of this identity, once it has
been effected in a subject which, being immaterial, does not suffer
from the opacity of matter. Another significant feature of Aquinas' philosophy of knowledge is the dynamic and unifying function which he assigns to the active intellect. Through the dynamic
finality of the intellect Aquinas can account for knowledge as a
single act, one unified process, which begins with the operation
of the external senses and proceeds through the abstraction of the
intelligible *species* from the phantasm to culminate in the objective
affirmation of the judgment. Transcendental Thomists have exploited these two aspects of Thomas' philosophy of knowledge
and have placed great stress on his insistence on the conscious nature of the process through which acts of knowledge and love proceed from the human subject.

As a consequence, they have been able to develop, in their dialogue with Kantian and post-Kantian philosophy, a cognitional
theory, an epistemology, and a metaphysics based on the human
subject's awareness of himself as spirit in the world. Although man's
knowledge begins with sensation and is dependent on the sensible
world for its representative content, man nonetheless can achieve
the free self-awareness which characterizes him as spirit because
he can unite an intelligible form with himself by abstracting it from

the phantasm, and distinguish it from himself by the objectivizing judgment or complexus of judgments through which it stands over against him as other in being. This process of identification and distinction in a single, unified act of knowledge is possible only because the human spirit is a dynamism which drives through and beyond every limited subject and object toward the unrestricted fullness of intelligibility and goodness. The existence of God, the absolutely unconditioned identity of being, knowledge, and love, as the term of the spirit's striving, is therefore a transcendental condition of possibility for every unified act of human knowledge. Awareness of this fact is the evidence which legitimates the Transcendental Thomist's claim to approach the world as a realist through a metaphysics of being and causality. The intellect manifests itself as the faculty of being because it reveals itself as the faculty of the divine.

God is not known through a cosmological proof based on the relationship of the constituted objects of the world to one another or to the immobile creative source of the contingent world of nature. The Five Ways of St. Thomas proceed, it is true, from the ontological relationships among the objective beings of the natural world to the First Cause of the universe required for their intelligibility. The hermeneutic, however, through which the mind of Aquinas is truly appropriated by the contemporary knower, reveals that the journey of Thomas' mind toward God which forms the dynamic core of his metaphysics is made by way neither of an ontological argument from the concept of a contingent being nor of a causal argument whose starting point is the physical objects of the sensible world. It proceeds rather through the discovery of God which is inseparable from a genuine understanding of the conscious and intelligible process of insight, conceptualization, and affirmation required for conscious emergence of a world of objects.[2] If this hermeneutic, which is one of the major contributions of Transcendental Thomism, is correct, Aquinas took a decisive step away from the cosmocentric Greek world and its preoccupation with objective natures and the necessary causes of their motion and moved into the modern world of the subject.[3] Aquinas' God is no longer the Pure Form which moves Aristotle's world of nature. God manifests Himself primarily as the Infinite Subject to whom man is essentially related in the free, intelligent, historical process through which man actualizes himself as a subject by allowing his world of objects and fellow-subjects to be.

This fundamental point, essential to a genuine retrieve of Aquinas' mind, has been missed by conceptualist Thomists, who look on abstraction as an unconscious process, and by existentialist Thomists, who claim that the intelligibility of being manifested itself to Aquinas in the sensible singular affirmed by the judgment rather than in the unified cognitional process which culminated in its affirmation. Thus for both the conceptualist and the existentialist Thomist, philosophical theology is the culmination of a metaphysics of potency, form, and act whose objective intelligibility has already been grasped through the mind's encounter with sensible reality. The causal influence of God is required, of course, to ground the existence and intelligible structure of the natural world, but its affirmation is not a condition of possibility for the mind's prior grasp of them. Consequently, philosophical theology is not contained, as an inseparable element, in the unfolding of a reflexive anthropology in which man discovers the essential relationship to God which constitutes his own being, since it is contained, consciously though implicitly, in the fundamental act through which, by knowing and choosing a world, he knows and chooses himself.[4]

METAPHYSICS AND SYSTEMATIC THEOLOGY

This difference in starting point and method between Transcendental Thomists and other modern disciples of St. Thomas might appear at first to be little more than another attempt to recast Thomas' proofs for God's existence in a form less vulnerable to the attacks leveled against them by empiricist and Kantian philosophers. As a matter of fact, the Kantian critique of metaphysics and philosophical theology was one of the motives which induced Joseph Maréchal, the founder of the movement, to write his *Le point de départ de la métaphysique*.[5] Transcendental Thomism however has gone far beyond Maréchal and, through its metaphysics, built on the movement of the spirit, has developed a philosophy of the knowledge and nature of God which has had a far-reaching and profound influence on Roman Catholic theology.

This great expansion of the Transcendental Thomist philosophy of God has been made in the theological syntheses of Bernard Lonergan and Karl Rahner. Although both have written major philosophical works to validate their epistemology and metaphysics, they address themselves to the problem of God in the context of Roman Catholic theology. Their concern is with the God of Christian revelation who, manifesting Himself to man historically in Jesus Christ, still manifests Himself today not only to the professing Christian who receives His word of revelation in the visible Church but to all men, since, because of the universal salvific will of Christ, they must have the capability of responding to it through an interaction of grace and implicit faith which it is the theologian's task to elucidate to the extent that this is possible. In the tradition of Roman Catholic theology, both these theologians clearly distinguish the natural order and the autonomous domain of reason from the supernatural order and the domain of faith.[6] Theology, which is an understanding of faith, must not be confused with philosophy, which is an operation of reason. Theology, however, is a science through which the believer endeavors by a rigorous and systematic reflection on his experience to reach a more adequate understanding of the mysterious God, who can never be completely understood, through analogy with the realities which can be understood. Theologizing is an indispensable activity even in a Church which claims to possess certain knowledge of God and His attributes through historical revelation and to propose it for belief through the authoritative teaching of her magisterium.[7] For men must think and act responsibly. They must inquire if and how an encounter with the mysterious God of revelation is possible and, if indeed it has occurred, how that encounter can provide modern man with an understanding of God which is at once coherent enough to be intellectually acceptable and significant enough for his own self-understanding to unify his comprehension of himself and his world and to guide his personal and social action. Clearly the contemporary theologian has no easy task, for both he and his readers are inhabitants of a civilization which is far removed, temporally and spiritually, from the one in which the historical word of revelation was spoken, and whose understanding of reality, formed by modern science, history, and psychology has become radically different.

Thus, like other contemporary Thomist theologians, Rahner and Lonergan have been confronted with a number of problems. Some of the more important ones can be listed under the following headings:

1. Man's knowledge of God

Does man's reflection on the essential relationship to God which manifests itself to his knowing and willing activity disclose, as the term of that activity, a God who (a) is capable of manifesting Himself to man in a free, historical word of revelation, and yet paradoxically (b) is capable of being present to the human spirit in such wise that even those men who have never encountered or accepted the message of the scriptures can still encounter Him as the God of revelation? And, on the supposition that a word of revelation was spoken by God to man at the time of Christ, how is it possible for that word to maintain through the vicissitudes of its varied expression in the history of human consciousness enough cognitional content to warrant the assertion that the act of faith through which the modern Christian encounters the God of revelation terminates at the same object as the act of faith of the first Christians? In the very process of human consciousness itself, can we find any reliable principles through which a genuine historical development in the knowledge of God can be distinguished from an aberration?

2. The coherence of the doctrine of God

Is the doctrine of God which is proposed by the Christian tradition truly intelligible? Has not the development of human consciousness, stimulated by modern science and contemporary philosophy, rendered the traditional problems connected with the nature of God and His relation to the world even more acute? Have not both the Triune God of conservative Christian theology and the infinite, a-temporal God of classical theism proved incompatible with our contemporary understanding of the processes of nature and the consciousness and freedom of the human person?

3. The relevance of the knowledge of God

How can God enter into the experience of contemporary man in a way which has any real connection with the needs, aspirations, and challenges which move him to action in the world? What difference does it make to contemporary man, as a moral and social agent, whether he knows anything about God or not?

A NEW APPROACH TO CLASSICAL THEISM: RAHNER AND LONERGAN

Facing the challenge presented to them by these difficulties, Lonergan and Rahner have reworked the whole theology of God's nature and relation to the world, using a metaphysics whose starting point is their philosophical anthropology. In doing so, they have shown their awareness of the difficulties against classical philosophical theology brought forward by Heideggerian and process philosophy. Nevertheless, their personal reflection on the dynamism of the spirit has convinced them that, although Being manifests itself in the knowing and loving event through which *Dasein* and its world of objective entities emerge into the light of truth, the Being, which transcends this world in which it manifests itself, cannot be finite and historical in the Heideggerian sense.[8] They are also unconvinced that God, as the highest entity, must be, like the other actual entities of the universe, processive. They agree readily enough with the neoclassicist theists that the metaphysics of God and the world must emerge from a reflection on the processive union of intelligibility, knowledge, and love which reveals itself in human experience. Nevertheless they do not admit that this metaphysics demands that God Himself, as the highest exemplification of being, must be in process.[9] The reason for their disagreement with both Heidegger and neoclassical theism is found, of course, in a different understanding of the dynamic relationship of the human subject to his world. With all metaphysicians in the Maréchalian tradition, they share the conviction that the dynamism of the mind, without which questions cannot be asked and sensible data be intelligently understood by insight and conceptualization and reasonably affirmed, is a real dynamism, the term of whose intentionality must be real absolute being. This Being, which transcends the subjects and objects of Heidegger's world, cannot be Nothing as Heidegger would have it. Limit as a negation, Rahner claims, requires a foreknowledge of a positive reality to make it possible. Consequently, unless the human mind has acquired an implicit knowledge of positively infinite Being in its transcendence of its world of objects, it cannot recognize them as limited as it does in every affirmation.[10] Furthermore, the Maréchalian metaphysics of knowledge, which grounds it in the ontological unity of knower and known in a single act, shows that there is no necessity to assert that the Divine Act must be in process in order to know. On the contrary, its function as the infinite intelligible, whose causal influence is required for any infinite process of knowledge and love to occur, proves that human experience demands that God not be in process.

It is understandable, therefore, that, despite the significant differences between the proof for God's existence presented by Rahner in *Spirit in the World* and *Hearers of the Word* and the proof given by Lonergan in *Insight*, God manifests Himself in all three books as the infinite identity of being, intelligence, and love without whose causal influence the insatiable drive of the human mind to know the limited realities of the universe through abstraction and affirmation would be unintelligible. Whether God be considered as the Absolute Horizon, consciously though unobjectively present to the mind as the necessary condition of its capacity to grasp finite realities as limited and still place them absolutely in the realm of being in virtue of the drive for the Absolute which moves beyond them (Rahner),[11] or as the content of the unrestricted act of understanding whose real existence the human knower must affirm as the absolutely unconditioned ground of the real world which has disclosed itself, through his own self-appropriation as a knower, as the object of his intelligent understanding and reasonable affirmation (Lonergan), God is the infinite, intelligible, free cause of the existence and action of His creatures. Novel and complex though the Transcendental Thomist proof for God's existence may be, as it certainly is in Lonergan's *Insight*, and intimate as is its connection with the original and diverse philosophical anthropologies which Lonergan and Rahner have developed in their major philosophical works, the God whose existence it establishes, as the necessary and inevitable consequence of its prolonged analysis of human knowledge and volition, remains unmistakably the traditional God of classical theism.

Nonetheless the relation of God to the world emerges in a new light because of the position which He assumes in Transcendental Thomism as the abiding Personal Mystery[12] whose presence makes possible the life through which the human subject creates himself by his involvement in the history of an evolving universe. In their development of this metaphysics of the divine presence, Rahner and Lonergan diverge from each other sufficiently to warrant a separate consideration of the unfolding of their metaphysics of God's relation to the historical human person.

RAHNER: THE ABSOLUTE MYSTERY

For Rahner man is capable of knowing the objects of the sensible world through the concept and the judgment because of the conscious, though unobjective, presence of Absolute Being in his intellect as the term of its dynamism. Through the very opacity of his knowledge, which makes it necessary for man to go outside himself to another being in sensation, understand it through abstractive insight, and place it in opposition to himself by the judgment in order to come to self-awareness, man knows that he is not pure spiritual self-presence as is Absolute Being. As one of many human knowers, whose knowledge is attained by abstracting forms from matter, he knows that he is not pure form but rather a composite of form and matter, a member of a corporeal species, linked, as his need for sensation shows, to the motion, exteriority, and time of the material universe. He is one of a race who makes himself, in company with the fellow-individuals of his species, in the temporal process of the universe. And, as he discovers his own freedom, he also learns that the process through which the members of the human race make themselves in society is not simply temporal; it is also historical.[13]

There is a difference between the unobjective knowledge which every man possesses of his own spiritual dynamism as a subject and the objective knowledge which he can express in the concepts which he abstracts from sensible reality. In the latter his knowledge of spiritual reality is indirect and, in the case of God, analogical. It is also affected by the differences in perspective inseparable from the varied place of diverse abstractive knowers in space and time and the position which each concept holds in the variety of cultural contexts which condition the knowledge of historical knowers in different epochs.

Man's knowledge of God, which perdures through history and the cultural vicissitudes of conceptual knowledge, is of God who exists in His unobjective presence as the Absolute Mystery, who can never be encompassed conceptually but whose preconceptual awareness is the condition of all objective knowledge. And, as the Absolute Mystery, God is known by love. For man, discovering his opacity and his need to question, realizes that he is not the absolute, self-grounding pure Spirit on whom he depends as the source of his being and knowledge. A finite, contingent being, however, can proceed from the Absolute Spirit neither by the intellectual necessity of rational deduction nor by the blind necessity of brute material process. Consequently the ground of both finite spirit and its world is the perduring free choice of divine love. But an act of love can never be understood from the outside. It can be grasped only through an interpersonal return of love by which the beloved enters into the lover and so understands him "from within." True understanding of the Absolute Mystery therefore can take place only in the act of free return of love through which the human spirit responds to God in love and *in the very process of freely loving Him understands Him.*[14]

This knowledge of the Absolute Mystery through conversion to Him in love, since it takes place on the unobjective level, may never attain adequate thematization on the objective level of the conceptual judgment. Conceptual affirmations of God, however, which are not conjoined with knowledge through love of the Absolute Mystery can scarcely be authentic. Nevertheless, authentic, unobjective knowledge of the Absolute Mystery is possessed by the human subject who, in loving submission to the value of the persons and objects of his world, responds to the Absolute Mystery as its source.[15] Therefore, it is clear that the ongoing task of giving explicit, thematic expression in analogous, historically and culturally conditioned concepts to our deepening awareness of the Absolute Mystery is an ongoing task for the philosophical theologian.

LONERGAN: INSIGHT AND PHILOSOPHICAL THEOLOGY

Lonergan views with considerable reserve Rahner's direct approach to God as the Absolute Mystery who reveals Himself as the unobjective Horizon of every act of affirmation.[16] For, in his opinion, the cognitional theory, the epistemology, and the metaphysics necessary for a scientific understanding of God and of His relation to the world in philosophy and theology require a much more detailed and careful elucidation of man's polymorphic consciousness and of the changeless cognitional structure which remains, as an unrevisable subject-pole, through all the revisions which the human knower has been forced to make and will still be forced to make in his scientific understanding of the world. Consequently in *Insight* God is reached as the term of the spirit's dynamism only after a long phenomenology of insight as activity in the first section of the book and an equally long validation of insight as knowledge in its second section.

In a paper of this length one can refer only in passing to the new metaphysics of proportionate being, which is the object of man's sensible experience, intelligent understanding, and reasonable affirmation, and to the metaphysics of transcendent being to which it leads. For our purposes at the moment it is enough to indicate that Lonergan's metaphysics, based on the isophomorphism between the cognitional structure of human knowledge (the dynamic unity of sensation, intelligent understanding, and reasonable affirmation) and the proportionate being which is its correlate (the intelligibly real unity of matter, form, and act[17]) reveals, as does Rahner's less highly developed philosophical anthropology, that man is an historical knower in a human community subject to the laws of historical development and retrogression[18] who reaches God through an act of knowledge and love which entails intellectual, moral, and religious conversion.[19]

This discovery is made gradually in the course of Lonergan's reflection on the role of insight in the conscious process of human knowledge stimulated by man's pure desire to know. From his recognition of the distinction between the act of insight into the phantasm and the subsequent act of conceptualization (which cannot be made by conceptualist Thomists who consider the abstraction of the concept an unconscious process), Lonergan leads his reader on to the further discovery of the higher viewpoint. A higher viewpoint is reached through an act of insight into a sensible datum—a mathematical operation, for example, or a range of empirical data—through which a new intelligibility is disclosed. In the formulation of this new intelligibility, as, for example, in the transition from arithmetic to algebra, a new and higher scheme of interrelated concepts emerges, under which the concepts of the lower scheme can be subsumed; and data which in the lower scheme remained unintelligible can now be understood in the explanatory knowledge of a higher science. His distinction between insight and conceptualization enables Lonergan also to make the important discovery of the inverse insight. Whereas direct insight discovered the presence of an intelligible form or correlation in the phantasm, inverse insight discovers the absence of an anticipated intelligibility of this kind which is significant because of its connection with another and important intelligibility.

By explaining the connection between direct and inverse insight with the heuristic anticipations which enable scientists to reach explanatory knowledge of the relationship between phenomena, Lonergan is able to account for the necessity of two diverse methods for the direction of empirical inquiry. Classical method directs its investigation of the ideal correlations between phenomena toward which all observed correlations converge. Statistical method, on the other hand, does not inquire into the ideal correlations between phenomena which, for the scientist, constitute explanatory knowledge of "the nature of" a thing. It concerns itself rather with the frequency with which events recur in the nonsystematic processes in which the recurring phenomena are not linked together by the ideal correlations which direct the heuristic anticipations of classical method. Statistical method was discovered when scientists were stimulated by the inverse insight that the ideal correlations are not present in nonsystematic processes to ask the further questions which led them to insight into another type of intelligibility. This new intelligibility is the ideal law which governs the statistically regular recurrence of events in a nonsystematic process. It is their probability, or ideal frequency (one in ten times, for example), from which the recurrence of events in a nonsystematic process cannot systematically diverge. Probability is the diverse form of intelligibility, discovered, like the intelligibility of explanatory correlations, by insight into sensible data, which directs the heuristic anticipations of statistical method.[20]

The scientist endeavors to arrive by his use of insight at abstract, explanatory knowledge of the relationship of things to one another. The man of common sense is concerned, on the contrary, with the descriptive knowledge of things as they are related to himself. His preoccupation is with the concrete world of practical daily life in which he lives and acts. Nevertheless, if he is to conduct his practical life intelligently, either individually or in society, the man of common sense must also constantly increase his store of insights and allow them to group themselves into the integrated clusters and complexes through which the man of action becomes the intelligent master of concrete situations. Unfortunately, however, the man of common sense who, as an animal, must contend with the drives and needs of corporeal existence, and, as a *persona*, find a satisfactory role to play before the audience of his fellowmen, is moved by more urges than the pure desire to know. Through their influence, conscious and unconscious, he often endeavors to prevent the emergence and recognition of unwanted insights, because their emergence, although it would satisfy the pure desire to know, might prevent the satisfaction of his biological needs or disturb the self-image to which he clings. Common-sense man's world of intelligible meaning is constituted through the interaction of two linked, but opposed, dynamic principles. They are the pure desire to know which moves him to seek insights, and the complexus of opposed desires, conscious and unconscious, which move him to flee from them. This is true of man both as an individual and in society. In human history the social world of common-sense meaning advances and retrogresses in intelligibility through the dialectical interplay of two linked, but opposed, principles of change—the pure desire to know, which moves men to seek insights and thus increase their grasp of real being through intelligent understanding and reasonable affirmation, and the individual bias of classes within a community or the general bias of the community as a whole, which moves men to prevent the emergence of the insights which would lead to an increase in their understanding and affirmation of the real. Thus culture and society, as social realities whose meaning is constituted by man, are subject to the dialectical interplay of two forces, rooted in the very structure of the human knower, through which their intrinsic intelligibility progresses or declines.[21]

Lonergan's extensive phenomenology of insight in the first half of his major work enables him in its second half to establish a metaphysics of central and conjugate form which is radically different from the hylomorphism of traditional Thomism. The emergence of a higher viewpoint which, as the phenomenology of insight shows, makes any conceptual science of nature revisable and consequently merely probable, eliminates a metaphysical science built on Aristotle's necessary science of nature. Furthermore, since the intelligibility of motion can be understood only through the use of both classical and statistical methods, the world of nature is not a world of cyclic necessity. It is a world of emerging probability. To understand its orderly growth, more is needed than a deductive science based on the necessary relations between fixed essences. The scientist and the philosopher will understand the world of nature only through the synthesis of classical and statistical methods which constitutes what Lonergan calls genetic method. Only thus will they be able to understand how the events of nonsystematic processes, through their cycles of recurrence, account for the emergence and survival of the constant correlations, the conjugate forms, which manifest "the nature of" the species whose central, or specific, forms emerge successively in the process of the world's evolution. The intelligibility of natural motion therefore excludes an Aristotelian universe in which motion is reduced to mere transition from one fixed form to another in an eternal hierarchy of changeless species. It demands a world whose emergence is not merely an evolutionary process but a process whose intelligibility is that of emergence probability, or, in other words, an evolutionary process, subject to the chances, failures, and vagaries whose absence would be incompatible with the presence of the nonsystematic processes which help to constitute it.[22]

Man, through his emergence in it, is part of the world of emergent probability. Even more, since the analysis of insight has shown that he is a biological as well as a spiritual being, it is inevitable that his conduct should manifest the dialectical opposition between his biological drives and his pure desire to know, and that, both individually and socially, his knowledge should manifest the consequences of their opposition. If, then, he is to be constantly faithful to the exigencies of the pure desire to know in his speculative judgments about being and in his practical evaluations and actions, he must struggle to overcome the opposition of his biological drives in a painful process of intellectual and moral conversion. And, for the majority of men at least, the power and light to undertake the process of conversion is found through a genuinely religious conversion.[23]

The converted knower, who has overcome the extrovertive influence of his biological drives and their resultant biases, will be able to understand that real being is the object of neither sensible apprehension nor imaginative construction. It is the object rather of intelligible understanding whose existence or occurrence can be reasonably affirmed when the absence of further relevant questions makes it clear that all the conditions required for its affirmation as an intelligible, virtually unconditioned, fact have been fulfilled. Consequently the converted knower can understand the "positions" concerning being, objectivity, and knowledge which enable him to free his scientific and common-sense knowledge from the "counterpositions" concerning them which underlie the aberrations introduced into human knowledge through the influence of man's biological drives.[24] Furthermore, once he has clearly understood that the real being of this world, no matter how often his scientific knowledge of it must undergo revision, must be the objective correlate of the unified process of his knowing through sensation, intelligible understanding, and reasonable affirmation, he knows that the real beings of the universe which he encounters in his experience must be real composites of matter and central and conjugate form and act.

It is only at the end of this long development in which, through his reflections on insight, Lonergan has established that the world of man's experience is a universe of emerging probability, whose intelligibility demands a metaphysics of central and conjugate form and act, that he feels ready to approach the metaphysics of God's transcendent being.[25] His reader can now appreciate that the unrestricted drive of the mind which raised the successive questions, whose answers constitute the phenomenology, epistemology, and metaphysics of *Insight*, is possible only because the real being which is the object of its quest is equally unrestricted in its intelligibility.

Being is the real whose nature has been understood by answering questions for intelligence (what is it?; how often does it occur?) and whose existence has been verified in the judgments through which questions for reflection (is it?; has it occurred?) receive their answer. For man's drive to acquire critically grounded knowledge through the intelligent and reflective process of the judgment is a drive toward the real or being in its unrestricted fullness. Man can always raise questions about what he does not know, and through his continuing urge to question, he is aware that he does not know all things. The unknown which he seeks to know through his endless inquiry is being, for outside of being there is nothing. And his questioning gives him the evidence that being is completely intelligible. For inquiry is a drive to know being by answering questions for intelligence and for reflection, and what is unintelligible can neither be understood by intelligence nor affirmed by reflection. Furthermore the complete intelligibility of being, since it is present only when all reasonable questions are answered, requires the existence of an unrestricted act of understanding. For, as Lonergan's analysis of the judgment makes clear, in our restricted acts of understanding, evidence sufficient to warrant its reasonable assent is had when the affirmer grasps through insight that the conditions necessary for the existence or occurrence of the object of his affirmation happen in fact to be fulfilled. No further relevant questions for reflection arise and consequently no further verification is needed. The grasp of evidence on which the judgment rests, therefore, since it is simply the awareness that the conditions necessary for the existence or occurrence of its object have been fulfilled in fact, is a virtually unconditioned ground, one whose

conditions have *de facto* been fulfilled, and not an absolutely unconditioned, necessary ground of intelligibility. As a contingent
fact, it is itself in need of further explanation. It does not provide
the answer to all reasonable questions. Since, however, restricted acts of understanding, as Lonergan's analysis of the judgment
shows, are restricted to the grasp of the virtually unconditioned,
no series of restricted acts of understanding, even an infinite series,
can constitute the understanding of the absolutely unconditioned
ground which is required for being to be completely intelligible.
Consequently man's ability to know real being through intelligent
understanding and reasonable affirmation demands as the absolutely unconditioned ground of its possibility the infinite identity
of being, knowledge, and love in an unrestricted act of insight whose
necessary characteristics are the attributes which classical theism
assigns to God.[26]

THE SIGNIFICANCE OF THE NEW METAPHYSICAL SYNTHESES

Lonergan's theory of the judgment as the grasp of the virtually
unconditioned is the basis of a proof for the existence of God which
is different from the proof proposed by Rahner. Rahner arrives
at his knowledge of God through a preconceptual awareness of
the Absolute Mystery as the condition of possibility for objective
knowledge through abstraction and affirmation. Lonergan reaches
God as the absolutely unconditioned ground for the complete intelligibility of being. Although both proofs reach the existence
of God as the term of the dynamism of the spirit as the condition
of possibility for human knowledge, Lonergan's proof is much
more complex and requires the whole development of the cognitional theory, epistemology, and metaphysics of *Insight* which un-
dergird it. His proof for God's existence is really the culmination
of the whole metaphysical system which he has worked out in his
major philosophical work.

Although Lonergan's metaphysical system is more original and
his grounding of it far more systematic and detailed, Rahner too
has produced a new metaphysics of nature, man, and society. As
a result both have developed a new philosophical theology in which

the world to which the God of classical theism is related is no longer the world of Aristotelian nature and science. It is an evolutionary
world in which man, as an individual and in society, creates himself through a process of development which is subject to the risks
inseparable from nonsystematic processes and human aberration.
Although God is always in some way present to the human spirit
as the term of its dynamism, the human knower's conceptual knowledge of Him is intrinsically historical and culturally conditioned.[27]
Individual and social conversion are inseparably connected with
the genuine historical developments or the aberrations of the knowledge which man acquires of himself and of his world through his
use of science and common sense.

Their new metaphysics of man and his world has enabled these
Transcendental Thomist theologians to rework, often in quite a
radical way, the philosophical theology of God's relation to the
world and of man's relation to God, especially in his knowledge
and moral action. Some understanding of its important contribution to classical theistic philosophical theology may be gained
through a brief consideration of the fresh approach which it has
enabled them to take to some of the urgent problems listed earlier.

NEW SOLUTIONS TO THE PROBLEMS OF
PHILOSOPHICAL THEOLOGY

1. *Knowledge of God*

The first of the major problems which we considered earlier was
the problem of how, through reflection on the essential relationship to God manifested in man's knowing and willing activity,
man can discover a God who can both manifest Himself in an historical word at a definite place in space and time and yet also be
accessible in that supernatural revelation to men who have not encountered that historical word through the Church or through
the scriptures. Rahner's metaphysics of the Absolute Mystery,
the understanding of whose free communication requires for its
accomplishment a free acceptance of Him by the human knower
in a process of knowledge in love, provides an answer to this problem. If, as a theologian in the Catholic tradition, Rahner can claim

that revelation is a work of grace, he has the positive datum which he needs to extend his metaphysics of the Absolute Mystery to the level of knowledge of God through revelation. For he can then say that, because of the salvific will of Christ, we know that the offer of grace has been extended to all men and that all have been called effectively to a supernatural end. God's calling them to this supernatural end, as an effective divine action, has as its term a real, intrinsic modification of man's being. A new structure of the human spirit, a supernatural existential, has been produced, through which its dynamism has been elevated to the supernatural order.[28] The Absolute Mystery which is the term of its dynamism is no longer God as a natural end to be possessed by the unelevated powers of intellect and will. He is rather the Triune God who will be possessed in the Beatific Vision when man's elevated nature reaches its full flowering after death. Because of the supernatural existential, the act of knowledge through love which permits God's free supernatural self-communication of His personal riches is man's acceptance of grace. It is his welcoming of the Uncreated Grace, the Holy Spirit who (with the other persons of the Trinity) sanctifies man through His indwelling in the soul.[29] It is more than that, for, since it is supernatural knowledge in love of the Absolute Mystery who is subsistently the Revelation communicated by God's historical word, it is in its own way a grasp of revelation through the supernatural knowledge of faith.[30]

Rahner's distinction between unobjective knowledge of God as the Absolute Mystery and objective knowledge of Him through conceptual affirmation can now be applied to his distinction between transcendental and categorical revelation.[31] Transcendental revelation is the unobjective supernatural knowledge of God which has become a possibility for every man because of the supernatural existential. Categorical revelation is the historical word of revelation spoken first through the inspired teachers of Israel and definitively through Christ and His Apostles which reaches the contemporary Christian through the scriptures and the teaching of His Church. Consequently both natural and supernatural knowledge of God comes in both its transcendental and its categorical form. Since man, as a spirit in the world, is a social and historical being, categorical knowledge of God is analogous and indirect, for its content of representation must come by abstraction from the sensible objects of his world. Furthermore, it is socially and historically conditioned and can therefore be more or less extensive and satisfactory as a thematization of the implicit transcendental awareness man possesses of the Absolute Mystery.

The presence of inadequacies in their explicit thematization does not mean, therefore, that men do not possess an implicit knowledge in love of God which has a deep and pervasive influence on their lives. As Rahner has indicated in *Hearers of the Word* and *The Concept of Mystery in Catholic Theology*,[32] the man who responds to his world of objects and fellow-subjects through a fundamental, free attitude of loving submission to their true value has arrived already in the very intentionality of that freely chosen, fundamental attitude at an implicit acceptance in faith and love of the Absolute Mystery who is the fundamental Horizon of his world. The deep experiences which come to men like this in their daily life, experiences of love, or devotion, of dissatisfaction, of transcendent, undefinable value, are, as the metaphysics of the supernatural existential shows us, experiences of grace and, in their way, experiences of God.[33] Indeed one of the greatest services which believing Christians can render to modern man is precisely the help which they can give him in clarifying these profound experiences through which he, as an anonymous Christian, encounters the Absolute Mystery.

The distinction between transcendental and categorical knowledge of God is not simply a means for Rahner to arrive at a clearer and more satisfying account of man's knowledge of God's existence. It is a necessary condition for most of the major elements in his systematic theology. The dialectic between the abiding, universal presence of the Absolute Mystery and man's thematic knowledge of God in the culturally conditioned concepts of judgments which are never isolated from their historical and social context appears in Rahner's Christology,[34] his theology of revelation, his explanation of the development of doctrine and theology,[35] his understanding of the role of the individual in the Church,[36] and in his reflections on the possibility of a fundamental theology in an age of irreducible philosophical pluralism.

The historical character of conceptual knowledge, however, presents the philosophical theologian with the problem of whether it is possible to make abidingly valid statements about God. This is a particularly acute difficulty for a philosophical theologian who is also a systematic theologian in the Catholic tradition. Such a theologian is aware of what Rahner calls the irreducible philosophical pluralism of our age and of the difficulty of correctly interpreting philosophical statements outside the conceptual systems in which they are located. His scriptural and patristic studies have also confronted him with the hermeneutical problem of properly understanding scriptural statements made in the context of world views which have long since ceased to be our own and into which modern man enters with great difficulty. From his experience as a theologian he understands that there has been a development both of theology and of dogmatic statements in the history of the Catholic Church. He must deal, therefore, with the problem of philosophical, theological, and dogmatic statements dealing with the relations between God and man.

Both Rahner and Lonergan are original and illuminating in their treatment of these problems. Lonergan's treatment, however, as we shall see, is more systematic and coherent because he has at his disposal the results of his long analysis of man's polymorphic consciousness.

The knower's unobjective grasp of the Absolute Mystery, Rahner believes, is an abiding datum of every human consciousness. Consequently, no matter how man's conceptual knowledge may evolve, or how much it may change under cultural conditioning, God's unobjective presence will remain, as a fringe, surrounding and making possible all objective statements. As long as men are knowers at all, it can be understood and thematized. Our conceptual knowledge is not so historical, therefore, that it excludes abiding statements about God. It is true nonetheless that as our theological statements become more extensive and affirmations about the interrelationship of God and man are multiplied, theology becomes more a work of conceptual reasoning and moves away from the fundamental characteristics of the Absolute Mystery which are evident from our reflection on man's fundamental awareness of Him. As a work of conceptual reasoning it becomes involved to a greater or lesser degree in the historical and perspectival nature of conceptual knowledge.

This fact eluded the attention of Catholic theologians as long as they remained convinced that one system of philosophy could express the nature of the real truly and adequately and serve as the metaphysical structure for the one adequate theology. Today, however, theologians are aware that the historical nature of our knowledge, the vastness of reality, and the existence of many complex philosophical systems have eliminated, in the practical order at least, the possibility of arriving at one philosophical system as their instrument for understanding reality. Under the influence of many philosophical systems, and in their dialogue with the positive sciences which today have more or less declared their independence from philosophy, theologians will carry on their more extensive speculations about the interrelationship of God and the world through many irreducibly distinct theological systems inside of which alone their statements can be rightly understood.[37]

This should not alarm the Christian who understands the nature of the word of revelation. As a definitive word of God spoken by Christ to historical and social man, it was spoken in a definitive society. The Church will not be superseded like the synagogue, and her social, magisterial authority will, through its official, social action, protect the word of revelation spoken to her. Although they are distinct from the magisterium, the reflections of theological tradition have played their part in the unfolding through thematic statements of the intelligible riches of the Absolute Mystery. Their continued fidelity to the word of God has been the result of a supernatural *a priori*, the continued welcoming of the Absolute Mystery in the knowledge and love which is faith and charity. That is why the development of theology—which often leads to the development of doctrine—like all personal knowledge, through which the inner depths of another are thematized, has not always followed the laws of logical development. Deepened personal knowledge does not always have to take the form of expanded conceptual thematization. It can also take the form of "return to the mystery."[38] In other words, it can turn back from a multitude of statements to focus its attention reflectively on the great traits of a rich personal reality which always elude complete conceptualization.

It is by such a return to the Absolute Mystery in the contemplation of the basic truths which thematize the fundamental structure of our relation to Him that Catholic theologians will find their unity of faith in an age of philosophical and theological pluralism.

Although Lonergan is willing to admit that God is the Absolute Horizon of the human knower's world, he believes that the cognitional theory, epistemology, and metaphysics vindicated in *Insight* are required to handle the problems connected with philosophical and theological knowledge of God.[39] This is particularly true of the problems with which the historicity of knowledge has confronted the contemporary theologian. One of the major contributions which *Insight* has made to epistemology and metaphysics is the clear distinction drawn in its cognitional theory between the level of intelligence and the level of reflection in human knowledge. The level of intelligence is the level of conceptual, scientific formulation. It is the level of theories, of hypotheses, of intelligible possibility proposed in answer to the questions "what?" and "how often?" The level of reflection, on which answers to the questions "is it?" "did it occur?" are given through the "yes" or "no" of the judgment, is the level of verification. Intelligible possibility is verified not as rational necessity but as intelligible fact, through reflective understanding's grasp of the virtually unconditioned—i.e., through its insight that the conditions required for its verification have been met in fact.[40] This new insight into the nature of the judgment is the discovery which enables Lonergan to see that metaphysics and theology cannot be sciences in the Aristotelian sense of necessary, deductive knowledge. Cognitional theory has made it clear that they too are sciences in the modern sense. They proceed, as modern science does, by insight into data leading to grasp of intelligible possibilities whose factual realization must then be verified. This new conception of the nature of metaphysics and theology has great consequences for the formulation of our knowledge of God.[41]

The perduring element in empirical science, whose formulations are subject to constant revision, is the scientific method which is operative in the making and revising of scientific theories. An analogous method, perduringly operative in metaphysical and theological reasoning, can be derived by reflecting on the cognitive structure of the human knower who enters into all acts of conceptual formulation or revision as the unrevisable performer of these acts. The act of human knowledge is an inseparable unity of insight into data, intelligent understanding, and reasonable affirmation. It is set in motion by man's pure desire to know, which, if unimpeded, allows the emergence of insights. Insights in their turn result in the higher viewpoints, revisions, and the discovery of new and higher sciences which Lonergan described in his phenomenology of genetic method. But the pure desire to know is impeded in its intelligible expansion if, because of man's biological extroversion, it finds itself linked to an opposed principle of cognitional change, the drive of man's other appetites which move him to flee insights.

Cognitional theory and epistemology, therefore, Lonergan believes, have placed at the disposal of the metaphysician and theologian a fourfold method—classical, statistical, genetic, and dialectic—which is rooted in the unrevisable cognitional structure of the human knower.[42] Its use will provide the operative norm through which genuine developments in human knowledge can be distinguished from aberrations. Under the influence of the pure desire to know, the human knower reaches certain basic positions concerning knowledge, being, and objectivity when he understands his own cognitional structure, becomes aware that being is the object of intelligible understanding and reasonable judgment, and sees that the evidence for being's objective affirmation is the knower's grasp of the virtually unconditioned.[43] Opposed to these truths are the contradictory affirmations which can be called counterpositions. Since both positions and counterpositions are basic affirmations about knowledge, being, and objectivity, their influence enters into the whole expansion of any philosophy. Counterpositions contradict the drive of the pure desire to know. Positions emerge from it and are the expression of its very nature. Through the influence of the pure desire to know, therefore, counterpositions and the incoherence which they introduce into philosophical expansions must inevitably be reversed. Positions, on the other hand, since they are in harmony with the pure desire to know, must lead to genuine developments in human knowledge.[44]

The dialectic between positions and counterpositions in the history of human knowledge becomes the means by which the metaphysician can see that the affirmation of God's existence as an unrestricted act of understanding is a coherent and valid answer to relevant questions which are so fundamental that the human knower cannot dodge them.[45] It is an answer completely in harmony with the basic positions. The opposing views, on the other hand, are not; and it is possible for the philosopher by tracing the influence of the counterpositions on the development of the philosophies in which they are found to understand the reasons which led to their acceptance.[46] Furthermore, the dialectic of positions and counterpositions will enable an exegete, through a reflection on their interplay, to anticipate heuristically a higher viewpoint from which a hermeneutic of the mythical statements emanating from a prephilosophical consciousness might be properly understood and their aberrations distinguished from the assertions which, being in harmony with the basic positions, have been integrated into the genuine development of theology.[47]

Lonergan is also convinced that conversion is as necessary to the philosopher as his mastery of the fourfold method. In fact, conversion is essential for his successful use of it. If he is to remain faithful to the demands of the pure desire to know, the knower must effectively and habitually overcome the other desires which move him to shun insights. Thus the fourth level of consciousness, the level of rational choice, evaluation, and effective freedom, has an essential function in the genuine development of metaphysics and theology. Like Rahner, Lonergan is convinced that intellectual conversion (for him, the faithful holding to the positions on knowledge, being, and objectivity) requires moral conversion. And since, again like Rahner, Lonergan believes that man's effective freedom is a work of grace, moral conversion implies religious conversion.[48]

He looks on theology, therefore, as a work of conversion, a constant turning to the God who is present through grace and who is grasped by faith. The theologian does not seek the absolute certitude of the magisterium, the unshakably certain "yes" or "no" of the Church's verification. Theology is primarily a work of the second level of cognitional structure. As a work of intelligent understanding, it seeks probability, clearer understanding. It pro-

ceeds as a probable science by insight into data, intelligible understanding, and reasonable verification.[49] Through the use of genetic
and dialectical method, it can trace the genuine development of
theology and detect aberrations. It is consequently a science whose
method, based on the invariant structure of the human knower,
should be an expression of the proper function of the four levels
of human consciousness under the impulse of the pure desire to
know.[50]

The description of this method, to which Lonergan's most recent book is devoted,[51] cannot be undertaken here. Since the
method is built on the invariant structure of human knowledge,
Lonergan is convinced that through its use many collaborators
can systematically combine their efforts and, by doing so, cope
with the problems of historical knowledge, scientific diversity, and
philosophical pluralism. Clearly then he is much more optimistic
than Rahner whose solution to these problems is simply to accept
theological pluralism as irreducible and urge a return to the Absolute Mystery. We can see, therefore, why Lonergan shows considerable reserve about Rahner's starting point. For it is the difference in starting point distinguishing *Spirit in the World* and *Hearers of the Word* from *Insight* which has led to the radical difference
between Rahner and Lonergan concerning the nature of theological method and the possibilities which it offers for the understanding of God.

2. The coherence of the doctrine of God

As modern man has become increasingly aware of the dignity and
freedom of man and of his responsibility for the development of
the world, dissatisfaction with the philosophical theology of classical theism has increased. A changeless God who is in no way affected by the history of the world seems to rob man's effort to improve
it of religious value and to deprive the process of human history
of its intrinsic value. A God whose omniscience and omnipotence
give Him complete knowledge of future events and causal dominance over them appears to be an absolute despot who in reality
deprives man of free control over his own acts. And a God who,
being both omniscient and omnipotent, is the creator and conserver

of a world in which moral and physical evils abound seems hardly a fit subject for religious worship. Although these difficulties have not moved the Transcendental Thomists to abandon or to modify their classical theism, they have induced them to employ their metaphysics of the human spirit to propose solutions which the modern reader will find more satisfactory.

a) *God's involvement in history.* Rahner has approached this problem as a theologian. God has changed and continues to change through His interaction with men in history, but He changes *only in His other,* i.e., in the humanity of Christ, to which He is personally united through the Hypostatic Union.[52] This statement, though unexceptional from the Catholic point of view, is hardly new. The novelty which it possesses in Rahner's work is in the metaphysics through which he works out its consequences for theology. This is the metaphysics of the real symbol.[53] In *Spirit in the World* Rahner had grounded the metaphysical possibility of the unified act of knowledge, in which sense and intellect cooperate to grasp the real through sensation, abstraction of the concept, and affirmation, in the successive emanation of the intellectual and sensible faculties from the soul.[54] The soul "expresses itself" by going over into its faculties. In other words it reaches its own intelligible and dynamic completion by allowing them emanation through its own quasi-efficient causality and, at the same time, sustaining them in their independent existence as its own proper accidents. The "other" through whose ontological procession a being reaches its fullness, Rahner calls the being's "real symbol." Thus the Son, through whose procession the Father expresses Himself in the Trinity, is the Father's real symbol. For the Father is Father only through the interrelationship between Himself and the Son.[55] Likewise Christ's humanity, through which He expresses Himself as man, is His real symbol.[56] For man is the only being whose ontological dynamism is such that he can come to the full flowering of what he is by nature when he enters into metaphysical identity with the Word of God as the real symbol through which He expresses Himself. For man is a spirit whose intrinsic drive is to unite himself in knowledge and love with the Absolute Mystery, and this union reaches its perfection when it reaches the heights of personal identity.

If, then, the Word of God wishes to express Himself in the created world through a real symbol, He must do so as man. But in becoming man He enters history. He is tied to the natural history of the world's evolution to which man as a spatio-temporal being is linked. And, more importantly, He is tied to the human history in which man, as a social being, makes himself by making his world. Through the theology of the real symbol Rahner explains how God has entered history and is changed and affected by it, although always in His other.

Although Rahner has confined his considerations to the Hypostatic Union, his theology of the real symbol has enabled other Thomists, especially Walter Stokes,[57] to extend his considerations to the involvement of God in human history not only in His human but also in His divine nature. Clearly God does not express Himself in creation in the full sense of the real symbol since creatures do not become one with Him in a metaphysical, personal union. Nevertheless, the ontology of the real symbol indicates that the more perfectly God expresses Himself in His causal grounding of a creature the greater is the "otherness" or the independence of the creature. Thus the more perfectly God expresses Himself in man, the freer man is. In the free act of creation through which God created man He created a society of incarnate persons who express their freedom socially and historically. He created persons with whom His relations would be conditioned by their acceptance of Him in love and whose response would therefore condition His ongoing relations with them. And, since man is social and historical in nature, his free response to God is conditioned by his relations with his fellow-men in the cultural milieu in which he lives. Thus, in the very act in which God creates other persons, He finds that His personal relations with them are conditioned by their response to Him, and that this response in turn is conditioned by the course of human history. History, then, does make a difference to God. In creating human persons, the very outpouring of His power, which is the source of their independence, makes Him in a sense dependent upon it.

b) *Divine providence.* Furthermore, just as the Transcendental Thomists are convinced that God's involvement in human history in on sense entails His mutability and that His infinite perfection would have remained unchanged whether He had created men or not, they are convinced that He remains the Lord of history through His omniscience and omnipotence. What is more, the resources of their new metaphysics make it possible for them to reconcile the classical theistic understanding of providence with human freedom and the fact of evil more satisfactorily than their predecessors were able to do. This is particularly true of Lonergan.

God, as the unrestricted act of insight, is the creative causal ground through whom the intelligible reality of every contingent being is founded. As their cause, He knows and wills them as they are. The world of contingent beings, as Lonergan's metaphysics has shown, is a world of emerging probability. It is a world in which natural species have emerged as nonsystematic processes fall into schemes of recurrence in which a happy combination of abstract laws and concrete circumstances makes further determinations recurrent and thus brings them under the dominance of intelligence. And, as man emerges, his own development falls into the historical interplay of the pure desire to know and the opposing desires which can be understood through the dialectical development of linked, but opposed, principles of change. Emergent probability is not a necessary process. It is intelligible rather as the one concrete probability out of many which was actually realized in the existing world. Since, then, it is an order which is neither necessary nor arbitrary, its ground must be in the reasonable choice of a rational consciousness.[58]

God can be this free cause of our world order. As an unrestricted act of insight, He can grasp every event in the series which led to the emergence of its intelligible pattern. He can do so because as first cause He cooperates with their action. Thus He not only knows the range of possible world orders and the possibilities which lie open to our own; He also knows each event in its relation to all the others. Thus He knows the history of the cooperation and interference of causes which determine the concrete order, among the many probable ones, which actually will be realized in our world.

To explain God's knowledge and control of world history, therefore, we need not fall back on the old theories about the futurables. We need no longer talk about God's knowledge of what men would infallibly do if placed in certain circumstances. Nor need we do injury to human freedom in our effort to defend God's foreknowledge through postulating a divine concurrence with the free act which predetermines it to a definite choice through physical premotion. Seeing the whole order of emerging probability as present to His timeless act of knowledge, God knows and dominates every event simply by knowing it as actual. Futurables and premotions which threaten human freedom become otiose.[59]

Physical evil also becomes more comprehensible. The order of emergent probability is one in which nonsystematic processes are at play. Inevitably, therefore, it is an order of evolution, risk, false starts. Yet it is an intelligible order of growing perfection and, as intelligible, it is a good. As a true good it is perfectly worthy of God's reasonable choice. It is also quite intelligible that man should emerge in such a world and that through man, a being linked to matter by his biological constitution and transcending it by his spirit, the universe should, in part at least, assume the free direction of its own history. But the inevitable concomitant of human freedom is the dialectic between biological desires and the pure drive to know and the stupidity, moral evil, and social suffering which are inseparable from it.[60]

For man is capable of basic sin. He can refuse to realize the intelligibility which it is his duty to contribute to the universe through his free choices. He can either refuse to perform the acts which he has judged to be reasonable and obligatory or perform those which he has judged unreasonable and forbidden. Yet, although basic sin is inherent as a possibility of our world order, God is not responsible for it. This is easier to see in Lonergan's metaphysics than in the older Thomistic systems. In the older systems, God, as the author of world order, viewing the possibles and the futurables, decreed to realize some and not to realize others. The world consisted, therefore, of the goods which God willed and the unrealized goods which God deliberately decided not to will. Thus, even though the older Thomists held that sin, as an evil, was a nonentity, they did not quite clear God of responsibility for it. He had allowed it to occur by deliberately deciding not to produce the opposite entity through His decision not to concur with the causes which would have produced it.

Lonergan's metaphysics of being enables him to take another tack. There is no causal connection between sin and any act either of willing it or of not willing it on the part of God. This can be seen when we understand correctly the status of sin as nonbeing. Basic sin is an empirical fact, true enough. Yet being is not brute, contingent fact. Being is the object of intelligent understanding and reasonable affirmation, and, as such, it is the real, outside of which there is nothing. Basic sin, however, is a complete surd. It has no intelligibility, for it is precisely man's failure to realize intelligibility by his free action. Since there is nothing to understand in it, there is nothing to be contained in God's unrestricted act of understanding. Sin, therefore, is not caused by God, for causality is procession of being with intelligible dependence, and there can be no relation of causality between the complete surd and God. Sin is an irrationality which God neither wills nor does not will, but forbids.[61]

3. The relevance of the knowledge of God

From what has been said above the relevance of the new philosophical theology of Transcendental Thomism is not difficult to see. It approaches man at the level of his personal, moral, and social experience. Its aim is to reflect on man's basic intellectual and volitional activity in science and common sense and on man's fundamental, implicit "experience of God and grace." Through its reflections it enables contemporary man to see how his fundamental experiences open out into a knowledge of God which finds its fulfillment in faith. Through its epistemology and metaphysics the believer can be led to understand and appreciate at their true worth the implicit faith and love of the anonymous Christian. Likewise the formal unbeliever not only is brought into contact with a presentation of traditional theism which he finds more credible but is enabled to see how the God of the philosophers, who is also the God of revelation, can be a source of light and strength to the man of good will. The Christian is placed in a better position to enter into fruitful dialogue with his contemporaries. He is no longer engaged in an endeavor to "prove" to them the existence of a God of whom they have not heard. He is engaged in company with them in clarifying the profound experiences through which God manifests Himself to all.

The world which confronts believer and unbeliever alike is the world of emerging probability. Man is called individually to foster its evolution by promoting the advance of intelligibility in the human community. Evils there are and will be, but man can work to make them fewer. And, as he does so, he will create himself by the use of natural and social sciences.[62] Thus, individually and collectively, he will promote his development as a knower and free himself to follow the pure desire through whose influence he commits himself to God. God and the world of science are not indifferent to each other. For to create himself, the Christian must leave behind the world of Aristotle and accept, albeit critically, the world of modern science. He need not be afraid to do so, for in his philosophical theology he has his corrective against the ideologies of the age.[63] The free man, whose pure desire to know relates him immediately and essentially to the Absolute Mystery, can never be subjected as a mere means to the manipulation of totalitarian society.[64] Since man knows that he is a spirit tied by matter to the laws of space and time, he knows that he cannot make his irrevocable commitment to God until the moment of death.[65] He must always be on his guard, therefore, and struggle constantly to maintain his openness to the Absolute Mystery. Free, responsible action, based on intelligent understanding and reasonable affirmation, will be placed only by the men who struggle to win effective freedom.[66] And this, the theologian knows, is a work of grace. The God who has been involved in human history from its beginning is involved in it now by His love and grace. And it is He who is the Absolute Future toward which the individual man stretches out in his historical activity and toward which the course of history tends.[67] For at death, in the free decision of love, man enters into immediate contact with Him. Our modern ideologies mistake some being inside the world for its Absolute Horizon as the meaning-giving term of its historical evolution. The world which man must create, however, points beyond itself to the Absolute Mystery whose love is the reason for man's being and whose promised help is the reason for man's abiding hope.[68]

NOTES

1. Bernard Lonergan, s.j., *Insight* (New York: Longmans, 1958), p. 677.
2. Lonergan attempts this hermeneutic in his historical study *Verbum: Word and Idea in Aquinas* (Notre Dame: University of Notre Dame Press, 1967). In both *Verbum* and *Insight* Lonergan contrasts Aquinas' view that the procession of both concept and judgment are conscious ones with the position of the conceptualist manuals that abstraction is an unconscious process.
3. See Johannes Baptist Metz, *Christliche Anthropozentrik* (Munich: Kösel, 1962).
4. See Karl Rahner, s.j., "The Dignity and Freedom of Man," *Theological Investigations* ii (Baltimore: Helicon, 1964). See also "Theologie und Anthropologie," *Schriften zur Theologie* viii (Einsiedeln: Benziger, 1967), pp. 43-65.
5. The most important of the five volumes of Maréchal's major work is the celebrated *Cahier* v: *Le Thomisme devant la philosophie critique* (Paris: Desclée de Brouwer, 1949). For an excellent selection of Maréchalian texts, see *A Maréchal Reader*, ed. Joseph Donceel, s.j. (New York: Herder and Herder, 1970).
6. See K. Rahner, "Philosophie und Philosophieren in der Theologie," *Schriften* viii, pp. 66-87 (trans. "Philosophy and Philosophizing in Theology," *Theology Digest*, 16 [1968], 17-29).
7. See Lonergan, "Theology and Understanding," *Collection* (New York: Herder and Herder, 1967), pp. 121-41.
8. This is the contention of Rahner's *Spirit in the World*, trans. W. Dych, s.j. (New York: Herder and Herder, 1968), esp. pp. 183-87.
9. *Insight*, pp. 658-65.
10. See note 8.
11. *Hearers of the Word*, trans. Michael Richards (New York: Herder and Herder, 1969), pp. 53-68.
12. See K. Rahner, "The Concept of Mystery in Catholic Theology," *Theological Investigations* v, pp. 36-73.
13. The vindication of man's basic capacity to hear a word of historical revelation, rooted in his metaphysical structure as an historical knower whose intellectual dynamism opens him to Absolute Being, is the theme of Rahner's *Hearers of the Word*.
14. *Hearers of the Word*, pp. 87-101, and "The Concept of Mystery," *loc. cit.*, pp. 53-59.
15. See "Bemerkungen zur Gotteslehre in der katholischen Dogmatik," *Schriften* viii, pp. 165-86, esp. pp. 179-83, and "Atheismus und implizites Christentum," *ibid.*, pp. 187-212. See also "Über die Einheit von nächsten und Gottesliebe," in *Schriften* vi, pp. 277-98, and "Anonymes Christentum und Missionauftrag der Kirche," in *Schriften* ix, pp. 498-515. For a discussion of Rahner's theology of the anonymous Christian, see Anita Röper, *The Anonymous Christian* (New York: Sheed & Ward, 1966).

16. See "Metaphysics as Horizon," *Collection*, pp. 202-20.

17. See "Cognitional Structure," *ibid.*, pp. 221-39, and "The Isomorphism of Thomist and Scientific Thought," *ibid.*, pp. 142-51.

18. See "Dimensions of Meaning," *ibid.*, pp. 252-67.

19. "Functional Specialities in Theology," *Gregorianum*, 50 (1969), 485-505.

20. *Insight*, pp. 103-39.

21. *Ibid.*, pp. 191-242.

22. *Ibid.*, pp. 431-87.

23. See "Theology in its New Context," *Theology of Renewal*, ed. L. K. Shook (New York: Herder and Herder, 1968), I, 34-46.

24. *Insight*, pp. 387-89.

25. *Ibid.*, pp. 634-85.

26. For a clear summary of Lonergan's proof for the existence of God, see Gary Schouborg, "A Note on Lonergan's Argument for the Existence of God," *The Modern Schoolman*, 45 (1968), 243-48.

27. See K. Rahner, "Philosophie und Philosophieren" (note 6) and "Zur Geschichtlichkeit der Theologie," *Schriften* VIII, pp. 88-110 (trans. "The Historical Dimension in Theology," *Theology Digest*, 16 [1968], 30-42). See also Lonergan, "*Existenz* and *Aggiornamento*," *Collection*, pp. 240-51.

28. See K. Rahner, "Concerning the Relationship of Nature and Grace," *Theological Investigations* I, pp. 297-319, esp. pp. 311-13, and *Hearers of the Word*, p. 10n8. For a discussion of Rahner's theology of the supernatural existential, see William G. Shepherd, *Man's Condition* (New York: Herder and Herder, 1969), esp. pp. 81-93.

29. See "Nature and Grace," *Theological Investigations* IV, pp. 165-88.

30. See "Die anonymen Christen," *Schriften* VI, pp. 545-54.

31. *Hearers of the Word*, p. 67n10.

32. See note 14.

33. See "Reflections on the Experience of Grace," *Theological Investigations* III, pp. 86-90, and "Gotteserfahrung heute," *Schriften zur Theologie* IX, pp. 161-76; and Lonergan, "Openness and Religious Experience," *Collection*, pp. 198-201.

34. See "Current Problems in Christology," *Theological Investigations* V, pp. 151-92.

35. See "Considerations on the Development of Dogma," *Theological Investigations* IV, pp. 3-35.

36. "Freedom in the Church," *Theological Investigations* II, pp. 89-107, and *The Dynamic Element in the Church* (New York: Herder and Herder, 1964).

37. See note 27.

38. See note 35.

39. See note 16.

40. *Insight*, pp. 271-78; 315-16.

41. See notes 19 and 23.

42. *Insight*, pp. 396-401.

43. *Ibid.*, pp. 328-32; 348-50; 375-84.

44. *Ibid.*, pp. 387-90.

45. *Ibid.*, p. 680.

46. *Ibid.*, pp. 680-86.

47. *Ibid.*, pp. 462-581.

48. See note 19.

49. See note 7.

50. See note 19.

51. *Method in Theology* (London: Darton, Longman and Todd, 1972).

52. See "On the Theology of the Incarnation," *Theological Investigations* IV, pp. 105-20, esp. pp. 112-20.

53. See "On the Theology of the Symbol," *ibid.*, pp. 221-311.

54. *Spirit in the World*, pp. 253-60.

55. See "The Theology of the Symbol," *loc. cit.*, pp. 225-30.

56. See *ibid.*, pp. 236-40.

57. Walter Stokes, "Is God Really Related to the World?" *Proceedings of the American Catholic Philosophical Association*, 39 (1965), 145-51.

58. *Insight*, p. 656.

59. *Ibid.*, pp. 661-65. See also "Gratia operans," *Theological Studies*, 3 (1942), 533-78, esp. 547-53.

60. *Insight*, pp. 666-69.

61. *Ibid.*, p. 666, and "Gratia operans," *loc. cit.*, 550-52.

62. See K. Rahner, "Experiment Mensch," *Schriften* VIII (trans. "Experiment Man," *Theology Digest*, 16 [1968], 57-69).

63. See K. Rahner, "Ideologie und Christentum," *Schriften* VI, pp. 59-76, and "Marxistische Utopie und christliche Zukunft des Menschen," *ibid.*, pp. 77-90.

64. See "The Dignity and Freedom of Man," *Theological Investigations* II, pp. 235-63.

65. See K. Rahner, "The Theological Concept of Concupiscentia," *Theological Investigations* I, pp. 347-83, esp. pp. 360-66.

66. *Insight*, pp. 619-33.

67. See K. Rahner, "Kirche und Parusie Christi," *Schriften* VI, pp. 348-67, and "Fragment aus einer theologischen Besinnung auf den Begriff der Zukunft," *Schriften* VIII, pp. 555-60.

68. See K. Rahner, "Zur Theologie der Hoffnung," *Schriften* VIII, pp. 561-79 (trans. "The Theology of Hope," *Theology Digest*, 16 [1968], 78-87).

8

Can We Still Make a Case
in Reason for
the Existence of God?

JOSEPH DONCEEL, S.J.

IT IS A REMARKABLE FACT that the many philosophers who, in the English-speaking countries, try to point out the weaknesses of the proofs of God's existence, always restrict themselves to the way in which these proofs were presented in the past. They seem to be unaware of the fact that the proponents of natural theology have done some thinking of their own. Admittedly many of the former "demonstrations" of God's existence contain weak spots, but something has been done about them. The theological agnostics do not seem to have heard of this. They continue blithely to refute the shopworn arguments, they flog dead horses.[1]

It is true that the modern approaches in natural theology have come mainly from the Continent, that they were presented in French and in German, that they have enjoyed little publicity this side of the ocean. Yet, we would expect professional philosophers to know of them. A perusal of the abundant English literature on the proofs of God shows that most philosophers seem never to have heard of them. That is why I shall attempt here to present these new approaches as clearly and as briefly as possible. Clarity and brevity may be difficult to reconcile with thoroughness and profundity. Philosophers who prize the latter qualities above the former are invited to refer to the sources from which I have borrowed my ideas.[2]

I do not expect to convert to my views those who claim that God's existence cannot be demonstrated, that no case can be made for it in reason. But it might be worth their while to turn their critical acumen away from the threadbare arguments they have been so zealously castigating and to direct it against these new attempts. They will, of course, hold their fire until they have thoroughly studied them, not in my admittedly simplified, but in their original, presentation. Thus they may force the natural theologians, who continue to claim that a reasonable case may be made for God's existence, to dig deeper still and to penetrate ever more profoundly into the heart of the matter.

Before we start on the new proof, a few remarks may be useful.

1) Why is it important to defend natural theology? Because if we give it up, we must admit that we can no longer make a reasonable case for the existence of God. We might find it useful or comforting to assert that He exists; such a belief may satisfy our feelings, provide us with a sense of security. But it is not reasonable. It cannot stand the test of intelligent scrutiny. I am not willing to embrace this kind of intellectual defeatism.

Many Christians seem to derive their certitude of God's existence, not from reason, but from faith. They firmly believe that God exists, but they assert that no reasonable case can be made for this belief, that it is a question of faith. Let us briefly examine this kind of fideism.

What do they mean by *faith*, by *believing*? Is it a natural faith and belief in their educators? Do they believe in God's existence because they continue to believe what their parents, their teachers, their priests or ministers told them about God? Or do they mean the supernatural "virtue of faith"? It is difficult to see how they might simply mean a case of natural belief. There are so many things they believed as children (the stork, Santa Claus, the existence of

Australia). Some of these beliefs have been abandoned because no evidence ever arose to bolster them; others have been retained because they were strengthened by new evidence or testimony. Why did they keep their belief in God? Is it not because they have met new evidence for it? And is this evidence not simply the fact that they found it reasonable to admit God's existence? It is obvious that most of us *started* to believe in God because, when we were very young, our parents told us about Him. But the reason why we continue to believe in Him is no longer the word of our parents. Something else has taken over in our mind. What is this something else?

Some Christians would say that it is what theology calls the supernatural virtue of faith, infused at baptism, and starting to operate on the conscious level with the awakening of the mind. This faith has undoubtedly a strong influence upon many a person's conviction that God exists. But to admit that it is the *sole* reason for this conviction brings up considerable difficulties. Supernatural faith consists in believing something *propter auctoritatem Dei revelantis*, because God Himself tells us it is true. In this hypothesis we would be convinced that God exists because He Himself tells us so.

This might be unobjectionable if we were able to meet God the way we meet John or Mary. Before meeting them we know what a human being is, and when they tell us that they are respectively John Doe and Mary Roe, we act quite reasonably in admitting this. But the case is quite different with God. We are supposed to know *nothing* about Him from reason or from experience; what we hear about Him from others *never* receives any experimental confirmation. Firmly to believe that He exists because He Himself— the utterly unknown—tells us He does seems to be a case not of faith but of gullibility.

We should rather say that, before welcoming God's revelation, we must somehow know that and what God is. "Before" does not imply any chronological, but only a logical and ontological, priority. As children we believed God's existence as we may have believed that of the stork or of Santa. But there is a great difference between these two kinds of belief. The latter have no root in our mind; soon they wither and are rejected. The former is deeply rooted in our intellect, and many people welcome it as soon as they have critically examined it. It can withstand doubts, denials, and difficulties. This is not an effect of the sole virtue of faith. As Professor Léopold Malevez puts it:

The act of faith refers definitely to an Absolute who is implicitly affirmed by our intellect. When we state, in the act of faith: it is God who speaks in Jesus Christ, we refer this word to the Absolute who is already written in our mind, we claim that it possesses the features of a God whose existence we naturally affirm. . . . It is on account of this relation to the implicitly affirmed God that the God of revelation and of faith assumes a meaning *for* *us* and becomes *our* truth. In other words: it is impossible to believe revealed theology without the "exercise" of a natural theology. This natural theology does not have to be explicit. . . . But it must have been "lived" implicitly by our reason. Otherwise the affirmation of the God of revelation would make no sense for us.[3]

2) The unsophisticated human mind naturally affirms the existence of God. It is rarely called upon to put into words the reasons why it holds such a view. If it were to do so, these reasons would, in all probability, be far from cogent. Does this mean that the ordinary people are wrong when they admit the existence of God? By no means. The real reason which makes them cling to this conviction is much deeper than they themselves are aware of or can verbalize. The task of the following pages is to uncover it.

The argument which lurks in the mind of ordinary people is, in reality, some kind of "egg and hen" argument. Every hen comes from an egg, every egg comes from a hen. There must have been a first hen or a first egg, and this first link of the chain must come from a Creator God. This way of arguing is far from convincing. Why might this series of antecedents and consequents not extend indefinitely into the past? Why should there be a first link in the chain? Suppose that we can demonstrate that there must have been a first link, and that God produced it. How do we know that God continues to exist, since He is no longer needed, once the process has been set into motion? Finally, why do we need an *infinite* cause to explain the first link, a *finite* effect? The "egg and hen" argument is totally inadequate.

Of course, few people nowadays would use such a simple way of arguing. The reason which many people consider sufficient to establish the existence of God is the fact that the world exists and that it must have a cause of its existence. This might be a good rational basis for holding the existence of God, provided it be well understood. Too many people, however, interpret it as meaning that God must explain the *origin*, the *first beginning* of the universe. This is the "hen and egg" argument again, enlarged to cosmic proportions. Instead of considering only one causal series—that of our domestic fowl—it considers all the innumerable causal series whose totality constitutes the universe. And it meets the same difficulties. It is not certain at all that the universe had a beginning in time. Even St. Thomas denied that our reason can demonstrate that there must have been such a beginning. It is not contradictory to hold that matter has existed from all eternity. If God is needed only to start off the cosmic show, there goes the foundation of the whole argument; the show never started, it has been going on forever. Suppose, however, that we can establish that the universe has started in time. We are once more in the presence of a finite reality. The universe is immense, it might be infinite in space, it is certainly not infinite in perfection; it is a finite reality, it might be better than it is. Why does it take an infinitely perfect cause to produce and explain a finite effect?

3) This leads me to my next remark. The weakness which I have tried to point out in the common-sense argument affects to some extent all demonstrations of God based on efficient causality or on teleology. It renders the *viae* or *ways* of St. Thomas obsolete for present-day purposes. Or, to put it more mildly: it shows that these ways are only ways to the real argument which Aquinas developed only implicitly in other parts of his work. Once we accept the value of the principle of causality, the *viae* lead us to a first cause. Furthermore, it is not difficult to show that they do not merely refer to a cause of *beginning*, to a phenomenal cause, to a mere antecedent. They do really reach a cause of *being*, a noumenal, ontological cause. In this case an infinite regression is excluded. They arrive at God, not as the one who started the universe, but as the one who right now continues to keep it in existence. But why should this ever-active cause of a finite universe be an infinitely perfect cause, one whose essence it is to exist?

This is rather obvious, yet it deserves a few moments of consideration. The arguments based solely on efficient causality and on teleology run into the following, very serious, difficulty. How can we ever hope to arrive at an infinite, necessary, absolute conclusion if we start from finite, contingent, relative premisses? The conclusion can never be stronger than the premisses from which it is drawn. In other words: how can we ever arrive at the infinite, if we start from the finite? There is no bridging an infinite gap. In such arguments we almost unavoidably make of God the highest link in a chain of causalities. And this the Absolute is certainly not. He is not a link, not even the highest link, in a chain of causes.

Moreover, the traditional ways hinge on the principle of causality. St. Thomas took it for granted, and rightly so. But great philosophers, Hume and Kant among others, have challenged the value of the principle. We should be willing to consider their objections. Too many textbooks have tried to demonstrate it by begging it. They claim that it is immediately evident (which it is) because it is analytic (which it is not).

Some authors try to demonstrate it as follows: Every contingent being is caused either by itself or by another being. But obviously not by itself since, in that case, it would confer upon itself a perfection which it does not possess. Therefore it is caused by another being.

It is easy to see that this merely begs the question. The disjunction is not complete. The major premiss should be: Every contingent being is caused either by itself, or by another being, or by nothing. This last possibility is not considered. The demonstration takes for granted, from the very start, that a contingent being is not caused by nothing, that is, is caused by something. But this is precisely the principle of causality which it is supposed to demonstrate.

The fact is that we shall not use the principle of efficient causality in our vindication. The reason has been mentioned above: even if we succeed in establishing the value of the principle against the onslaughts of Hume and of Kant, it cannot bring us higher than a finite cause. From finite effects it is impossible logically to infer an infinite cause.

I shall use the principle of final causality. Not, however, as it is used in the teleological argument, where an attempt is made to show that the finality of nature supposes an infinitely wise Creator. The principle of final causality will be applied, not to the realities outside of us, but to the motion of our own intellect. I shall try to show that our intellectual knowledge is possible only because, in its every act of knowledge, our intellect intends the knowledge of the Infinite. This intending of the Infinite, this *Vorgriff* or anticipating grasp of the Absolute, is a condition of the possibility of our intellectual knowledge.

It is important to notice this shift from the usual approach, from God "demonstrated" as the efficient cause of the universe to God "necessarily affirmed" as the final cause of our intellectual dynamism. It was first suggested by Joseph Maréchal, taken over and elaborated by Karl Rahner. As Rahner puts it: we speak more of affirmation than of causality, we pay more attention to our own intellect than to the things out there. We rely not so much on the metaphysics of being as on the metaphysics of our knowledge of being. We do not say: the beings which actually exist require, as a condition of their existence, the existence of God. We say: the affirmation of the beings which we know demands as a condition of its possibility the affirmation of God's existence.

That is why, rather than using the cosmological or the teleological argument, I shall try to arrive at God by using a refurbished form of the ontological argument.[4] Everyone is familiar with this clever way of reasoning, which has a long and brilliant career in the history of philosophy. It was first used in the eleventh century by Anselm of Canterbury.[5] For clarity's sake, we might summarize it in the following syllogism:

> The greatest conceivable being exists in reality.
> But God is the greatest conceivable being.
> Therefore God exists in reality.

The minor of this syllogism is undeniable. God is undoubtedly the greatest conceivable being, than which a greater one cannot be thought of. But what about the major premiss? This one does not seem so obvious. St. Anselm established it as follows: If your greatest conceivable being does not exist in reality, it is not the greatest conceivable. You may then conceive a greater being, namely the one you were thinking of, to which you add real existence.

This, and only this, is the greatest conceivable being. And it obviously exists.

The difficulty with this line of reasoning is that it remains exclusively within the realm of concepts, of mere possibles, within the ideal order. It is undeniable that the greatest conceivable being must be *conceived* as existing in reality. But it does not follow at once that it exists in reality.

God's existence is a fact, the fact of facts. Facts should not be demonstrated, they must be established. We notice or perceive them, or we notice something which implies them. Logic alone, concepts and syllogisms alone, cannot lead us to God. We may need them, to be sure, but they will never do as our starting point. We must start from a fact, from experience, from an undeniable fact in our experience. I intend to start from such an undeniable fact of experience: the fact that I think and that I want to know.

Leibniz has presented the ontological proof in another way.[6] We may summarize his approach as follows;

> If God is possible, He exists.
> But God is possible.
> Therefore God exists.

Most people's reaction on hearing this elegant bit of sophistry is to concede the minor premiss and to deny or to question the major. They admit that God is possible, but they fail to see why it is evident that if God is possible, He exists.

In fact it would be wiser to admit the major premiss and to question the minor, to request a demonstration of the minor. Most metaphysicians readily admit that if God is possible, He exists, not because His existence derives from His possibility, but because His possibility implies His existence. Since I shall need this important idea as a step in my vindication, we must have a closer look at it.

There are two kinds of possibility: intrinsic and extrinsic. A being is intrinsically possible when its definition contains no contradiction. A square circle is impossible, a square island is possible. A being is extrinsically possible when it either exists or can be made to exist. A square island is extrinsically possible. Although there actually may exist no perfectly square island, God or the "Seabees" might bring one into existence.

Let us first consider the extrinsic possibility of God. It is clear at once that God is extrinsically possible only if He exists. For if He did not exist, nothing would be able to make Him exist, He could never possibly exist. Therefore the only way for God to be extrinsically possible is to exist. In this sense at least, it is evident that if God is possible, He exists. Or, to put it more modestly: He who affirms that God is possible has also affirmed that He exists.

It is somewhat more difficult to show that God's intrinsic possibility too implies His existence. For this purpose we must first agree to some extent on what we mean when we speak of God. It seems to me that we would have to agree at least on this: that if God exists, He exists necessarily, He is not a purely contingent being, who happens to exist, but might as well not exist. Such a being would not be the God we are speaking of. At least, He is not the being I am speaking of. He is not the being for whose existence I am trying to make a case in reason. The God I mean is a being who, if He exists at all, exists necessarily. But a non-existing necessarily existing being is as contradictory as a square circle. Such a being is (intrinsically) possible only if He exists. Hence, if God does not exist, He is not (intrinsically) possible. And, by contraposition, if God is (intrinsically) possible, He exists.[7]

The major premiss of Leibniz' is true. The difficulty with his argument is that he takes the minor premiss for granted, that he simply affirms the possibility of God, or rather that he tries to establish it by a priori considerations, by a simple examination of the concept of God. There seems to be no contradiction in the concept of an infinitely perfect, necessarily existing being. But we have no adequate concept of such a being, so that, although we do not notice any contradiction in its concept, there may lurk a hidden contradiction in it. There is no establishing the possibility of God a priori, by a mere examination of concepts. The only way of establishing that God is possible is either to demonstrate that He exists or—and that is what I shall try to do—to point to an undeniable fact of human experience, which implies the possibility of God.

So my claim is that, if I discover such an undeniable fact of experience, one which implies the possibility of the unlimited, infinite, necessary being, I shall have made a reasonable case for the existence of God.

Here is how I would try to go about this. Whenever I know anything at all, I know at once that this thing is finite, limited. The awareness of the limitation of every object I know is of paramount importance in my vindication. It is impossible to know a limit as limit unless one be already beyond this limit, either in fact or, at least, in desire. The human intellect is not beyond every limit; in fact, it is limited in many respects. So, it must be beyond any limit in desire, in striving. Its dynamism drives it beyond any limit. It is aware of the finiteness of all its contents; therefore it must be striving past them. Without this urge to proceed beyond any conceivable limit, it would not be aware of the universal limitation of all the objects of experience.

Do we really know all realities we know as limited realities? What about the universe? Even the universe is known to us as a limited reality, not necessarily limited in time or space, but at least limited in perfection, in goodness. The universe as it is right now might be in a better shape than it actually is in. It is limited, finite. Being aware of this, we are already beyond it.

It follows that the human intellect continually strives beyond any limit whatsoever. I say: any limit whatsoever. This is important. It is the limit as such which is unacceptable to the intellect, not simply this or that or the next limit. Any limit, the limit as such. Hence it is erroneous to claim that our intellect goes off in an *indefinite* quest, that it gets lost into what Hegel called the bad or spurious infinite. It is the limit as such, not this or that limit, which is rejected by the intellect. In transcending any limit, we are at once, in desire or yearning, poised beyond any limit, pointing toward the unlimited. In transcending the limit as such, we keep aiming at, anticipating, affirming the Infinite.

Another way of showing this is to point out that in every human action, every time we know some reality, we implicitly affirm of the object of this activity that it is. The word is puts the stamp of reality on that which we know. We say of things around us: This is, that is. In fact, the predicate is is too wide for all the realities we attribute it to. Nothing in our experience strictly speaking is, without any further qualification. It is this or that, it is a man or a dog or a tree. We continually use, we cannot not use (either explicitly, or at least implicitly) a predicate which is too wide for all the subjects we predicate it of. If we give this some thought, we easily become aware of it. And with some more reflection, especially upon the fact that we are also aware of the limitation of everything we know, we might reach the insight that what our intellect is really after in every one of its activities is: to meet and to grasp a reality which fully deserves the predicate IS, a reality which is not merely this or that, a reality which simply IS, without any specification, determination, negation, or limitation. This reality is Being Itself, *Ipsum Esse*, as Aquinas used to call it. It is the Infinite, it is God. The word IS which every human being, in all human languages, uses either explicitly or at least implicitly, is the indelible mark in human speech and in human thought of the transcendent finality of the human intellect. It shows that whatever we know or want as human beings is known or wanted as projected against the horizon of Infinity.

Suppose now that we admit that in every human action man implicitly intends the Infinite. Does it follow that the Infinite, that Being Itself, exists? People have been known to strive for things which do not exist and will never exist. That is undeniable. What the striving of my intellect certainly implies is the possibility of the Infinite Being. If this being is not possible, if it is contradictory, then I keep striving *naturally*, irresistibly, congenitally, toward the impossible. But this is hard to admit. That a diseased mind may occasionally pursue impossible or contradictory goals may be true. This is one of the reasons why we call it diseased. But that the human mind would universally, always, of its very nature, act in this way is excluded. An impossible goal is one which not only does not exist, but cannot exist. To tend toward the impossible is to tend toward nothing, not to tend at all. To tend congenitally toward the impossible would introduce a living contradiction within the core of man's being.

It follows that the undeniable fact, known in direct personal experience by every human being, of the dynamism of his intellect, implies the possibility, hence the existence of the Infinitely Perfect, Unlimited Being whom we call God.

We shall now have a look at some of the typical features of this vindication; next we shall examine at least a few of the many objections which may be presented against it.

1) It is easy to see why we call it a vindication, rather than a demonstration. A demonstration in philosophy starts from presuppositions about which both parties in the discussion agree. These common presuppositions refer generally to the basic laws of human thinking. In the present case, however, the disagreement concerns precisely one of these basic laws itself: our claim that in every affirmation man affirms the existence of God. No common presupposition can be previous to this claim. Therefore we cannot demonstrate it in the usual meaning of this word.

But there can be a vindication of it, which looks like the procedure used by Aristotle to establish the first principles of logic and metaphysics, in the books Gamma and Kappa of the *Metaphysics*. It is some kind of argument *ad hominem*, with this peculiarity that the *homo* in question is every man, man as man. Some authors call this way of arguing *retorsion*, an attempt to show that the one who denies what I hold contradicts himself in his very act of denying. A "retorsion" is in fact the pointing out of a transcendental necessity.

A couple of examples may make this clearer. When someone tells me that only scientifically established statements are certain, he contradicts himself since what he says has not been and cannot be scientifically established. Thus he affirms in the same breath that what he says is certain and not certain. If someone tells me that whatever we affirm is affirmed and is true only within a certain framework, he contradicts himself implicitly, since what he says embraces absolutely every assertion, within all possible frameworks. Of his own affirmation he holds that it is true only within a certain framework and in all frameworks.

In these two examples the contradiction is not explicit, it does not occur between terms used in the assertion. It resides rather between what is affirmed and the act of the mind by which it is affirmed. In the first example the *act* of affirming implies a certitude which is denied by the *content* of the affirmation. In the second example the act of affirming embraces a range which is denied of it by the content of the affirmation. In both cases my imaginary opponent denies implicitly what he affirms explicitly. My only defense against him consists in making this "lived" contradiction visible ("retorsion").

Something similar occurs in our vindication. I claim that the person who denies God's existence explicitly affirms it implicitly in his very denial. This denial is an affirmation, an activity of his intellect whose dynamism transcends every limitation and intends the Infinite. I admit quite readily that the implicit, "lived" contradiction is much more difficult to show in the present instance than in the two cases explained above. Even there I expect to meet intelligent people who claim that they do not see any contradiction, either explicit or implicit. This is true *a fortiori* of our present, more fundamental, instance. Anyway, my purpose here is not to press my defense, but to explain what I mean by a vindication and how my approach differs considerably from the usual "demonstrations" of God's existence.

2) It is important to notice *how* we reach God in this vindication: as the ultimate end of the dynamism of our intellect, as the reality which we try in vain to grasp (*Vorgriff*) every time we grasp anything at all intellectually. The affirmation of this ultimate end is a condition of the possibility of our every act of knowing. God is co-affirmed implicitly in everything we affirm explicitly. He is never really an object of our knowledge, but that which makes all objects of our knowledge possible as such. He is, as Rahner puts it, not the "what" but the "whereunto" of our knowledge. We never really know Him, we only co-know Him, we know Him only as the background, the horizon, the "whither" of all our knowledge. We never see Him directly, but, as it were, only out of the corner of our eye. When we turn our gaze upon Him to see Him more clearly, what we perceive is no longer Him, but some idol. In this sense and only in this sense is it true that the dynamism of our intellect aims at nothingness. What I intend in all my knowledge is not a thing, no-thing, since it is the condition of the possibility of all things in my knowledge.

Yet we cannot speak of God, we cannot think of Him directly, without turning Him to some extent into a thing, into a *what*, without transcending even Him, as spoken of in our words or conceived in our mind, toward our *whereunto*. Whenever we think or speak of God, we make Him finite and we turn Him into a pseudo God. But we are aware that we are doing so.

The great Scholastic philosophers of the past knew of this. That is why they insisted so much on the analogical nature of our knowledge of God. They claimed that what we know and say of God is true only to some extent. It always has to be corrected. In modern language we might speak of an unavoidable dialectical tension between the mental picture we have of God and what we really mean when using it, between an element of representation, which is always deficient, and an element of signification, which can never be fully represented and verbalized, although we can speak of it only if we represent and verbalize it.

3) It is easy to understand why this approach does not bother overmuch with Hume's and Kant's attacks against the principle of causality. These attacks were aimed at the principle of *efficient* causality. We do not use this principle in our approach. Instead we use the principle of final causality. God is known by us as the "final cause" of our intellectual dynamism, of what Lonergan calls our "pure desire to know."

This principle may also be called the principle of intelligibility. It might be stated as follows: Whatever is not intelligible by itself, is intelligible only by being referred to that which is intelligible by itself. The very fact that we are aware of the limitation of whatever we know, that our intellect is at once beyond it in its desire to know and to understand, implies that no object in our experience is intelligible by itself. Every one of them requires a complement of intelligibility. We *live* this complement through the dynamism of our intellect. We make it explicit when we affirm God as the source of all intelligibility. The principle of intelligibility corresponds to the traditional principle of sufficient reason. The principle of efficient causality is only a partial application of it.

Should we not demonstrate this principle before using it in our vindication? It cannot be "demonstrated" any more than the existence of God and for the same reasons, as explained above. It can only be vindicated, in exactly the same way in which we vindicate our right of affirming God's existence. Practically the two vindications coincide. We *live* the principle and the affirmation before we can express them in words. Our only way of establishing their validity is to try to show that those who deny them in words use them in their knowledge. In other words, we must use "retorsion" and try to show that, like the existence of God, the principle of intelligibility can be denied only through an affirmation which implicitly affirms it.

4) Let us finally draw the attention upon the fact that this vindication shows that we do not really *arrive* at God's existence; we do not discover the reality of God by starting from the reality of the objects of our experience. We have mentioned the serious objections which may be raised against such a way of proceeding. How can the knowledge of finite realities lead us to the knowledge of an Infinite Reality? How can we ever hope to bridge the infinite gap between them? The fact is that we do not have to bridge it, we do not really arrive at God. We start with Him, we are with Him from the beginning. He is already in our mind when we know our first object, when we perform our first intellectual activity, since it is His attraction which makes possible any object in our mind. This was not made sufficiently clear in the traditional demonstrations. They gave the impression that we had first to know a certain number of realities before being able to look out for the Supreme Reality. If that were possible, Kant would be right, the affirmation of God's existence might be subjectively unavoidable, but it would objectively have no value. God is not merely the Ideal under which we organize all the data of our experience; He is the condition of the possibility of there being any data at all. We reach God at once or never at all.

SOME OBJECTIONS AGAINST THIS VINDICATION

We shall now consider some of the objections which may be raised against this vindication. It is, of course, impossible to consider all objections or to consider those we take into account as thoroughly as they deserve. Few topics in philosophy have been more hotly and constantly debated, and we harbor not the slightest illusion that we are offering the decisive solution. Our considerations are intended as a contribution to the continuing discussion

on this very central topic. Most of the objections we shall consider stem somehow from Kant. He remains the greatest adversary
of all those who admit theoretical reason's ability to reach God.

1) Thus Kant practically denied the existence of any intellectual
dynamism. He simply ignored it. He frequently used expressions
which refer to the dynamic aspects of our knowledge. But in fact
he paid no attention to their implications. He contented himself
with a very thorough investigation of the static aspects of human cognition. He showed how the sense data are "informed"
by the forms of space and time, how the resulting phenomena are
subsumed under the categories and referred to the transcendental
Ego. But he considered only the *result* of this gradual invasion
of the data by increasing intelligibility, while paying no attention
to the very *activity* of the mind which brings it about. If he had
more carefully adverted to the various syntheses in the *making*, and
not merely studied these syntheses *as made*, he might have modified some of his agnostic views. There seems to have been another
blind spot in Kant's outlook. He claimed that his statically conceived knowledge is restricted to the phenomenal order, without
adverting to the fact that the very awareness of this restriction,
of this limitation of our knowledge, implies that something in it
is already beyond this limit.

It is difficult to see how one can deny the reality of man's intellectual dynamism. Man not only knows, he wishes to know more
things and to know more about the things he knows already. The
whole history of the sciences and of philosophy is a witness to man's
urge for more and more knowledge. Nor is this urge restricted
to the few great searchers of all times. It is to be found in every
normal human being. Each meets problems, asks questions, is aware
of his ignorance, displays a steady desire to know more and more
deeply. Even the skeptic who doubts everything or the suicide
who gives up the struggle of life has reached his stance because he
had the feeling that he would never reach the answers he wanted.
It seems very difficult, in the light of this evidence, to deny that
the human intellect is essentially a dynamic, striving power.

2) A much more serious objection comes from those who claim that
man's intellect, whose dynamism they admit, does not tend to-

ward the infinite, but toward the indefinite. Man wants to know, to know ever more. There is no final end to this drive. The only end is precisely the progression of knowledge itself. Man's basic dynamism does not strive for the knowledge of a fully satiating final object, it merely desires ever more knowledge for knowledge's own sake. There is no end in sight or intended. The only purpose is the unimpeded continuation of the flow of knowledge.

This is a serious objection which contains a good deal of truth. I am willing to admit that scientific knowledge, as opposed to philosophical knowledge, heads for the indefinite. Its horizon is the world, an open horizon, calling for ever more knowledge and unable ever to totalize it. One of the main functions of science is to discover the antecedents which explain the present state of affairs in some segment of the universe. These antecedents follow upon others, which derive from others, and so on, *in infinitum*. This kind of infinite is indeed the indefinite, the bad infinite of Hegel. That is why science as such cannot establish the existence of God.

It is impossible to discuss here in detail the problem of the relation between science and philosophy. Opinions about it diverge considerably. To me it seems that science advances horizontally and philosophy (or, at least, its central part, metaphysics) advances vertically. Science tries to explain the phenomena by discovering how they came about, what came before them in time; metaphysics tries to understand them by referring them to the principle of all intelligibility. Science is not possible without metaphysics, metaphysics cannot exist without either scientific or everyday knowledge. The relation which exists between everyday or scientific knowledge on the one hand and metaphysics on the other is the same as that which obtains between a material and a formal cause, roughly speaking between body and soul. Metaphysical knowledge is the soul of all human knowledge: it animates, permeates, vivifies all scientific (or everyday) knowledge. When a scientist studies the nature of genes, he tries to discover their components and antecedents (horizontal knowledge). But he is aware— at least unthematically—that these substances under his microscope are real, are finite (vertical knowledge), and he refers them, *ipso facto*, implicitly, to the infinite substance.

A whole book might be written to explain this concept of the relation between science and metaphysics and to defend it against possible objections. What precedes, although admittedly quite inadequate, will have to do within the restricted scope of this article. I am only trying to explain why, while admitting an indefinite progression in scientific knowledge, I maintain that, in its ever-present metaphysical component or "soul," the dynamism of our intellect does not get lost in the indefinite, but points toward the Infinite. It radically rejects any limit as such, hence it is poised at once toward the Unlimited as such. There are no intermediate stages. There is no gradual passage from one affirmation to the next one. The awareness of the limitation *is* identically the affirmation of the Unlimited.

No thinker has insisted more upon this immediate passage from the finite to the infinite than Hegel. For him the finite is so intimately related to the infinite that it may be said that the finite is infinite. The finite is an *infinitized finite* (*das verunendlichte Endliche*).[8] The limited can be properly understood only in direct relation with the unlimited. That is why for Hegel it is not necessary to demonstrate that God exists. His existence is immediately evident, and the philosopher should concentrate his efforts on the investigation of God's nature. Hegel's *Logik* is basically such an investigation.

The trouble with Hegel is not that he fails to establish the existence of God but that he seems to endanger the existence of man as a being distinct from God. This is neither the time nor the place to discuss the difficult problem whether or not Hegel is a pantheist, and if he is, what kind of pantheism he embraces. There is no doubt that some of his utterances seem to imply pantheism in the strictest sense of the word. But we find other statements in his work which make us refrain from hasty conclusions.

But when Hegel writes " . . . man knows God only in so far as God knows Himself in man. This knowledge is God's consciousness of self, but at the same time it is God's knowledge of man: and this knowledge of man by God is man's knowledge of God,"[9] and when a serious Hegel scholar comments "The thought which thinks infinity is infinite thought, and infinite thought is the thought of God Himself,"[10] a distinction seems to be called for. When we think God, we obviously think the Infinite. Hegel claims that only an infinite mind can think the Infinite. Maréchal, on the other hand, admits that a finite mind may think the Infinite if this mind, although finite, has an infinite capacity, a dynamism which strives toward the Infinite.

> Why should a finite intellect not be objectively infinite, that is, infinite as a capacity of objects? It is true that this blending of finite and infinite would be contradictory for every hypothesis but one. . . . This hypothesis supposes that finite and infinite are reconciled through the natural finality, through the basic tendency of the intellective power. A tendency which is necessarily contingent as existence and finite as a subjective essence (*tamquam res quaedam*) may, on the other hand, be infinite in its objective capacity and absolute in the necessity it imposes upon the becoming orientated by it. The objective capacity and necessity of a tendency are measured only by the range and the necessity of its ultimate end, while the existence and subjective essence of it depend on conditions which are necessarily limiting and contingent. The first of these conditions, as may be demonstrated, is the reception of a *natural motion* proportioned to the ultimate end.[11]

Although Lauer claims that "to say that, when man thinks, God thinks in him, is not to say that God is man or that man is God,"[12] I find it difficult to understand how, if my most intimate activity *is* God's activity, my being too would not be God's being.

Thus I agree with Hegel where he claims that man's thinking passes at once from the finite to the Infinite and that man's awareness of the limitation of all objects of his experience does not lead him astray into the bad infinite, into the indefinite. But I do not explain this fact by claiming that God thinks Himself in man. Man can think the Infinite, not because that which thinks in him is the Infinite, but because his finite intellect is drawn by the Infinite and responds to this attraction by pointing toward, aiming at, preapprehending the Infinite. Man's knowledge of God is admittedly very imperfect. This obvious fact is difficult to understand in Hegel's conception; it is much easier to explain in the dynamic interpretation of Maréchal.

3) The next objection brings us back to Kant. He admitted that, even in the domain of theoretical reason, man necessarily affirms the existence of God. But in his opinion this affirmation has no

validity: it leads to God only as supreme Ideal of reason in which all the lines of human thinking converge as in a virtual, not an actual, focus. This Ideal has a useful function in human thinking: it helps man to organize his thoughts by lining them up in the direction of this supreme peak. But the peak itself is purely problematical, we have no right, in theoretical reason, to affirm its existence. In other words, Kant admits a subjective, not an objective, necessity in man of affirming God's existence. Man cannot help having the idea of God, somewhat as he cannot help see the sun "rise and set." But, in the domain of theoretical knowledge, this idea of God does not represent a reality any more than man's impression of the sun rising and setting pictures the real state of affairs in the field of perception.

What must be shown therefore against Kant is that the affirmation of God's existence is not only subjectively but objectively unavoidable, that it is an *a priori* condition of the possibility of any objective knowledge. Man affirms God's existence not only after having known many objects in his experience; he would not know any object as object at all if he did not simultaneously affirm the existence of God. He knows them only through an activity of his mind which affirms this existence. The affirmation of the Infinite is not only a regulative, it is a constitutive element of human knowledge.

Both Maréchal and Rahner have tried to establish the constitutive function of the affirmation of the Transcendent. Each has done it in his own way, which will be briefly presented here.

Maréchal insists on the need of explaining the objectivity of human knowledge, as opposed to its immanence. The word *objectivity* has many possible acceptions. Here it means simply the fact of being an "object in consciousness," the fact of being opposed to the subject, at least in his mind, the fact of being not-I, at least not the knowing-I. When man knows some reality, this reality is somehow in his mind (immanence) but it is in his mind as distinct from it, as opposed to it, as facing it, as objectified by it. The problem is often overlooked by people who have a rather naïve conception of knowledge. They consider the spatial distinction between subject and object sufficient for the objectivity of our knowledge. Animals perceive this spatial distinction, and for sense knowledge as such it seems to be the only "objectivity" available. That is why the knowledge of animals (so far as we can conceive it) is not objective in the strict sense. Animals do not perceive objects as objects. They do not know that what they perceive is not-I. They are, as Scheler put it, "ecstatically immersed in their environment." That is why they are so perfectly adapted to it. But that is also why they do not speak. There is nothing to speak about; there are no objects.

Others explain the objectivity of human knowledge through some kind of awareness of our intellect's passivity with regard to what it knows. There is no difficulty in admitting such a passivity in our material senses. But this passivity does not yield more than the spatial objectivity which is present in the knowledge of animals. It is very difficult to see how our immaterial intellect as such can be passively affected by material objects.

With most of the leading thinkers of all times, Maréchal excludes this possibility. He claims that the object of any intellectual knowledge can be known as object, as not-I, only because the intellect causes these objects or because it strives toward them. When we cause something or when we strive toward it, we know that this thing is not-I. Except for the so-called "artifacts" man does not cause the objects of his knowledge. The objectivity of his knowledge can therefore be explained only by the fact that the mind strives toward these objects, intends them. It can be explained only by the dynamism of the intellect. Thus the dynamism is an *a priori* condition of the possibility of any object in consciousness. But we have seen that this dynamism coincides with the affirmation of the Infinite. Hence the affirmation of God's existence exercises in human knowledge not only a regulative, but also a constitutive, function. It is only because every time he knows something man is always already beyond it through the infinite openness of his mind that he possesses "objects" of knowledge. The affirmation of God is not only a psychological necessity, it is a logical necessity.

Rahner proceeds in a different way, which I hope not to over-simplify by explaining it as follows. Of all objects I get to know, I claim implicitly that they are *something which*. . . . Further characteristics are supplied, which come generally from sense perception. Thus a dog is something which has four legs, barks when excited, and so on. Now, whenever we *perceive* in a given individual such a complex totality of sense data, we *conceive* it at once as universal, as capable of being indefinitely reproduced in other individuals. In other words, we are aware that these data only *happen* to be embodied in the present individual. They might also have been embodied in another one. We call the thing *a* dog, not *the* dog, even if we know of no other dogs. We call every reality we know *a* reality, *a* being, *some*thing. This supposes that, as soon as we know any reality, we know it only as part of, sharing in a wider, reality. This is true of absolutely all real or conceivable limited reality. Thus the wider reality toward which our intellect transcends whatever we know is one without limits or boundaries, the Unlimited, Infinite Reality. It is only because we have this anticipating grasp of the Absolute, because we pre-apprehend the Infinite, that we can say of everything we know that it is *some*thing. And it is precisely our power of calling whatever we perceive *some*thing which transforms our perceptions into concepts, our sensing into thinking. We would have no concepts, no ideas, we would be unable to think and to speak, we would have neither language nor civilization, we would be confined to the animal level of knowing, were it not for the fact that whatever we know is known by us against the Infinite horizon of Being, of God. Hence the intending of this horizon, the (implicit) affirmation of God, is the *a priori* condition of possibility of all human thought and action. It is not only psychologically, it is also logically necessary for man to affirm God's existence.

4) We must have a closer look at another important step in our vindication. It was argued as follows. If the dynamism of our intellect aims at the Infinite Being, this being must be at least possible. Otherwise we would have to admit that man necessarily, congenitally, of his very nature, is but a striving for the impossible. This would be absurd, hence it is inadmissible and false. The dynamism of the human intellect implies at least that the Infinite Being is possible.

Not everyone will admit this. More and more people seem to be reaching the conclusion that human life is absurd. Is Sartre's claim that man is *une passion inutile* not based on his conviction that man is always looking for a synthesis of the *en-soi* and the *pour-*

soi, a synthesis which would be identically God? Sartre claims that such a synthesis is contradictory and that God is impossible. Thus man is for Sartre a being who is always yearning for the impossible. Human life is absurd. It is not easy to answer such an objection. It involves more than intellectual considerations, it comes from the heart rather than from the head. We may, nevertheless, point out some of the difficulties involved in it.

What do we mean when we say that something is absurd? That it makes no sense, although it should make sense. It is not enough for a thing not to make sense for it to be called absurd. A handful of "Scrabble" letters taken out of the bag makes no sense, but no one calls them absurd. No one calls decorative painting absurd, but many people feel that most modern painting is absurd, because they expect it to make sense for them, and it does not. We understand what is meant when people say of reality or of life that it does not make sense. But their claim that it is absurd implies that it should make sense, that they expect it to make sense. Why should it? What is it in man which demands of life that it make sense, which leads him to the bitter conclusion that it is absurd? Is it not the principle of intelligibility, which is like the very breath of his mind? Without an implicit affirmation of this principle (and of its consequences) it is difficult to see how anyone might call life absurd.

It is easy to claim that life is absurd, but it is not easy to avoid contradictions if one makes this claim. For if life is absurd, human life, and especially human intellectual life, must be absurd too. Should it not follow then that all statements made by the intellect, including the one about life's absurdity, are absurd? But this may be an unfair way of treating the objection. The absurdity might be predicated only of the deepest (*ex hypothesi* admitted) yearning of the human intellect, but it would not be extended to the particular statements made by the intellect. The basic urge of man's mind would be absurd, its activities would remain sound. The tree is dead, but its fruit is fine! This is, to say the least, a rather strange conclusion.

The objection may assume another form which might lead to a clearer understanding of the very peculiar nature of our vindication. Your vindication, so goes the objection, begs the question. You claim that man's dynamism cannot lead him to the impossible or to the contradictory, because this would be absurd. Hence you suppose that reality is not absurd, that it makes sense. And you also admit that life makes sense only if God exists. Therefore you suppose from the start that God exists. Obviously a vicious circle, a case of begging the question.

It is true that, in a certain sense, my vindication contains a circle; only it is not a vicious circle. It is the circle which is contained in any "retorsion." Man's highest certitudes cannot be demonstrated, in the strict sense of the word. They are not based on sense experience, and it is impossible to establish them by appealing to higher principles, since these certitudes are precisely the highest of all principles. All the truths of metaphysics contain each other. It is impossible to establish one of them without taking the others for granted. In this sense, every metaphysical demonstration implies a circle. Metaphysics might become dazzlingly evident only if we were able to establish all its truths together, in one fell swoop. But we are unable to establish a complex truth without analyzing it. And by analyzing it, we seem to weaken the case for it. The more we analyze, the weaker does the evidence look, unless we see to it that our analysis be at every step compensated by a corresponding synthesis. No wonder that *analytic* philosophers can see no way of making a reasonable case for metaphysics and for the affirmation of the existence of God!

Are we then powerless before those who deny these certitudes? Not quite. But our only defense will assume the form, objectionable to many, of a personal challenge to the discussion partner. You do not accept these basic certitudes. All right, deny them. I shall try to show you that you affirm them in your very denial. You cannot deny them without an implicit contradiction. Something similar happens in the present instance. You claim that I beg the question by assuming from the start that reality is not absurd, that it makes sense. What if I do? I have the right to assume this, because every human being naturally does it, because you do it too. By engaging in a discussion with me, you admit implicitly that reality makes sense. The purpose of a discussion like ours is precisely to discover this sense. There can be no meaningful discussion with a person who does not admit that things make sense. Such a person can avoid contradictions only by keeping silent.

We must remember what was said above. The affirmation of God's existence is the *a priori* condition of the possibility of any intellectual knowledge. Hence as soon as I start out on my vindication, I have already implicitly affirmed this existence. I would be unable to say or understand anything without this implicit affirmation. We do not reach God at the end of our discussion, we start from Him, and our argument consists simply in becoming aware of this and trying to make the others too aware of it. In this sense I beg the question from the very start, but so does my interlocutor.

By way of conclusion, a couple of remarks may be useful, one about the cognitional, the other about the volitional aspect of our vindication.

1) What makes this vindication unpalatable to many people is that they get the impression that it consists simply in words, words.[13] They would like to *see* that it is really so, that God really exists. They feel that they are merely talked into admitting it without seeing it. What these people are asking for is an *intuition* of the divine essence. Only a mystical experience of the highest order might provide them with such an intuition.

We use some kind of intuition in our argument, namely, the intuition of the dynamism of our intellect. We have tried to show that this intuition implies the affirmation of God's existence. The affirmation, not the intuition. Man's substitute for the missing intuition is *unavoidable affirmation*. He does not see the supreme truths, but he cannot not affirm them, he continues to affirm them even in the very acts by which he tries to deny them. He does not *see* that God exists, but he cannot not affirm it.

Sartre has rightly insisted that man is condemned to freedom. He is free, but he is not free to be free, he is necessarily free. Whether he likes it or not, he cannot help being a free agent. He will deny or destroy his freedom only through some free act. A similar necessity rules man's intellectual life. Man is *condemned to affirm* the great metaphysical truths. He cannot not affirm them. The core of his intellect *is* this affirmation. One of these basic truths is the existence of God. That is why man might be called *an embodied affirmation of the Absolute*.

It would, of course, be much more satisfactory if we had the intuition of God. Might we not say, however, that our very regret about being restricted to a necessary affirmation, our very awareness that we do not enjoy the intuition of God, that our knowledge of Him is very limited, is one more indication that something in us is already beyond this poor substitute, that our intellect is, as Maréchal puts it, "a faculty in quest of its intuition."

2) It might surprise some readers that I claim that man is an embodied affirmation of God, that this affirmation is a condition of the possibility of his very thinking. How can anyone make such claims when so many great philosophers and thinkers deny the existence of God?

This is a serious objection which directs our attention to the volitional and free aspect of the affirmation of the Transcendent. On the unconscious, unthematic, prereflective level, this affirmation occurs necessarily, without any freedom. It is my contention that on this, the transcendental level, no one does or can deny the existence of God. With the truth of this contention my whole case holds or collapses.

But this unconscious, transcendental, "lived" affirmation of God has to be conceptualized and verbalized. We must become aware of it and express it. This occurs consciously and freely. Here man uses concepts, words, the categories of his mind. That is why Rahner calls it the *categorial* level. On the categorial level the affirmation of God's existence implies a free commitment.

Many philosophers admit some kind of distinction between man's intellect and his will, between man's knowing and his loving. This distinction is rather obvious in everyday life, where we may know many things without loving or hating them. Ultimately, however, these two powers derive from the one ground of man's spiritual soul. Now the affirmation of God's existence is such a profound and central concern of man that, at the depths where it takes place, the two spiritual powers are not yet distinct. This affirmation (or denial) is made by man σὺν ὅλῃ τῇ ψυχῇ (with his whole soul). At this depth, knowing is loving and loving is knowing. Hence only he who loves God, who welcomes the dawning awareness of Him in his mind, will be able to grasp the truth of the statement by which His existence is affirmed and to see the validity of the vindication of this affirmation. A circle again, to be sure, as with all the deepest realities in man. But not a vicious circle.

Seeing the truth of the affirmation of God's existence supposes an option, an option for meaning, for sense in the universe, for the basic goodness of life. It supposes an act of confidence, of trust, of faith in the ultimate meaning and bountifulness of existence. Without such an option the categorial affirmation will never emerge, although the transcendental affirmation remains undisturbed.

This does not imply bad faith in the atheist. Man cannot help admitting some Absolute. If the choice were restricted either to admitting totally or to rejecting totally God, man would have a choice between only two Absolutes: God or himself. Rejecting God, he would make an Absolute of himself, he would idolize himself. There is, however, a third possibility. The man who does not want to idolize himself will make some other being into an Absolute. This other being may be either the other or the Other, either his fellow-man or God. Countless professed atheists are not self-adorers. For them the Absolute is the others, the human race, mankind. Many of them reject the Other because they feel that He does not care for the others, or interferes with their full development. To me it looks as if these thinkers were unable to conceptualize God as the "whereunto" of the dynamism of their intellect. Having turned Him into a "what" they have rightly rejected Him. But the very reasons which induce many of them to reject this kind of God seem to show that, short of conceptualization and verbalization, they are groping for Him and anonymously worshipping Him.

If a short theological remark be allowed at the end of this philosophical paper, I should like to note the following point. We have seen that the categorial acceptance of God happens consciously and freely. As a free act of man in the present world order, it falls under what Rahner calls the "supernatural existential," which might be defined very simply as "God's standing invitation to man to accept divinization." In other words: when a person affirms that God exists, he performs a free and meritorious act, which stands strongly under the influence of God's grace, which might be impossible without the influence of this grace. This free affirmation is, in fact, the first conscious step taken by man toward the full and free acceptance of the proffered divinization.

NOTES

1. For a striking critique of this mentality, see W. N. Clarke, s.j., "A Curious Blindspot in the Anglo-American Tradition of Antitheistic Argument," *The Monist*, 54 (1970), 181-200.

2. They are mainly: Joseph Maréchal, s.j., *Le point de départ de la métaphysique* (Brussels: Édition universelle, 1927-49), 5 vols., especially Volume v, *Le Thomisme devant la philosophie critique* (a summary and translation of the main passages into English may be found in *A Maréchal Reader*, ed. J. Donceel, s.j. [New York: Herder and Herder, 1970]); Karl Rahner, s.j., *Geist in Welt. Zur Metaphysik der endlichen Erkenntnis bei Thomas von Aquin* (2d ed. rev. J. B. Metz [Munich: Kösel, 1957]; *Spirit in the World*, trans. W. Dych, s.j. [New York: Herder and Herder, 1968]); Karl Rahner, s.j., *Hörer des Wortes: Zur Grundlegung einer Religionsphilosophie* (2d ed. rev. J. B. Metz [Munich: Kösel, 1963]; *Hearers of the Word*, trans. Michael Richards [New York: Herder and Herder, 1969]); Gaston Isaye, s.j., "La finalité de l'intelligence et l'objection kantienne," *Revue Philosophique de Louvain*, 51 (1953), 42-100.

3. L. Malevez, s.j., "Le croyant et le philosophe," *Pour une théologie de la foi* (Paris: Desclée de Brouwer, 1968), p. 34.

4. Hegel held that, if a proof of God's existence were needed at all, this proof would have to be the ontological argument. See his *Lectures on the Philosophy of Religion*, trans. E. B. Speirs and J. B. Sanderson (London: Kegan Paul, 1895), III, 155-367. See Quentin Lauer, s.j., "Hegel on Proofs for God's Existence," *Kantstudien*, 55 (1964), 443-65.

5. *Proslogion*, ch. II-IV. The most important texts about the Ontological Argument are available in *The Ontological Argument from St. Anselm to Contemporary Philosophers* ed. A. Plantinga (Garden City: Doubleday, 1965). The text from St. Anselm is found on pp. 3-27.

6. From *The New Essays Concerning Human Understanding*. See Plantinga, *op. cit.*, pp. 54-56.

7. See Charles Hartshorne, "The Necessarily Existent," in Plantinga, *op. cit.*, pp. 123-35. See also J. N. Findlay, "Can God's Existence Be Disproved?" *ibid.*, pp. 111-22, especially pp. 121-22.

8. *Logik*, ed. Georg Lasson (Leipzig: Meiner, 1932), I, 134.

9. *Philosophie der Religion*, ed. Hermann Glockner (Stuttgart: Frommann, 1928), II, 496.

10. Quentin Lauer, s.j., "Hegel on Proofs for God's Existence," p. 457.

11. Donceel, *op. cit.*, p. 225.

12. Lauer, *loc. cit.*, p. 448.

13. Of course, the objection too will be presented and defended by means of words!

9

Law, Obligation, and God

JOSEPH V. DOLAN, S.J.

FOR ALL THE CURRENT INTEREST in the nature and source of moral obligation, it is not a new problem in ethics. Long before the *Critique of Practical Reason* made it central, it had been a point of contention between Suarez and Vasquez, and representatives of the Scholastic tradition continue even today to resolve it differently.[1] Outside that milieu it has been raised in different contexts and with different preoccupations—those of psychology, value theory, jurisprudence, and, most notably, analytic philosophy to which it owes its popular designation as "the is-ought question." For the most part, contemporary ethical and legal theory, owing largely to an *a priori* positivist stance, is forced to conclude to the non-objective or non-transcendent character of obligation. However, these recent approaches, with their exploration and close analyses of moral experience, have helped to illuminate what R. M. Hare has called "one of the dark places of ethics,"[2] and they should be of help for avoiding the dead ends to which some of the earlier treatments led.

In his probing book *Reason in Ethics*, Stephen Toulmin concludes that there is no room within ethics for the question: why ought one to do right?[3] It is what he calls a "limiting question"—like "why is scarlet red?"—which can only be parried with another:

what else "ought" one to do? This is in one critical sense true, viz., if it were taken to mean: "I don't honestly see, or am not sure, that I ought to do right. Can you help me to see that I ought to?" For that is just what "right" in its ethical sense means. One who does not thus understand "right" cannot understand "ought" either and so cannot meaningfully pose the question.

However, there is a sense in which the question is significant and even urgent—the sense, that is, in which it would be posed by one impressed with the theoretical case for moral positivism in any of its several forms (existentialism, naturalism, Freudianism, legal positivism). Here a person who has formed the judgment that some particular action was "right to do" and experienced an obligation to perform it is now reflecting on the genesis and implications of that experience and wondering whether there are objectively verifiable grounds which warrant it—making the obligation, so to speak, de jure—or whether the necessity experienced as moral has a merely psychological origin, say as the product of the superego or as a survival in the collective unconscious. If that be the case, the "ought," however deeply imbedded in nature, is a tyrant without genuine authority, and we may then deal with it as with any neurosis or mere de facto condition of nature and can start the elaboration of a liberating morale sans péché. Ought we— I mean really and truly ought we—to do what is "good," i.e., what, perhaps because of a collective neurosis, we are compelled to judge as good?

One immediate objection to the serious entertaining of such a question will be that any attempt to prove one ought to do right would involve either a begging of the question or a commission of the so-called naturalistic fallacy in passing from is to ought, from neutral fact to morally weighted value. For in order to conclude that we ought, "ought" would either have been surreptitiously assumed as validly grounded in one of the premises from which we argued, or else have been gratuitously intruded into the conclusion.

Here again distinctions are in order, and everything depends on what one understands by "prove." It is true, as we will be insisting, that one who has had no experience of "ought" and does not in some real sense already judge with unassailable conviction that he ought to act rightly will never be brought to this perception by any appeal to "facts" or non-moral considerations. That is the reason for Aristotle's insistence that a man coming to the study of moral science should already have made good moral judgments.[4]

But the experience of obligation is itself a fact, and it cannot be excluded *a priori* that perhaps in the final analysis the only accounting or sufficient reason for this phenomenon might indeed be the "fact" that obligations are real and that there are moral values with valid claims upon us, just as cognitional sense experience is explained by the existence of real material objects to whose perception our faculties are proportioned. It is this line of reasoning which we shall pursue as one part of our treatment—"one part," for it appeals to the metaphysical principle of finality, which is not universally received. Or, in other words: it supposes that reality, including man and human activity, is radically intelligible, makes objective sense, and is not, as the Sartrean existentialist would have it, absurd.

The phenomenology of our moral experience and moral-value responses has been thoroughly and penetratingly done elsewhere and, whatever the opposing inferences drawn from them, the descriptions substantially agree.[5] Here we need only recall the radical and irreducible difference between "ought" (or "should" or "must") as expressive of duty and obligation—of a categorical moral imperative—and the milder evaluative "ought" (or "should" or "must") which we frequently and lightly use but which is merely hypothetical and morally neutral. I translate different kinds of internal judgments in saying "I ought to be more honest" and "This summer I really ought to read *War and Peace*." Ordinarily only the first would reflect the experience of obligation. If we keep this difference in mind, it should be clear that the "feeling" of obligation (as it is frequently called, though it is in fact a judgment)[6] could not originate through any extrapolation from, or reinforcement of, a non-moral experience. It is an *Urphänomenon*.

It is indeed curious that despite the wide, though not unanimous, agreement since Hume on the fruitlessness of any attempt to deduce *ought* from *is*, it is taken for granted that non-moral perceptions or prescriptions have by some magical psychology given birth to the sense of obligation. Alexander Sesonske in *Value and Obligation*, for example, asserts that "our tendency to feel bound by com-

mitments we have made, to feel as authoritative judgments of obligation referring to these commitments, results, of course, from
the conditioning we receive from early childhood, with rewards
and punishments being meted out as we do or do not honor our
commitments."[7] We are not told how these morally neutral consequences (they are only painful or pleasant) induce the awareness of an "authoritative" imperative. Similarly in *The Language
of Morals* Hare explains:

> It is easy to see how, if we have been brought up from our earliest years
> in obedience to a principle, the thought of our not obeying it becomes
> abhorrent to us. If we fail to obey it, we suffer remorse; when we do
> obey it, we feel at ease with ourselves. These feelings are reinforced by
> all those factors which psychologists have listed; and the total result is
> what is generally called a feeling of obligation.[8]

Here it appears that we have the naturalistic fallacy in reverse,
and the inadequacy of these causal accountings becomes manifest
when we try to imagine a possible technique for communicating
or instilling the notion of obligation. How, for example, is a parent to *teach* a child with no prior grasp of the meaning of "ought"
that he ought, as a matter of moral obligation, not to tell lies or
to ring doorbells? What would "naughty" mean to him at the
level of pre-moral experience other than the quality of those actions which upset Daddy and are followed by one or another painful consequence like chastisement or the temporary withdrawal
of affection? And if this is all he means in "obediently" writing
a hundred times "I must not tell lies," he is not recording the judgment which Sesonske and Hare are proposing to account for. He
is at the superego stage of moral development, and parent and teacher must wait for something else to occur within the child before
their own "do" and "don't" take on any genuinely moral import.[9]

It is probably because recognition of the good as moral value
is part of our natural endowment and a genuine first principle that
we can overlook its necessity as condition for making particular
moral judgments or for assimilating those we are taught.[10] Its
role here is parallel to that of the principle of identity (or of contradiction) in the operation of speculative reason. Both are starting points. Without his own native insight into the axioms of geometry, to which only attention need be called, a pupil cannot

be taught the Pythagorean theorem. For one does not teach by injecting his own ideas into another mind; he presents considerations
to the pupil in such order that the light of an "interior truth" already present can be brought to bear on them. Only then—when
a pupil does his own seeing that $a^2 + b^2 = c^2$—has he been properly taught. This is the point which Plato artfully exploits for his
own purpose in the *Meno* where an untutored slave boy, without
being "taught" but simply by being questioned in the right way,
is brought to recognize, in virtue of what he already knows, the
incommensurability of the diagonal and sides of a square.[11] As
Augustine notes, we are all, in a sense, our own teachers.

> For do masters profess that it is their own thoughts which are to be heard
> and retained and not rather the disciplines themselves which they judge
> they convey by their speech? For who is so idly curious as to send his
> son to school just to learn what goes on in a teacher's mind? But when
> those disciplines they profess to teach—including those of virtue and
> wisdom—have been expounded through words, then those we call pu-
> pils, consulting as best they can an interior truth, consider within them-
> selves whether true words have been uttered. So it is thus they learn;
> and when they find within themselves that truth has been spoken, they
> applaud, not realizing they are praising themselves who are learners as
> much as their teachers, provided these, too, realize what they are saying.[12]

He then notes perceptively:

> But men are misled into calling teachers those who are not. This, be-
> cause it is most often the case that between the spoken word and the mo-
> ment of knowledge there is no lapse of time. And because the inward
> learning follows so swiftly upon the speaker's admonition they judge
> that knowledge has come externally from the one who admonished.[13]

Moral education, the inculcation of principles through word or
example, can awaken and promote development of the moral sense
and, where there is question of particular applications, a clumsy pedagogy can pervert it. But, ironically, even to accomplish this
distortion—for example, to induce assent to the morality of racial
discrimination—an original recognition of moral value and obligation must be there to distort, just as an inept teacher can lead
his pupils to wrong conclusions in geometry only if they first perceive the axioms.

The point of this reduction is that we make moral judgments of obligation not because we have been taught to, but for the simple reason that we are people; people are and cannot help being to this extent moral animals. What we are to conclude from this fact depends, of course, on our larger view of reality and on our basic metaphysical options. If natures, including man's, are recognized as stamped with intelligibility and "meant" to be what they in fact are, then true natural activity is finalized and natural potencies are not "inane." The "ought," rooted as it is in nature, will then make sense only if there is a realm of moral values which correspond with and define it. And if man cannot but judge that good ought to be done, it must be because he ought in truth to do it. To draw the parallel with speculative intellect again: the reason we cannot assent to manifest contradiction is that the mind is a faculty of the real and reality is consistent with itself.

But, as we intimated earlier, this style of argument will hardly prove congenial to most contemporary philosophers and would most likely be rejected out of hand as a priori and dogmatic. Dialogue need not be broken off, however, for the peculiar features of the "ought"—its radication in nature and irreducibility to a non-moral judgment—suggest the possibility of an effective ad hominem argument aimed at pointing out a basic inconsistency on the part of the moral positivist (as distinct from the position of positivism itself). True, this would not directly and of itself establish the falsity of the position or the validity of obligation. Nevertheless, it would achieve something more significant than a mere debating point. For it may serve a further maieutic purpose of revealing the occasion for the inconsistency, which is the mistake one here makes about his own state of mind.

One approach suggesting itself, though not without its uses, would not be to our present point, and we touch on it only to mark its difference from the one we are taking. It would be to wait during conversation for an inevitable unguarded expression of commendation, disapprobation, or indignation, which would betray a judgment on some action as objectively due or undue. But no positivist has ever claimed exemption from the tendency to make spontaneous ought-judgments, and so he could disown this one just as another "can't help." Or else he could advance reasons "within ethics" of the sort which would soon involve us in another long exchange over emotivism, hedonism, utilitarianism, and their manifold subspecies.

Our proposed procedure would be to engage in a preliminary out-of-court dialogue which should as a matter of fact make subsequent argument on the issue of positivism itself superfluous. It requires only that before matching reasons for or against the validity of the "ought," each of us allow a methodic, not necessarily real, doubt that he has read the moral experience correctly as to its implications. We could then put the question: "Just suppose that by some surprise reasoning I should manage to convince you that there are real objective obligations. Would you—as a matter of principle and not just by yielding to inner compulsion—commit yourself to honoring them?" It should be remarked in the first place that we are not asking whether he would agree that real obligations ought to be honored since that is just how they are defined. We are asking him what he would decide to do. Secondly, the question is not unfair. Answering it affirmatively does not require that he even momentarily renounce his positivist stance, for he can meaningfully and really declare what he would do given the actualization of a condition he knows to be unreal, e.g., if he enjoyed better health, or even one he is absolutely convinced is unrealizable, e.g., that Christianity should be found out to be a hoax.

He could conceivably answer no. But since presumably he is a "man of good will" and his objection to obligations arises from a difficulty with the evidence adduced in their support, such actual resolute attitude of *non-recevoir* would surprise. In any case, such a refusal of subjection would have to proceed from some spirit of *ressentiment* indicating problems of an idiosyncratic rather than philosophical kind. Moreover, the refusal would itself be a choice which, like any other, would have to be resolved in some absolute value of his which it would be fascinating to trace down and identify. But this would take us down another path.

Presumably, then, he will answer yes. But why? The reason is not, as might at first appear, that otherwise he would be illogical; there is no logical entailment involved at all, for action is never the formal logical consequence of the acceptance of a fact. Only

in the loose sense am I "illogical" if while recognizing my obligation to be honest, I nevertheless decide to steal. I would be
illogical only if I were at the same time to claim that my stealing
was not immoral. Actions should of course conform to conviction,
but they need not; otherwise wrongdoing would be impossible.[14]
Actions are choices which conclude a practical, not merely speculative, syllogism. As such they are resolved in the will's natural
orientation toward the apprehended good, an orientation specified
by an effective direction of practical intellect. The good in the
present instance would be the good of observing moral obligations.

A prospective obligatory action—doing penance, for example[15]—
would depend for its actual coming-to-be on the conviction of the
obligation, though it would not be completely guaranteed by it.
But the special point to notice, and on which this argument turns,
is that a choice is being made now. "Yes, I will—or propose to—
honor bona fide obligations" signifies an actual, not hypothetical,
decision. The choice is rationally motivated but it cannot finally
rest on a judgment of speculative reason alone, and certainly not
on the tautological one: if obligations are real, they ought to be
honored. No amount of "ifs" can of themselves issue in action even
when the condition is verified. They must be linked to an actually operative unconditional judgment of practical intellect which
can, through the will, supply the power for choice (which is an
action) and direct the will in choosing here and now what one will
do when and if.[16] Here and now one must judge that here and
now—not just later on or on some hypothesis—he is obligated to
the good and to do what he is shown to be right. This is the judgment which is verbalized as "good must be done and evil avoided."
It is the *principium* or starting point of all deliberation.[17]

The inescapability of this principle[18] might be highlighted by
supposing a reverse situation where it is asked whether we, for our
part, in the hypothesis of proof that obligations are illusory, would
work to overcome our past conditioning and commit ourselves
to the existentialist ethic of absolute freedom in the manner of Simone
de Beauvoir's "genuine man." The answer would of course be
yes, but it would not mean that the principle "good must be done"
had been put aside; the principle itself requires that we do our best
to free ourselves from pseudo-obligations.

If, then, we attend carefully to the conditions required on part of both speculative and practical intellect for deliberation and choice, we find the moral positivist involved in formal inconsistency, i.e., between two convictions, and not just what might be termed a practical inconsistency of conviction with conduct. For while explicitly asserting he is bound by no transcendent obligation, his considered choice is made on the basis of an actual present judgment that he is. He might protest that all we have shown is that even he finds it psychologically impossible, in the process of decision, to escape the illusion that he is objectively bound even though reflection convinces him he is not. But this is just what he has been asked to do: to reflect carefully on a choice. If he is now objecting that the controlling judgment made under these controlled conditions remains itself uncontrolled by objective reality and that he cannot endorse it as warranted, what reasons have we, or he himself, for taking any of his judgments seriously? After all, conclusions in any discourse of reason can be no more rational than the principles in whose evidence they participate and resolve.

What our *ad hominem* has established, for whatever it is worth, is that in fact there exists no actual moral positivist. He has as much reality as his counterpart, the professed universal skeptic. Or else we must redefine him as one who is able to conclude on theoretical grounds that he has no obligations through oversight of his own affirmation that he does. Perhaps a brief examination of some of these grounds may prove enlightening.

It was noted at the outset that moral positivism is implicit in the general theory of positivism which recognizes no reality beyond what can be verified by the techniques of natural science. And one is hardly likely to scrutinize moral phenomena with great diligence or be alert to possible disclosure of realities, such as moral values, which he is firmly convinced are spurious. This, we think, accounts in major part for the readiness to accept the standard but amazingly superficial explanations of moral experience which appeal to totemism, atavism, community pressure, and the superego. All these solve the problem by suppressing it and obliterating the characteristic feature of that experience which gives rise to the is - ought problem in the first place. They can, as we saw, account for particular judgments and distortions, but not for the phenomenon of obligation itself.

There is another way in which moral positivism comes about through entailment. We have been discussing the judgment "good must be done" as a principle of practical reason. But we may also consider it as a judgment of speculative reason affirming that there are real obligations. Taken this way, it is not a first principle but a conclusion which can be challenged, and so it needs defending by speculative intellect (as this essay itself will witness). Now, in the truth of the conclusion that there are real obligations, there are other conclusions involved as well, some more evident than others: that God exists; that the will is free; that there are realities transcending matter; that the human soul is spiritual and immortal. But these are not so evident in themselves that no plausible arguments can be brought against them. Yet, though we will not here attempt to develop the reasoning, most would appreciate that the denial of any one of them will involve the denial of any real or intelligible moral order. Hence one who is an atheist, a determinist, a naturalist, or materialist is only being consistent in denying the reality of obligation.[19] But it should be noticed that he does not come to this determination on the basis of a faithful analysis of moral experience. On the contrary: constituted as we are in such a way that the intellectual habits developed in one area affect our approach to others, such an analysis would most likely, though not necessarily, be hampered.

Finally, we must point out a hazard in any attempt to analyze the "ought." One of the several difficulties with moral reasoning arises from the peculiar nature of moral judgments and their corresponding ought-statements. They are not subject to verification in the same way as fact-judgments, even those of a metaphysical kind. They seem like ordinary judgments because the language in which we translate them can be cast in the logical form of is-statements which affirm a relation of subject and predicate (e.g., X *is* an action which ought to be done). But a practical judgment is not, as such, a perception but a prescription; that is to say, it is a movement and direction or judgment *per inclinationem*. Its truth, therefore, is of a different and elusive kind, harder to fix the harder we peer at it.

The difficulty lies in the common, almost unavoidable, tendency to regard *evidence* as univocal. Because we do not "see" that we ought to pay our debts in the same way we can be said to see a conclusion in mathematics, we can begin wondering whether the judgment is "true." But "ought to be done" is not that kind of object with that sort of visibility. It does not stand for something already there, so to speak, established and to be beheld; it stands for something *to be done* and realized, something which is not yet but should be. Of course, granting the truth of one ought-premiss on which an ought-conclusion depends, we will see its *consequence*, and because this is what goes on in ordinary ethical reasoning, we may think we see the oughtness itself, until we are pressed for proof. But a moral judgment can be true in only one way: by conformity with the first principle of practical reason (which is the ultimate sense of the formula that reason is the norm of morality). The first principle itself operates in a sort of psychological penumbra.[20] It is not, as ethics books sometimes suggest, a major premiss of the moral syllogism any more than is the corresponding principle of contradiction in the case of speculative reasoning. Its evidence is indeed ultimate but in its own order of *practical* truth—truth to be done and lived. The good man, in the Gospel expression, "does the truth." A moral judgment is already a kind of prompting, which explains the evident relation between the kind of persons we are and the moral judgments we make, and the language "good is to be done" is really, though somewhat poorly, translating an initial movement of man, through intellect and will, toward the "good."

Now, whatever the problem with their evidence, ought-statements are intelligible in that they have meaning for us and so, for what they prescribe (and, in prescribing, imply), can be valid or invalid (and true or untrue) depending on their conformity not with a fact but with an objective exigency (or, if the expression satisfies, the "fact" of exigency). It would be arbitrary to deny them their proper validity simply because they cannot be tested by criteria suited to fact-statements or truths of speculative reason.[21] To dismiss them as non-rational and reductively emotional is to overlook the special function of practical reason which also judges. Indeed the primordial sense of *judge* (*jus dicere*) applies to a function of practical intellect.

We can no more withhold the judgment that good must be done and evil avoided than we can resist the principle of contradiction. In one case we may be properly said to *see* and in the other not, but neither principle is within our power. We do not judge them but judge according to them and so we have as much evidence and authority for the one as for the other. They are equally axioms, standing on their own, and their only warrant is the intellect's own soundness. We are at the mercy of the mind and its first principles. If it distorts reality in prescribing that good must be done, it can distort also in proclaiming any other "self-evident" truth.

We cannot help remarking here the curious revenge of metaphysics on the positivist. Committed to fidelity to the data of experience whose evidence alone he will accept, he is finally found out rejecting the content of whole areas of experience and these the most meaningful of all—the ones which place him in contact with moral values such as justice, honesty, and courage, which engage him at the very core of his personality. For only in terms of these do we qualify a person as simply good or bad, as possessing or lacking integrity or "wholeness." These values are immediately experienced as highly intelligible "phenomenological essences," that is, not as abstract notions but as concrete manifestations of realities not reducible to other categories or explainable through them. These value-experiences, in other words, are not just feelings passively undergone like hunger and thirst. They are meaningful "intentions" which put us in new and original relation with their objects. Yet, by violent effort against the spontaneous response of nature, they are resolutely written off as so many "stubborn lies" to satisfy the Procrustean demands of an *a priori* "verification principle" and a rationalist system for which they prove too large and generous.[22]

So far we have been dealing with one type of challenge to the reality of obligation. We have next to treat with another which contests it in the name of morality itself. Supposing, then, that the "ought" has been reflexively vindicated in the only manner possible where a first principle is in dispute, we wish now to explore the role of obligation in our moral life and to see what are its implications. Does it have a proper place there or is it more appropriate to an infantile stage of development? Is not all genuine morality beyond obligation, a morality of aspiration rather than *une morale de pression*? Is a man really good in behaving well because he is obliged to? (Or, on the other hand, can he be called good if he were to act for any other reason than because it is his duty?) Finally, we must ask whether obligation connotes a personal God, relating us to Him in such wise that all morality is ultimately religious. *Religion* and *obligation* most probably have a common etymology. This would mean that where moral decisions have to be made, we are being addressed by an Other to whom we are "responsible."

These are not all new questions but the contemporary stress on subjectivity, on the uniqueness of the person and of moral situations, has focused attention on them. Most believers would agree that their most, or even only, significanta wareness and realization of God's presence in the world is had through the experience of value, aesthetic or moral, rather than through an impersonal cosmological argument attaining Him as an abstract Prime Mover or Necessary Being.

What has come to be known as the deontological argument, which infers God's existence from the fact of moral obligation, has in fact a long history. Cicero used it in the *De re publica*, and it seems implied in the Epistle to the Romans where Paul points to the operation of conscience among the Gentiles based on their natural discernment of right and wrong.[23] It became popular with Scholastic philosophers and theologians during the nineteenth century, though they do not expound it uniformly.[24] It is likely, though arguable, that the influences of Kant and the radical interpretation given the notions of law and duty in his moral theory were the chief occasion for this concern.

The argument as commonly presented runs this way: only from a personal being possessing the original and absolute authority of Supreme Legislator can the moral law derive its universally obliging force and man-made laws their own binding power. For evidently no impersonal non-moral cosmic force, but only an all-wise, provident, and omnipotent God can legitimately prescribe our conduct, witness our deliberations and decisions, warn through the inner voice of conscience, and, some would note, vindicate the moral order with the adequate rewards and sanctions. "Without God everything is permitted."[25]

The reasoning is not without coherence. However, its elements must be carefully sorted, especially since we are dealing with terms like *law* and *obligation* which shift meaning at different stages of the discourse and whose analogical character must be respected if we are not to stumble into circuitous reasoning and falsify the quality of the very experience for which the argument proposes to account. It is important, then, to determine what notions of law and obligation are operative and to decide which is cart and which is horse. How do we know that there is a moral law in the first place? Because we are obliged? But does the awareness of obligation itself not depend on prior recognition of a law and so of a lawgiver? And in any case, we have to ask whether the obligation springs from God's will in accord with the principle "whatever has pleased the prince has the force of law"; and if it does, would we then know, apart from revelation, that God has obliged us at all? For on such supposition He could have willed not to. Or if He "had to," because of the intrinsic goodness or evil of a possible action, then He Himself would seem to be obliged. But since there is no will superior to His, obligation would arise independently of any will and so have its source in impersonal reason. But how can reason, which merely sees, effect a binding of will?

Law and obligation appear to be correlative notions. However, the basis of the correlation is often misunderstood because of a prior confusion of the differing senses of the terms *law* and *obligation* themselves. Our English *law* is of Scandinavian origin and has the root meaning of *laid*, the sense latent in the expression "positive law." But we have other closely associated words like *legal, legislation, obligation*, which derive through the Roman Law tradition from *ligare*, to bind. Binding is a most prominent aspect of law, and dictionaries include the notion in the first of the many meanings of the term proposed—and this even where the etymology does not call for it, as in the German *Gesetz*. Laws are imposed; they do not coax or counsel, they command. And they are onerous. We have no laws prescribing attendance at musicals or coffee-breaks. They prescribe or ban the sort of action we would otherwise be likely to omit or perform.

On the other hand, it seems clear that constraint, for all its prominence, is not an essential element of law at all and that laws would still be necessary even in a community of public-spirited citizens for whom no coercion is needed. The essential function of law is to direct, as signified in such synonyms as rule, regulation, order, measure, directive—all of which connote a function of reason. Law is defined as an "ordinance of reason" not merely in that it should be reasonable but in that it proceeds, even when it is bad law, *from* reason since only reason can order, measure, rule. Law originates as an act of the legislator's practical reason prescribing the means judged suitable for promoting the common good of the body politic. Its necessity is predicated not on the need to compel the recalcitrant, but on the presence of free and intelligent agents whose activity must be coordinated and authoritatively directed.

Obviously, since a law must be communicated to direct effectively, the legislator must will its enactment, promulgate it, and enforce it when necessary. In the actual state of affairs, along with the inherent directive power must go the physical thrust to compel the subject's conformity where his own reason will not suffice. Positive law needs "teeth." Moreover, since the selection of determinate means, which need not be the only or the best ones at hand, reflects a prudential judgment, the law will be, in the proper and thoroughly respectable sense, arbitrary. But since arbitrary judgments are not objects of demonstration and since there will frequently be plausible reasons to advance against the merits of even sound ones, "arbitrary" has come to acquire an additional pejorative sense (now in fact the prevailing one) of capricious and willful.

All this encourages the subject at the receiving end of legislation to regard law as a product of will, as an alien force restraining liberty and reflecting not so much objective reason as established power. It will seem at best a necessary evil. This will be especially so when he judges a law unreasonable and must obey it anyhow, or when law has been debased to an instrument of a corrupt will to power on the part of an individual tyrant or group. Legal positivism in its form of social Darwinism has in fact developed this outlook into a formal theory of law. "The *ultima ratio* not only *regum* but of private persons is force."[26]

Another point to notice about laws: although they originate in acts of counsel, deliberation, and choice motivated by the common good, they have to be framed in impersonal statutes coldly and precisely formulated with an eye not to personal individual situations but to the general run of cases. Because of the emergence of unforeseen, though generally expected, contingencies, they will not always fit concrete situations nicely, and so, when they are strictly applied according to their letter, may even work an injustice for which equity and epicheia—an appeal above the written statute—must provide the remedy. The justice accomplished by the legal order is approximate.

These are somewhat commonplace observations which must be made to appreciate the falsification of consciousnses resulting from an understanding of moral or natural law based on a definition proper only to the positive or civil law.[27] It is then conceived as a kind of celestial *corpus juris* or code of particular imperatives, another law among laws, burdensome, restrictive, and extrinsically imposed through fiat of another's will as source of its binding power. Yet all that natural law has in common with civil law, its analogue, is the fact of its being formally constituted as an ordinance of reason directive of action. And, insofar as it is natural, it is a prescription of the moral agent's own reason ordering his own actions (including enjoyable ones) on the basis of his own perception of good and evil. He is in this respect his own legislator, "a law unto himself." And even when he experiences himself as morally constrained or obligated by this law, the pressure arises from his own persistent judgment, while resistance and reluctance are traceable to irrational dynamism not yet assimilated to reason and opposing his decrees.

These distinctions may help to evaluate some of the current criticism of natural-law ethics for its legalism. But now it might seem that our distillation of the notion of law has resulted in its evaporation. For by resolving natural law in the agent's own reason we appear to have eliminated the element of obligation. We are left in that case with a system of independent morality where man is no longer under authority. Natural law becomes a mere *lex indicativa* or *norme pilote* whose content could indeed be determined objectively by the normality of function for human nature, as the "law" of an acorn's activity is determined by its internal structure and the objective conditions for attaining oakhood. But it would not be a genuinely prescriptive law since its necessity would be only hypothetical just as the necessity of winding one's watch is not absolute but dependent on the necessity of telling time. Whence the absolute categorical necessity for man to pursue any particular or even final end? Can genuine obligation exist where there is no superior and binding will? And then the problem returns: how do we know that there is such a will?

As in the case of law, here, too, etymology betrays us into a notion of obligation which defines it in formal opposition to freedom. Yet we have only to substitute the equivalent "ought," as we always can, to recognize that there are all sorts of "obligatory" actions which are performed willingly and gladly. We are in fact obliged to a suitable amount of recreation, and there are even neighbors we spontaneously love. Indeed the sign of a moral virtue is the case of performing good acts, and a just man will find it impossible to steal where the thief is "free" to. It is true that we ordinarily speak of obligation or of "having to" only with respect to actions which are onerous and conflict with inclination. But, as we have already remarked, this conflict is generally recognized as a result of what Augustine describes as the schism within a man's own household. It is by the machinations of this foreign self, not by obligation, that freedom is compromised. On the contrary, in a perspective of human action distinguishing what is accidental and what is essential, obligation will be seen to exist in the inner logic of freedom, that is to say, not just as pressure brought to bear from without on an inherently wayward force in need of fencing, but as giving freedom its own final intelligibility, summoning it to authentic exercise and realization.

This diagnosis will of course make little sense in the absence of a metaphysics of the will and its tendency. Where freedom is viewed solely in political terms or as a simple datum in isolation from its origin and end, it comes to be defined in its dictionary sense as indetermination, without inherent direction, and without significance apart from the value of its exercise.

Brief inspection of the simple mechanics of human action alone should manifest the illusory character of this notion of freedom. Choice, being rational, supposes deliberation or a "weighing" of alternatives with at least implicit reference to a standard of value.

But deliberation must itself be powered by desire for a good which choice aims to realize. That standard itself may have been the object of a previous choice or commitment, but since deliberation is, absolutely speaking, prior to choice and since the process cannot regress to infinity, the first deliberation must originate in a natural indeliberate movement of the will—in a wanting which is not in will's own power.[28] Though it is man's specific tendency and defined as intellectual appetite, will is *natura* before it is *ratio*.[29] Choice only prolongs and determines a natural tendency of the will and is possible only where an object appears as a concrete partial realization of a good which man already wants and cannot help wanting.

We can make no sense of freedom of choice where it is not recognized as based on this natural non-free thrust of the will toward the good and ultimately to an Absolute Good as final cause and completion of human tendency. Freedom, at both start and finish, resolves in nature. It is essentially of the order of means and cannot itself be man's absolute value. This means that we must make what may seem an oversubtle distinction between freedom of choice and liberty, for the terms are not simply convertible.[30] The first is a mere capacity for self-determination whereas liberty is an achieved state of self-possession. The "power" to choose a merely apparent good supposes either darkened vision or unruly appetite. It evidences a defective freedom or "captive liberty" just as the capacity to contract pneumonia, which is predicated on the presence of physical life, witnesses at the same time to defective vitality. On the other hand, a just man's inability to steal is the result of a genuine liberty too luminous to be deceived.

Although it is admittedly paradoxical, this resolution of freedom in nature should prove a scandal only for a romantic doctrinaire liberalism. Not all necessity is constraint since that to which it is determined can also be loved. Or to put it the other way around, love induces its own necessity. *Trahit sua quemque voluptas.*[31] The contrary of liberty is not nature or necessity but violence or the involuntary.

It remains only to delineate a bit further the character of this non-constraining necessity-of-will tendency to identify it as the same moral necessity we know as obligation. At the same time,

in obviating some likely objections, we may find a perhaps surprising compatibility among what are usually considered rival and
mutually exclusive solutions to the problem of obligation—those
which ground it respectively (*a*) in reason or *recta ratio*, (*b*) in the
necessity of man's final end, and (*c*) in the divine will or in the eternal law.[32] Their dovetailing depends, however, on a deeper sound-
ing of these formulas than is evident in standard expositions.

It might be questioned, for example, whether in reducing obligation to a natural tendency of the will we have not lost sight
of the original problem. Have we uncovered anything more than
a physical and therefore non-moral hypothetical necessity, one rooted in a mere *de facto* inclination of a faculty for its proportionate
good? Have we not made the leap from *is* to *ought*?

It is true that some recent Scholastic accounts of obligation, through
their preoccupation with safeguarding the objectivity or intrin-
sicism of the moral order and avoiding any taint of voluntarism
and subjectivism, seem content with an analysis which in effect re-
duces ethics to the philosophy of nature by resolving obligation
into a "necessity of the final end" which is uniform with the rest
of nature.[33] Man "has to" seek happiness as the acorn has to strive
toward oakhood. Perhaps the fact that we are involved with an
immaterial faculty and that the implementation of the necessity
through particular actions is not physically determined encourages
the belief that we have shown a genuine *moral* necessity to pursue
the end. The tacit assumption appears to be that natures "should"
(in some sense) achieve their ends and that since in the case of man
the necessity is not physical, it must therefore be moral.[34] But *moral*
is not defined simply as *nonphysical*. For that matter, it is precisely because man is not physically necessitated, as are the "closed"
biologically determined natures about him, that the existentialist
and secular humanist argue that man has carte blanche to determine his own ends and his own moral order. Wrongdoing could
be at most defined as unreasonable, not as reprehensible.

It is here, we believe, that the notion of value and the phenomenology of value-perception and response can be illuminating. Thus
far we have been at pains to insist that will is nature before it is reason. Now it must be pointed out that it is nature of a special kind
in the world of nature; it is also spirit, an appetency for the good

as apprehended by intellect.[35]   And intellect is a faculty of the real. It perceives "objectively." It recognizes a good not only as perfective of a subject and thus, under this precise formality, founding a merely hypothetical necessity; it also perceives the good as value, as important in itself and, according to the category of value involved, calling for acknowledgment in its own right. Some values will be discerned *a priori* as moral, irreducible to any other category (aesthetic, cultural, scientific), addressing themselves to a personal center and engaging our liberty in a unique way. The command leveled by intellect on will with respect to them will then be categorical.[36]   Thus reason, through connatural recognition of a moral value (or, in the Scholastic formula, "reason informed with the natural law") is indeed the norm of morality and an immediate, though not ultimate, source of obligation. It is not, in other words, a Kantian autonomous reason. Having privileged access to the realm of values, it prescribes, as it were, on a delegated authority whereby man is constituted "minister of providence."[37]   This is the sense of the classical definition of natural law as "the rational creature's participation in the eternal law" which may itself be considered as the divine practical intellect.

> And so after saying: *Offer up the sacrifice of justice*, the Psalmist (as though some were asking what the works of justice are) continues: *There are many who say "Who shall show us what is good?"* In answer to this he says: *The light of your countenance, O Lord, is sealed upon us*, as much as to say that the light of natural reason whereby we distinguish good and evil, which is the function of natural law, is nothing else but the impress upon us of the divine light itself.[38]

Of course, even love of a value for itself supposes attraction and so must answer to some appetite. It must spring from the will as nature and have some reference as a good of the person. But it is a good for the subject because it is a value and not the other way around. Or, in von Hildebrand's language, the importance of the value is the *principium* and love and desire are *principiata*.[39]   How else could acts of courage and justice be shown to benefit the person? Indeed the opposite would appear true were it not for the connatural recognition that justice and courage enhance the person precisely because of their transcendent dignity as values.[40]   With-

out involving ourselves any more deeply with the problem of disinterested love or with the protests raised since the time of Kant
against a eudaimonist ethics, we can simply note that although
man, like all finite natures which go from potency to act, must by
metaphysical necessity seek his own perfection, he is that special
kind of nature which is also spirit. As such, he finds his own self-
realization in self-transcendence and in the "psychic gift of self"[41]
in the service of values and of the Absolute Value or Person to whom
they ultimately refer (for the source of meaning and intelligibility
will be itself intelligence).[42] Augustine, in a notable passage, gives
fine expression to this idea of the ultimate sense of the moral order
as an *ordo amoris*. Having concluded that man's final happiness must
consist in possession of the Sovereign Good through loving union,
he continues:

> But if it be virtue which leads to the happy life, I should say it is noth-
> ing other than supreme love of God. For that designation of virtue as
> fourfold, so far as I can see, is made on the basis of the different prompt-
> ings of love. So these four virtues . . . I should not hesitate to define
> thus: temperance is love offering itself wholly to what it loves; courage
> is love serenely enduring all things for its sake; justice is love at its com-
> plete service and so ruling rightly; prudence is love wisely discerning
> between what helps and what hinders. But we have said that this is
> love of not just any object but of God who is the sovereign good, su-
> preme wisdom, and perfect harmony. So we may again define them
> and say that temperance is love keeping itself whole and uncorrupted
> for God; courage is love calmly supporting all for God; justice is love
> serving only God and so ordering well whatever is subject to man;
> prudence is love correctly discerning between what assists us toward
> God and what holds us back.[43]

Provided happiness, or beatitude, be understood in this objective
sense, not as mere immanent perfecting of man but as the term of
tendency toward God as Supreme Value to whom love and adoration are due, the necessity of the final end is a source of obligation.
But in saying this, we must be careful to respect the autonomy of
individual moral values and not view them as instruments for attaining final happiness even as an objective value.[44] Although there
is a hierarchy in the order of moral values—justice, for example,
outranking temperance[45]—they are not subordinated even to each
other as means to end. Justice does not oblige because it is indis-

pensably connected with our final happiness so that one could say "I must be just so as to save my soul." Even Aristotle, who is often chided for a utilitarian view of morality, recognized this when he ranked justice first among the moral virtues and went on to add, in one of the few poetic passages in the *Nicomachean Ethics*, that is was "more admirable than either evening or morning star."[46]

However, in granting moral values this rightful dignity, we should beware of a tendency to hypostatize them as so many Platonic forms. They are not substances but qualities, and have no other existence than as "accidents" perfecting a human subject. They are prismatic reflections of the Absolute Value in whom they are found *eminenter*, who is their source, and with whom they are identified in ultimate realization. This is the meaning of the formula that the divine essence is the ultimate source of morality, and human nature the proximate one.[47] That is why all genuine love of moral values is an implicit love of God even when His existence is unrecognized, and why love of values is the only path to authentic knowledge and love of Him. We can generalize St. John's reasoning: "How can he who loves not his brother, whom he sees, love God, whom he does not see?"[48]

Finally, from these considerations we can see how obligation is grounded most ultimately in the divine will.[49] Certainly there is always the danger of being led astray by the rational distinctions we are compelled to make, on the model of our own psychology, between intellect and will in God and between both of these and the divine essence itself. God's will is not a neutral tendency or amoral power,[50] but is by definition holy,[51] that is to say, indefectibly adhering to the absolute good He Himself is, and the source of all created love of it as well. There is no possibility, as with created wills, of defection to any lesser apparent good. Thus all element of arbitrariness is excluded in saying that morally evil actions have their full quality of *moral* evil or sinfulness because they are forbidden.[52] Violating the divine will, they violate the original law of love—or right tendency.[53]

Only where man himself is regarded as the absolute value is there an indignity implied in this "heteronomy" of the eternal law.[54] Obligation goes hand in hand with man's dignity as sharer in a realm of values. We are obliged because God, who is absolute, "useless," and overflowing good, has created persons in His own image to love and possess that Good as He Himself loves and possesses it. Thomas Gilby mentions the happy oversight of a stonecarver which has a gravestone confess the deceased's hope in a life "of blissful immorality."[55] While we are still "under the law" and the press of obligation, we can forget that truth is finally glad. To pursue a suggestive thought of St. Thomas in the *De veritate*: Law is a consequence of God's joy in Himself. *Ex hoc enim quod Deus seipso fruitur, alia in se dirigit.*[56]

NOTES

1. See Claude Desjardins, *Dieu et l'obligation morale* (Montreal: Desclée, 1963).

2. *The Language of Morals* (New York: Oxford University Press, 1964), p. 75.

3. (Cambridge: Cambridge University Press, 1964), p. 162.

4. *Nicomachean Ethics*, I, 1094B27ff.; 1095B3ff.; 1098B1ff.

5. Besides Max Scheler's celebrated *Der Formalismus in der Ethik und die materiale Wertethik* (Bern: Francke, 1954), we have chiefly in mind D. von Hildebrand's *Christian Ethics* (New York: McKay, 1953); J. de Finance, *Essai sur l'agir humain* (Rome: Gregorian University Press, 1962); Hans-Eduard Hengstenberg, *Grundlegung der Ethik* (Stuttgart: Kohlhammer, 1969); A. C. Ewing, *Ethics* (New York: Collier, 1962); A. Sesonske, *Value and Obligation* (New York: Oxford University Press, 1964); C. Nink, *Metaphysik des sittlichen Guten* (Freiburg: Herder, 1955).

6. Thus Hare, *op. cit.*, p. 165. It is true that moral judgments are often accompanied by feelings, and this is what tempts some to consider them as simply emotive. It appears, too, that an explanation of the feeling is taken also to account for the judgment itself.

7. P. 91. For a similar explanation, see S. de Beauvoir, *The Ethics of Ambiguity*, trans. B. Frechtman (New York: Citadel, 1968), p. 36. C. D. Broad, *Five Types of Ethical Theory* (Ottowa: Littlefield, 1965), p. 36, is more tentative.

8. P. 165.

9. See Aristotle, *Nicomachean Ethics*, VII, 1147A21.

10. This does not mean that we have innate actual knowledge of the good or that it is had independently of a concrete moral experience.

11. 82Aff.

12. "Num hoc magistri profitentur, ut cogitata eorum, ac non ipsae disciplinae quas loquendo se tradere putant, percipiantur atque teneantur? Nam quis tam stulte curiosus est, qui filium mittat in scholam, ut quid magister cogitet discat? At istas omnes disciplinas quas se docere profitentur, ipsius virtutis atque sapientiae, cum verbis explicaverint; tum illi qui discipuli vocantur, utrum vera dicta sint, apud semetipsos considerant, interiorem scilicet illam veritatem pro viribus intuentes. Tunc ergo discunt: et cum vera dicta esse intus invenerint, laudant, nescientes non se doctores potius laudare quam doctos; si tamen et illi quod loquuntur sciunt." *De magistro*, Chap. xiv, *Oeuvres de St. Augustin*, ed. F.-J. Thonnard (Paris: Desclée, 1952), vi, 116. English translation my own.

13. "Falluntur autem homines ut eos qui non sunt magistros vocent, quia plerumque inter tempus locutionis et tempus cognitionis, nulla mora interponitur; et quoniam post admonitionem sermocinantis cito intus discunt, foris se ab eo qui admonuit, didicisse arbitrantur." *Ibid.* English translation my own.

14. Wrongdoing is taken here simply to mean acting contrary to one's conviction. I realize that some would eliminate the problem raised by such possibility (the problem of moral weakness or ἀκρασία) by defining conviction in such a way as to make action opposed to it a psychological impossibility. I am supposing that it is not.

15. I instance this sort of action because unlike other acts of justice or of courage, for which one might have reasons of a utilitarian kind, only moral or religious ones would seem to motivate it.

16. "Sicut nihil constat firmiter secundum rationem speculativam nisi per resolutionem ad prima principia indemonstrabilia, ita firmiter nihil constat per rationem practicam nisi per ordinationem ad ultimum finem." St. Thomas Aquinas, *Sum. theol.*, i-ii, q. 90, a. 2, ad 3. J. A. Stewart remarks: "There can be no πρᾶξις without a fixed *point d'appui* . . .; no κίνησις (ἡ γὰρ πρᾶξις κίνησις) without a fixed principle of conduct ἡ καθόλου δόξα ἡ ἠρεμοῦσα. In other words, animal motion (including moral action) implies a definitely constituted organism (or character) and a stimulus received by that organism (or character) from the environment." *Notes on the Nicomachean Ethics* (Oxford: Clarendon Press, 1892), ii, 20. This extensive note on 1139A17 along with that on 1147A28 is valuable for an understanding of the "physiology" of the practical syllogism.

17. "Omnis operatio rationis et voluntatis derivatur in nobis ab eo quod est secundum naturam. . . . Nam omnis ratiocinatio derivatur a principiis naturaliter notis, et omnis appetitus eorum quae sunt ad finem derivatur a naturali appetitui ultimi finis; et sic etiam oportet quod prima directio actuum nostrorum ad finem fit per legem naturalem." *Sum. theol.*, i-ii, q. 91, a. 2, ad 2.

18. See Gilbert Ryle, "On Forgetting the Difference Between Right and Wrong," *Essays in Moral Philosophy*, ed. A. Melden (Seattle: University of Washington Press, 1958), pp. 147-59.

19. See Paul Ramsey's essay "On Living Atheism: No Morality Without Immortality," *Nine Modern Moralists* (Englewood Cliffs: Prentice-Hall, 1962), pp. 1-34.

20. The expression is George Warnock's who uses it in a slightly different connection in *Contemporary Moral Philosophy* (New York: St. Martin's Press, 1967), p. 53.

21. See Ewing, *op. cit.*, p. 118.

22. See von Hildebrand, *op. cit.*, especially the "Prolegomena," pp. 1-19, and Chap. ix, "Relativism," pp. 106-28.

23. 2:14.

24. The different approaches are explored in Desjardins, *op. cit.*

25. Not because the universe would be left unpoliced, but because, as Sartre well insists in *L'existentialisme est un humanisme* (Paris: Nagel, 1946), unless they proceed from a creative act, existences are deprived of intelligibility. For a fine treatment of this thought, see J. Pieper, *The Silence of St. Thomas* (Chicago: Regnery, 1965), pp. 45-67.

26. Oliver Wendell Homes, *The Common Law* (Boston: Little, 1881), p. 44. In another place, Justice Holmes states: "Whatever body may possess the supreme power for the moment is certain to have interests inconsistent with others which have competed unsuccessfully. The more powerful interests must be more or less reflected in legislation; which like every other device of man or beast, must tend in the long run to aid the survival of the fittest. . . . The fact is that legislation in this country, as well as elsewhere, is empirical. It is necessarily made by means by which a body, having the power, puts burdens which are disagreeable to them on the shoulders of somebody else" ("The Gas-stokers' Strike," *American Law Review*, 7 [1873], 582, quoted in *The Mind and Faith of Justice Holmes*, ed. Max Lerner [New York: Modern Library, 1954], p. 50).

27. De Finance in his *Ethica generalis* (Rome: Gregorian University Press, 1959) would in fact make natural law itself the primary analogate: "Non videtur ergo nimis satagendum esse ad ostendendum quatenus lex aeterna aut naturalis definitionem legis genericam verificet. Melius et profundius ex ipsa lege naturali essentiam legis cognoscimus quam e converso" (p. 175).

28. See *Sum. theol.*, i-ii, q. 10, a. 1.

29. "Voluntas dividitur contra naturam, sicut una causa contra aliam; quaedam enim fiunt naturaliter, et quaedam fiunt voluntarie. . . . Sed quia voluntas in aliqua natura fundatur, necesse est quod modus proprius naturae, quantum ad aliquid, participetur a voluntate; sicut quod est prioris causae participatur a posteriori. Est enim prius in unaquaque re ipsum esse, quod est per naturam, quam velle, quod est per voluntatem. Et inde est quod voluntas aliquid naturaliter vult." *Ibid.*, a. 1. See also note 17.

30. See J. Moroux, *The Meaning of Man* (Garden City: Doubleday, 1961), Chap. vii, "Spiritual Liberty," for a fine development of this point.

31. St. Augustine cites this line from Virgil's *Eclogues* (ii, 65), in a rich passage of his commentary on St. John's Gospel, Tract. 26, on the relation

between love and necessity: "Non obligatio sed delectatio. . . . Quid enim fortius desiderat anima quam veritatem?" Of course, good moral theory, as Aristotle points out, should tally with the facts, and this may seem to romanticize the moral life, which even the magnanimous may find to involve choices which are hard, painful, and tragic. In such cases the summons of the value will be felt as obligation, and the "delight" will be only "according to the inward man" since it entails the sacrifice of other genuine and precious goods. But even there reason is being true to itself and its ideal, and the forgoing of lesser loves is explained only by one which is absolute. See Y. de Montcheuil, "Dieu et la vie morale," *Mélanges théologiques* (Paris: Aubier, 1946), p. 151.

32. For a treatment of these classical positions with their different shadings, see Desjardins, *op. cit.*, and, more briefly, de Finance, *Ethica generalis*, pp. 105-28; 147-58.

33. To cite two prominent examples: A. Sertillanges in his appended notes to the treatise on beatitude, in *Somme théologique*, ed. Revue des Jeunes (Paris: Desclée, 1951), esp. pp. 263-75; D. Mercier, *Theodicée* (Louvain: Inst. supérieur de phil., 1911), p. 55, cited by Desjardins, *op. cit.*, p. 30. Mercier in fact denied the possibility of arguing from obligation to a divine legislator.

34. Thus V. Cathrein, *Philosophia moralis* (Freiburg: Herder, 1911), contrasts physical and moral necessity: "Homo utpote libertate praeditus non potest hac ratione scil. necessitate physica adigi ad recti ordinis custodiam sed solum necessitate *objectiva* seu *ex suppositione finis* quatenus cognoscit recti ordinis custodiam sibi esse necessarium, *si certum aliquem finem consequi velit*" (p. 157; final emphasis added). He is here parsing St. Thomas, *De veritate*, q. 17, a. 3, which as an explanation of moral obligation is open to the same objection we are noting. So, too, in *Contra gentes*, 148, St. Thomas distinguished obligation as *necessitas finis* from *necessitas a coactione*.

35. See de Finance, *Essai*, p. 115.

36. That is, where the value reveals itself as exigent. Some will "invite," by appeal to magnanimity, to action "over and above the call of duty." See de Finance, *Essai*, pp. 299-304; von Hildebrand, *op. cit.*, pp. 277ff.

37. *Sum. theol.*, I-II, q. 91, a. 2.

38. *Ibid.*

39. *Op. cit.*, p. 99.

40. See Philippa Foot, "Moral Beliefs," *Theories of Ethics*, ed. Philippa Foot (London: Oxford University Press, 1967), pp. 96ff.; von Hildebrand, *op. cit.*, pp. 184-90.

41. J. Nuttin, *Psychoanalysis and Personality*, trans. G. Lamb (New York: New American Library, 1962), p. 242. This whole section on "basic needs" brings out the importance of these metaphysical considerations for a sound asceticism and moral pedagogy.

42. Resuming a point made in note 25: Plato in *Laws*, x, 888Dff. brings out the connection between atheism and the theory that might is right.

43. *De moribus ecclesiae*, Chap. xv, *Oeuvres de St. Augustin*, I, 174. English translation my own. See de Finance, *Essai*, pp. 191-98 (Le dépassement absolu).

44. See von Hildebrand, *op. cit.*, pp. 271-81; also his *Transformation in Christ* (Garden City: Doubleday, 1963), Chap. IX, "Striving for Perfection."

45. *Sum. theol.*, I-II, q. 66, a. 4; q. 141, a. 8.

46. 1129B28. See also 1097B2. Thomas cites him approvingly in *Sum. theol.*, II-II, q. 59, a. 12, although in a. 3, ad 2 he presents its obligation as springing from a *necessitas finis* (as opposed to a *necessitas coactionis*): "quando scilicet aliquis non potest consequi finem virtutis nisi hoc faciat." Perhaps an exegesis of *finis virtutis* to mean the value of the virtue itself can save it from an instrumentalist interpretation.

47. *Sum. theol.*, I-II, q. 71, a. 6.

48. 1 Jn 4:20. See de Montcheuil, *op. cit.*, p. 151; G. Nossent, "Dieu et la morale," *Nouvelle Revue Theologique*, 90 (1968), 801-11.

49. The manuals usually formulate the thesis on obligation of the natural law as deriving from the will of God against Vasquez who grounded it in rational nature itself. For holding that its obligation did not depend on God, Vasquez is considered to be a forerunner of modern rationalism. Suarez strongly criticized his confrère in his *De legibus*, II, 5 (See *F. Suarezii opera omnia* [Paris: Vives, 1856], V, 100-102; and H. Rommen, *The Natural Law*, trans. T. Hanley [St. Louis: Herder, 1946], pp. 63-72). Perhaps as presented by Vasquez there is a germ of rationalism in the system. He may, however, have perceived in dim fashion that "convenientia cum natura rationali" carried with it the weight of obligation not because of any autonomy of reason but because (as we would put it) values have their intrinsic *honestas*, and so oblige.

50. "Impossibile est Deum velle nisi quod ratio suae sapientiae habet. Quod quidem est sicut lex iustitiae, secundum quam eius voluntas recta et iusta est. Unde quod secundum suam voluntatem facit, iusta facit: sicut et nos quod secundum legem facimus, iuste facimus. Sed nos quidem secundum legem alicuius superioris. Deus autem sibi est lex." *Sum. theol.*, I, q. 21, a. 1, ad 2.

51. *Ibid.*, q. 36, a. 1.

52. See *ibid.*, I-II, q. 71, a. 6, and ad 4.

53. Thus though right can be defined as appetite in accord with right reason, right reason can be defined as that which is in accord with right appetite. See de Finance, *Essai*, pp. 306-11.

54. See Kant, *Foundations of the Metaphysics of Morals*, trans. L. Beck (Indianapolis: Bobbs-Merrill, 1959), p. 62.

55. *Summa theologiae*, ed. Thomas Gilby (New York: McGraw-Hill, 1966), XVIII, 144, appendix 5.

56. "Dicendum quod per eandem naturam aliquid tendit in finem quem nondum habet et delectatur in fine cum habet iam; . . . Fini ergo ultimo non competit tendere in finem, sed seipso fruitur. Et hoc licet proprie appetitus dici non possit, est tamen quoddam ad genus appetitus pertinens, a quo omnis appetitus derivatur. Ex hoc enim quod Deus seipso fruitur, alia in se dirigit." *De veritate*, q. 22, a. 1, ad 11.

I O

A Metaphysical Argument for Wholly Empirical Theology

ROBERT C. NEVILLE

THE ENCOUNTER OF CHRISTIANITY with the world's other religions is shaking Christian theology to its foundations. As if the blows of critical philosophy, positivism, and historicism had not been enough! Some thinkers have predicted the end of Christian theology and the development of a single ecumenical perspective toward which all religious traditions converge. This prediction seems plausible to me.

But Christian intellectuals have encountered serious alien philosophico-religious traditions before without losing integrity, and often the alternatives were more vital than Christianity's present competitors. One thinks of the encounter of the Church Fathers with Greek thought and piety, and of the introduction of Islamic texts into medieval Latin Christendom. In these cases and others Christianity did not just melt away like Sambo's Tiger into a stack of pancakes and butter. Its theology transformed itself to handle the challenges of the alternatives, but with enough continuity to sustain community ties.

What I want to recall about these crises is that one of the chief tools of transformation was speculative philosophy—"metaphysics," if that term can be allowed a generous interpretation. The *first theme* of this paper is that speculative philosophy is at the center of a rational response to the present encounter of Christianity with the world's religions.

A *second* and contrasting theme should be introduced immediately. No religion, Christian or otherwise, has ever wanted to claim that its main tenets are speculative constructs, even when they are intellectually expressed. The tenets are not constructs of *any* finite kind, however their expressions are "constructed" and culturally relative. Rather, religion's tenets are *given*. They come from experience.[1] The experience might be a matter of formal revelation, as in some kinds of Christianity and Islam. Or it might be an historical experience, as in Judaism and some Indian religions. Or it might be pure individual experience, conditioned by some discipline, as in Hindu and Buddhist sects and in much Christian mysticism (this was William James's primary conception of religious experience). Only Confucianism, of all the major religions, derives its tenets from what it claims to be only the wisdom of a man, and the *religious* elements of Confucianism are not so much in the Confucian intellectual tenets as in the sensibilities of respect and shame claimed to be primordial experiences.[2] Theology is at base empirical. If any theological tradition ever meant to claim that some *religiously* important tenets were "truths of reason," it was an aberration from what seems the more general religious situation. My second theme is that the religiously important claims of theology are empirically grounded.[3]

The key argument I shall use to develop these themes involves defending the truth of a certain speculative hypothesis about God and the world. The hypothesis itself is metaphysical, and its ultimate justification as an *hypothesis* is of course empirical. Furthermore, one of the virtues to be claimed for the hypothesis is that it is general enough to be true *no matter which* of the major religions of the world is true. This puts it *prima facie* in a favorable position to provide the context in which conflicts between the world's religions can be discussed. But the most helpful characteristic of the hypothesis is that it exhibits how and why the religiously interesting aspects of the relation between God and the world are *contingent* facts. As contingent, they are therefore to be known empirically in various other senses of empirical knowledge.

Briefly put, the hypothesis is that God creates everything having a determinate character. This includes His own character as creator; apart from creating, God has no determinate character. What He creates of the world may, depending on one's cosmology, be divided into (a) metaphysical conditions for the rest of the world, and (b) contingent facts which might have been other than they are under the same metaphysical conditions. But both are contingent, even the metaphysical conditions. God's own character includes not only His being a creator, but also His being *the* creator of *this* world, with its metaphysical and cosmological features; He is also creator of this historically unique world, if indeed this is religiously important. So the religiously important aspects of God are to be gleaned from examining what He has made.

The first thing to do is to establish the truth of the hypothesis, or at least to adduce the best arguments in its favor. Philosophers will look for dialectical arguments first, but I have given many of these elsewhere.[4] In keeping with the theme of this paper, I want here to justify the hypothesis by reference to the world's religions. In the discussion immediately following, I shall cite "evidence" for the hypothesis which will mean one or both of two things. Minimally I hope to show that the main claims of the various religions are special instances of the general hypothesis; although the religions' claims may conflict with each other, they all illustrate the general hypothesis. Maximally I hope to show that the general hypothesis illuminates the religious claims themselves; more particularly, that it resolves conflicts between claims by showing that on a higher level they are either compatible or identical. For claims responding to the maximal hope, the encounter of Christianity with the world's religions is pure profit since the common experience is enriched by different traditions. Where the minimal hope alone is realized, then we must simply look to experience to see which of the conflicting claims is best. The strategy in presenting evidence will be to deal with notorious "problems" for hypotheses like the above —for instance, the problem of calling Buddhistic "Emptiness" divine; a more systematic presentation of evidence cannot be attempted in a short essay.

After the development of the speculative hypothesis, I shall discuss the senses in which it supports the empirical basis of theology, and examine the importance of speculative philosophy in preserving experiential concreteness in religion (and life).

I. THE SPECULATIVE HYPOTHESIS

For present purposes, the speculative hypothesis can be exposited in terms of three propositions.

A. *All determinate things are created by an indeterminate ground.*

Explication. To be determined is to have an identity different from the identity of something else. The proposition thus says that everything with an identity is created. Creation does not mean the *causal* determination of one thing by another. Cosmological causation occurs between determinate things. Creation, rather, is the granting of reality to all determinate things from outside the system, a point determined only by the act of creating. Such ontological "causation" does not merely give existence to things whose natures are determined by cosmological causation, but grants reality to the whole society of determinate things together.[5] The dialectical defense of the proposition, in fact, takes the form of showing that there could not be even one determinate thing unless it exists together with the other determinate things, and that anything which could be related to the determinate thing must be created with it.[6] The togetherness of the created order is not temporal simultaneity but the mutual relative determination of related things. Time itself is something created. The creator cannot be determinate; if it were, it and its creations would have to be created by yet another creator, and so on.

Evidence. In religious terms this proposition expresses the doctrine of creation *ex nihilo.*

The first creation story in Genesis 1-2:4 is central to both Judaism and Christianity. This centrality is familiar enough that it need not be spelled out. Of course, there is no one, consistent interpretation of the creation story. It is particularly controversial to say that the creator is indeterminate and that everything determinate, including what the Augustinian tradition has called the "intelligibles," is created.[7] But even in the interpretations giving a determinate antecedent character to the creator, the character counts for something religiously only because of the creative "word."

Hinduism is even more internally diverse than the Judaeo-Christian tradition. But analogues to creation *ex nihilo* can be found throughout. The ancient creation hymn from the *Ṛg Veda*, for instance, claims that before creation there was neither being nor non-being; I interpret this to mean that there was nothing determinate, one way or another.[8] The hymn closes with the thought that the origin of creation is mysterious; perhaps it is understood from the vantage point of highest heaven, but then perhaps not. The later Upanisadic tradition distinguished the world of appearance from the qualityless Brahman on whom the appearances depended.[9] Even the character of Brahman as God was a matter of appearance. "Appearance," of course, does not mean mere illusion, but evanescence, insubstantiality. The realm of *māyā*, appearance, is the *play* of the Gods, in more popular expressions.[10]

Early Buddhism paid less attention to cosmology and cosmogony than to the spiritual life, but later developments of *Mahāyāna* Buddhism clearly affirmed that the world of characters or *dharma*s is ontologically non-existent. What this usually means is that everything determinate is dependent on something else, and ultimately there is nothing substantial to depend on.[11] The final ontological truth is that everything is Emptiness. Although we live in the world of *dharma*s, our home is in Emptiness; and the Mahāyāna moral of the Emptiness doctrine is that there is nothing more than the contingent world of *dharma*s. *Nirvāṇa* is *saṁsāra*.[12]

Three caveats regarding this interpretation should be expressed here.

1. The Western doctrine of creation has often been taken to mean that the created world is given existence of its own, distinct from God if not over against Him. This interpretation would make it embarrassing to cite, as I have, doctrines of an "apparent" world dependent on a qualityless ground as examples of creation. But the metaphysical status of the created world *per se* is not at issue here. The issue is whether the determinateness of the world is dependent on an indeterminate ground. The examples I have cited, and many others, illustrate this thesis. I suspect also that a careful interpretation

of what is meant in the Indian and Chinese doctrines of the world as appearance would reveal less of a difference from Western conceptions than the language might indicate.[13] At any rate, my claim is that the concept of the world as created or contingent upon a source other than itself is more general, although it is illustrated by the Western conceptions of the existential status of the world.

2. A similar qualification should be given to the Western concept of creation: creation should be approached from the standpoint of the world. Although some of the mythological elements in Hinduism and Buddhism refer to the creation of the world in a sense plainly analogous to Western conceptions of creation, more sophisticated expressions do not. For instance, some doctrines hold merely that the world is insubstantial and that beyond the world is Emptiness. Others say that the world is an appearance *of* Brahman or the Buddha nature, and that the relation of qualityless ground to its appearance is not necessarily like that of an agent to what he creates. Indeed, the term "creation" may well have been pre-empted by use in connection with an *agent*. But in the speculative theory presented here I do not want to limit "creation" that way. Creation may be by an agent, or it may be the arising of the world from Emptiness. I use the term "ground" in an attempt to be neutral at this stage. One of the main points to be made later is that the question of what kind of ground creates the world is an empirical one. Lest they think this makes undue compromises with language in order to benefit from Eastern theology, readers should remember that the mystical tradition in the West, exemplified best perhaps by Jacob Böhme, has asserted that the world is created from the depths of non-being.[14] And the term "ground" was made an essential element of establishment Christian theology by Tillich. I mean to have creation understood from the point of view of the created things, not the creator.

3. One final qualification to the above citation of evidence should be expressed. It might be claimed that some forms of Hindu or Mahāyāna Buddhism believe that the world is insubstantial or "nonexistent," and that its defective reality is contingent upon nothing. On this belief, the ultimate reality is nothing and the proximate reality *appearing* to be something is *only* apparent. It would not

be consistent with this belief to say that the world depends for its merely apparent reality on some creative ground. I am not persuaded that this belief is held as an empirical point by any religious group. Most forms of Hinduism and Buddhism intend to claim that the things of this world are defective merely in their lastingness, their basic unity, their self-sufficiency, or their causal basis. But let us consider two strong candidates for exception to this claim.

Advaita Vedānta is often interpreted as holding that all determinate differences are merely apparent and that at base all is indeterminately one. Therefore there are no appearances to be contingent upon a ground. But the conclusion denying appearances does not conform to the texts. The *Vedānta Sutra* claims Brahman is that from which the origin, subsistence, and dissolution of the world proceed.[15] Commenting on this, Śaṁkara says plainly that Brahman is the cause of the world. He distinguishes, however, between causes within the world *which can be objects of the senses*, and Brahman which *cannot* be an object of the senses. The conclusion he draws is that the relation between the world and Brahman is not an empirical one because Brahman is not empirical, but one known from scripture.[16] I would conclude, in turn, that this can be an example of the more general thesis that everything determinate is created (i.e., caused by Brahman) and that the creative ground is indeterminate (i.e., not an object of the senses).

A second position seemingly denying the dependency of the world is the Mādhyamika Buddhist doctrine that a thing cannot be said to exist; nor can it be said not to exist; it cannot be said both to exist and not to exist; and it cannot be said neither to exist nor not to exist.[17] The conclusion is that the world is inconceivable, and that it does not make sense even to deny its existence. But this logical dialectic is not itself a religious or theological view of the origin of the world; it is in fact about intelligibility. And it is preparatory to the religious experience of Emptiness, interpreted by Nāgārjuna to mean that *nirvāṇa* is identical with *saṁsāra*. According to this position, it is unintelligible to talk about causation at all, not to mention ontological causation. If, however, someone were to find a way which *is* intelligible, Mādhyamika Buddhism would not propose the thesis that the world is not created.

I have pushed the discussion of creation about as far as possible without turning to a more explicit consideration of the nature of the creative ground. What is an indeterminate ground? This brings us to the second proposition.

B. *The indeterminate creative ground of the world is God.*

This proposition has two controversial elements. The first is that the creative ground is indeterminate, a point mentioned but left undeveloped in discussion of the first proposition.[18] The second is that the ground is divine, worthy of being called God or given a religious interpretation.

Explication. According to the concept of creation sketched above, the creative ground must be indeterminate. If it were determinate, the relation between it and what it creates would need a ground prior to the ground in the relation, leading to an infinite regress. Arguments for this thesis, based on an interpretation of the contingency of determinateness, are given in superabundance in *God the Creator.*

Taken at face value, however, the statement that the ground is indeterminate might seem to be a non-statement. To say anything about a subject, even that it is indeterminate, is to assert a determinate character of it, and it would seem that this contradicts the very claim of indeterminateness.[19]

In light of this criticism it is necessary of course to spell out qualifications. Let me mention two.

1. Both the intellectual and religious contexts in which it makes sense to say "the ground of the created order is indeterminate" involve a progress through stages of reflection about the character and contingency of the world. Intellectually, the dialectic moves back from ordinary experience, seeking more nearly ultimate causes or explanations of intelligibility. Religiously, the meditation seeks feelings or appreciations of more nearly ultimate origins and foundations of transitory experience. Because the quest moves up an ordered series of one-way dependencies, the terminus is always viewed in light of its relation to the series. But because the order of movement is from the more dependent to the less, the terminus

by definition must be seen as that which is in no way dependent. The series depends on the terminus, but not the other way around. So if dependence derives from determinateness, the ultimate ground on which all else is dependent, but which is not dependent itself, must be indeterminate. Now this fact itself derives from *the order of dependent relations*, not from any determinate character in the ultimate ground.

The ground, however, is not indeterminate in all respects. With respect to its relation to its dependencies, it has the determinate character of being ground or creator. The cash value of the *ordered* relationship of dependence is that the ground could not be *ultimate* ground if that determinate character were in any way derivative from its independent *nature* and not from its *relations* with dependents. To say the ground *creates* the dependents, and with them its own relational character as creator, is not to say anything about a prior nature in the creator, only about the creative act. The point of all this is that it is improper to consider the meaning of a statement like "the creative ground is indeterminate" outside the context of the intellectual or religious quest for origins. And *in* this context, it is quite clear why in one sense the ground must be indeterminate and in another sense why it is determinately related to its dependents as their creator.

2. The second qualification is to spell out the logic of the dependency relationship. In itself, apart from created things, the ground is indeterminate because all determination is created. In relation to created things, the ground is determinate as creator. To be indeterminate is to be no thing. Apart from the creation relationship, therefore, the ground can be called Non-being as well as Being. Emptiness as well as Pure Act. But the ground is *not* apart from the creation relationship. Because there is a created order, the ground *is* creator, and that is not nothing. In speaking of the ground in relationship to the world, it is false to say that it is indeterminate except in the sense that relationship itself springs from an indeterminate source. So whether the ground is to be called indeterminate or determinate is a function of whether it is being considered (*a*) as the condition for the relationship between it and what it relates, or (*b*) as implicated in that relationship.

Explication of the second element of the proposition, namely, that the ground of creation is divine and to be called God, is fairly simple. Something is worthy of worship and may be called God if it is apprehended as the ultimate condition of the world. "Ultimate *condition*" means that which affects, causes, or sets the context for everything else. "*Ultimate* condition" means that which itself is conditioned by nothing else. The creative ground is the ultimate condition of the world.

Evidence. It is commonly believed that Western theology, including Judaism, Christianity, and Islam, interprets God as definite, personal, and active in history, whereas Eastern theology, including Hinduism, Buddhism, and Taoism, interprets God as indeterminate, empty, and removed. Some have even suggested that the Eastern God should not be called God precisely because He is Nothing. But I believe this basic observation is mistaken. The different emphases of Eastern and Western theologies are better understood with a model derivative from our speculative theory.

Consider the Upaniṣadic distinction between qualityless (*nirguṇa*) Brahman and qualified (*saguṇa*) Brahman. The former is the utterly incomprehensible absolute. The latter is Brahman in relation to the world it creates and is often personified as the God Īśvara. This corresponds to our distinction between the ground of the created order considered out of relation to that order, and the ground considered as implicated in it through creating. But the Hindu way of making the point separates the two sides with different names, admitting the relation between them.

Now I suggest that this is a dominant orientation in most Eastern theology. Western theology by contrast deals with the two sides together and distinguishes them only when forced by logic or a religious need for mystical, pure transcendence.

The logic of the *Tao-te ching*, especially in the first stanza, exhibits the Eastern orientation. Distinguishing being and non-being, Lao-tzu notes that this is a determinate relation and that they depend on each other. So therefore both are produced by a nameless ground.[20] Mahāyāna Buddhism in its turn also maintains a strong contrast between the Emptiness of the ultimate condition and the salvific character of its apprehension by persons. Consider the distinction between the *dharmakāya* on the one hand and the *saṁbhogakāya* and *nirvānakaya* on the other. The first is the indeterminate essence of pure being about which nothing can be said; the second and third are spiritual and earthly realities about which much can be said. The latter two are manifestations of the first. (The relationship between them is such, however, that the Pure Buddhahood of the *dharmakāya* is loving, and its love is located in the *saṁbhoga-* and *nirvānakayas*. Therefore the distinction between the abysmal transcendence and the relative transcendence is less sharp in Mahāyāna Buddhism than in Taoism or the Upaniṣads. This is why Buddhism is often said to be closest of the Eastern religions to Christianity.) Buddhism joins with the other Eastern religions in emphasizing the remoteness of the Absolute to the extent that religious piety populates the relative transcendence with a pantheon of gods and mythological figures.[21] There is no fear of idolatry because the transcendence and ultimacy of divinity itself are protected by remoteness from any transcendence implicated in the world.

Western religions, by contrast, emphasize the *connection*, rather than the distinction, between the absolute and relative sides of divinity. On the one hand they fear the idolatry resulting from the merely relative transcendence of the creator. On the other hand they are suspicious of otherworldly mysticism. The model of God as an individual agent, I submit, has been attractive in the West because it seems to render the *connection* between (*a*) internal action *ab initio* and (*b*) external relations in which the action is conditioned determinately. Nevertheless, when setting limits to the analogy of God with an individual agent, Western theologians have recognized the dialectic distinguishing the indeterminate transcendence from the relative and determinate transcendence. The Christian trinitarian controversies wrestled with this. Even Thomas Aquinas, for whom the Trinity was a mystery, philosophically speaking, called God Pure Act. *Actus purus* is a far cry from any ordinary individual agent, much closer to the Eastern Brahman shining forth in the glories of the world.[22]

The strains in Western religion best paralleling the Eastern distinction of the sides of God have often been on the fringes of orthodoxy—Sūfism, cabalistic Judaism, medieval German mysticism. But although orthodoxy has been wary of radical breaks between worldly religion and the mysticism of complete transcendence, it has also been unwilling to deny those two sides.

The conclusion I want to draw from this part of the discussion is that religions of both East and West acknowledge the essential integrity of a distinction between (*a*) God as creator of the world, and thereby determinately related to it, and (*b*) God as indeterminate *in se*, transcendent of any relation to the world. Moreover, whereas the Eastern religions tend to emphasize the difference between the two sides, Western religions emphasize their connection.

Basic agreement on metaphysical matters is more to be expected than not, logic being less culturally relative than most things. Experience of the world, however, and therefore the flavor of salvific activity, marks a more significant difference between Eastern and Western orientations. The religious quest in the East has often meant an attempt to transcend the vicissitudes of the world, and it follows the path of the dialectic of dependence traced above. As a result, the last step of appreciation of the ultimate condition is taken as most important, and God on the side of ultimate indeterminateness is religiously more significant. Whereas this path has also been followed in the West, there has been an emphasis on God's reverse movement from aseity to involvement with the world. God acts, makes covenants, reveals Himself, and saves. God's action—and therefore the divine nature as constituted by His relating to the world—is often religiously more significant for the West. This Western bias finds its closest Eastern parallel in the Buddha's love in Mahāyāna Buddhism. There is also an analogue, albeit greatly intellectualized, in the doctrine of *jen* in Neoconfucianism.

I do not mean to slough over the hard problem of whether the Emptiness of "atheistic" Buddhism can be called divine or be interpreted as a religious category. But it is difficult to locate exactly where this problem lies. It does not lie with the kind of Mahāyāna Buddhism I have been describing; for there the Emptiness is the Pure Buddha who, in connection with his fulgurations in the world, is very worshipful indeed! Nor does the problem lie with the orthodox Theravada Buddhists who would eschew any kind of cosmological speculation, for they would *not deny any claim* about God; they would resist only the suggestion that the Buddha be deified. The problem may lie, however, with Zen Buddhism or with forms of Theravada Buddhism emphasizing the ultimacy of Suchness. Religious life, for these religious outlooks, involves attaining, and organizing one's life around, the insight that things are simply their presence to themselves, and nothing more. There is no ultimate meaning to life or the cosmos, or any interesting origin.

I admit that this is the most difficult religious style to catalogue as an instance of our speculative hypothesis. If our hypothesis is somewhat weakened, however, the cataloguing is less difficult. Suppose we say all diversity is the *manifestation* of an ultimate reality. Then we can latch on to the fact that Suchness manifests itself in all determinate forms. Suchness itself is indeterminate. The determinations of the world are all such as they are, but their reality consists not in the different identities but in the fact that each is such as it is. Now the Suchness does not create or cause the manifestations. But it is the passive condition for their existence. And more importantly the Suchness is the ultimate condition of things, which, when apprehended, shakes a person to religious awe and peace.

With this last qualification to the evidence for our hypothesis, let us pass to the third proposition.

c. *God's character is derivative from His creative act.*

Explication. This proposition has two main specifications. *First,* God has the character of being creator as such. The religiously interesting elements of this character have to do with mystical experience and the appreciation of lordship and supremacy. Most of the major religions of the world are in fair agreement about this character and this kind of religious experience, however widely they disagree over what symbols are appropriate and what conclusions can be drawn. *Second,* God has the character of being creator *of this world,* and all His actions, revelations, and personality traits depend on how one interprets the general character of the world and its historical events. The major religions are in fairly profound *disagreement* about this second aspect of the divine character. The first aspect of God can be called His ontological character, the second His cosmological character; in most religions, the salvific, as well as the theological, question deals with both.

Evidence. The religious experience of God's ontological character has been well described by Rudolf Otto in *The Idea of the Holy.* There he treats the "creature feeling" in the apprehension of the numinous before treating the character of *mysterium tremendum.* I take it that God's ontological character as creator is religiously experienced in terms of the dual meaning of transcendence discussed in the last section. A person experiences God by feeling himself to be dependent and God not to be; the experience of God as having aseity distinguishes Him as "Wholly Other," to use Otto's phrase. Otto draws his evidence for this religious experience from the major world religions, and I do not need to rehearse it here.

The issue for this proposition, however, is whether the ontological character of God is experienced as *derivative from the divine creative act,* not whether the experience of God as numinous means the experience of Him as creator. There seems *prima facie* logical reason to deny the proposition. The numinal character of God is His aseity, not God as creating; therefore how does it make sense to say that the numinal character derives from the creative act?

On this logical level, however, there is a clear answer. God's aseity, His supremacy, His numinous quality, all depend on a contrast with His relations, and that contrast derives from the creative act. God could not intelligibly be said to have independence in Himself were He not independent of the world. This is not merely a distinction of reason. God would be neither in Himself nor relative to another if there were no others around. Because God is in fact relative to the world as creator, and this relativity requires ontological independence on His part, He has aseity and relativity *both,* by derivation from His creative act. Similarly with supremacy: God is not supreme unless He has a world to lord it over. If one adopted an Aristotelian concept of creation in which God would have the potential to create without creating, God's supremacy still would depend on relativity, this time to potential creatures. God's numinous quality, directly apprehended in religious experience, is a quality of revelation. He is numinous in a context and to properly equipped apprehenders. Of course, the *reason why* He is numinous is that He is transcendent creator, and this in fact is what is apprehended in ontological religious experience. But if there were no creative act, God would not be creator, and would have no transcendence to manifest.

Is there experiential ground to support this, as well as logical ground?

In Western religions, where "creator" language is at home, it is fairly clear that God makes Himself creator and that He has no character except what is revealed in His creative self-manifestations. In the most ancient Judaism, God's character stemmed from what He did—in fact, from how He proved Himself against the local competitors. In more sophisticated forms this doctrine became that of God's creatorship as such, and this reached fine expression in Job's whirlwind. In Christianity, the claim of incarnation raised the question of what God's role is, apart from relation to the world. The Trinitarian controversies reflect the deep experience of the Church, and I think their result was a doctrine of God as *essentially* triune, and this in reference to the created order. The rejection of both monarchianism and economic trinitarianism marked the denial that God has a deeper nature apart from the Trinity of which Christ is a part. The rejection of subordinationism marked the denial that Christ, obviously an element in creation, is less an essential part of the divine nature than the Father or Spirit.[23]

In Eastern religions, it makes little sense to wonder what the ultimate condition might be apart from the world of conditioned things. But it is quite clear that the absolute side of God, the quality-less Brahman, the *dharmakāya*, cannot be said to have any character whatsoever except insofar as it stands in contrast to the qualitied side. Therefore, God's ontological character depends on the contrast, and the contrast itself is a determinate (and merely apparent) character.

2. The *cosmological* character of God stems directly from the way in which He is reflected in the world. The interpretation of this depends in turn on the way in which the world is interpreted as reflective of God.

It is enough by way of evidence to cite some correlations between interpretations of the world and the concept of God. For Western scholars the first correlation coming to mind is that of the war-god Yahweh with the nomadic Hebrews in contrast to the fertility-gods of the agricultural inhabitants of Canaan.[24]

In a comparison of Eastern and Western religions, the difference in time sense is usually cited as significant. The Western image of time is linear and the Eastern (at least Indian and Chinese) is not.[25] So whereas gods are personified in both traditions, only in the Western is there an emphasis on a god having a single career. The God of Western religions has one unique career dealing with the world, and this means that each event in the world, because each is uniquely relative to God, has an irreplaceable quality about it. In Eastern religions the gods can assume many forms, have many incarnations, and be fairly indifferent to when and where they are.

A second contrast is in the ontological importance accorded time, the Western tradition giving it great ontological importance, the Eastern relatively less. So whereas both traditions admit that the fundamental divinity is somehow above time (however much He may enter it) the Western divinity must *essentially* be able to relate to time. The Eastern divinity can be—in fact should be—essentially indifferent to time. This difference reinforces the Western preference for a personal model since a person can assume a position in time by deliberate acts. It also reinforces the Eastern preference for a nonpersonal model at the ultimate level since a personal model would *have to* assume a stance toward temporal events.

This completes what I want to say in expressing general empirical evidence for the speculative hypothesis of God. Of course, much more can be said. If the evidence is to be coercive, much more should be said. I am especially aware of the dangers of the lack of qualification implicit in talking about religious "traditions" as such; comparing Eastern with Western religions is an even more treacherous task. In every religious tradition there are elements of every other, and some illustrations of this have been given above. The attempt has been made, however, to characterize religious traditions by their dominant strands. Admitting the inevitable distortions in such attempts, I believe the above discussion has shown how the major world religions lend the empirical weight of their funded experience to the speculative hypothesis of God the creator.

II. THE EMPIRICAL TASK OF THEOLOGY

The conclusion to be drawn from the speculative hypothesis is that theology is empirical in a variety of senses. Now I want to spell these out.

1. The speculative hypothesis is empirical.

The ultimate test of any hypothesis is empirical, and metaphysical ones are no exceptions. There are, of course, non-empirical processes in the formulation and expression of hypotheses. An hypothesis is discovered or invented by an act of imagination which has no rules.[26] Its internal articulation, clarification, and empirical predictions are formed by logical, not empirical, considerations. But whether the hypothesis is *true* depends on whether it interprets experience well.

One of the differences between philosophical and scientific hypotheses is that the former have no "critical experiments." They are so general that empirical probations at best make them only more or less plausible. A philosophical hypothesis is tested primarily by being lived with and judged whether it enlightens and fructifies experience. Furthermore, the difference between the generality of philosophical hypotheses and the particular relativity of the cultural forms in which their confirming or disconfirming instances are found is so great that it is difficult to determine what is important and what is not. At least philosophers are adept at defending their hypothesis against apparently disconfirming evidence by saying "I really did not mean that." If the cosmonaut sent to find God reported "She's Black," the Yahweh hypothesis no doubt could be altered to accommodate that evidence.

In a speculative theory about God as creator, there are four general areas of empirical reference. The first is that the theory must be plausible in general experience, that is, in experience broader than just religion. In the long run, the experience not of one man but of a whole society or tradition reveals whether a theory is worth much in terms of cutting at the natural joints of life.

The second area of empirical reference concerns the justification of the theory of God as a legitimate kind of knowledge. The only ultimately satisfactory claim that a kind of knowledge is possible and respectable is an empirical demonstration of instances of it. In philosophy this demonstration usually comes down to showing that something called by another name is really the kind of knowledge alleged in the case. Tillich's discussion of ultimate concern is a familiar example of this with respect to the knowledge of God as ground of being.

The third empirical reference important for philosophical theology is the field of religious phenomena. I do not mean by this the historical comparison of structured and integrated religious traditions. Rather I mean the more universal phenomena which enter into different connections in different contexts, things like prayer, mysticism, priesthoods, birth, death, and initiation rituals, conceptions of the "religious problem" (e.g., sin, suffering, transience) and of the "religious solution" (e.g., salvation, release, dissolution into the ultimate). Any hypothesis about God must be able to make sense of these fairly pervasive phenomena without explaining them away.[27]

The fourth empirical reference is the making of a claim for universality with respect to comparative religions. This is what I have attempted to sketch above for my hypothesis of God the creator.

All these areas of empirical reference are empirical in unusual senses. Even the appeal to phenomenology and to the history of religions touches not unwashed facts but rather phenomenological and historical classifications of facts. But all are empirical in the sense that the theory is brought to the bar of given evidence, evidence not constructed by the stipulatory powers of the hypothesis itself or by the purely formal truths of logical intuition.

2. *The particular character of God as determined by His creation is empirical.*

One of the strongest elements of plausibility in the divine-creator hypothesis as it was developed above is that it is general concerning the more concrete ideas about God over which religions disagree. As far as the hypothesis is concerned, God could be Yahweh, the Trinity, Allah, Brahman, the ontological Buddha, Suchness, or Nothing. On this level of generality the hypothesis directly addresses a profound experience of divine transcendence and mystery. But some of the more interesting religious claims are more concrete and conflicting between religions.

The issue of whether God is ultimately personal or impersonal is a vitally important question. Admitting that "person" is only an analogy, how seriously one takes the analogy determines the significance of prayer, historical revelations, and a variety of other religious elements making sense only in terms of a personal God. The issue is an empirical one. We distinguish impersonal movements from personal actions by peculiar patterns and styles of behavior; the question of robots illustrates the distinction by being a borderline case. Is this world God created one exhibiting the marks of a personal product?

Of equal importance with the "person" question is the issue of historical revelations. The "general" character of God is often discussed under the rubric of "general revelation," that is, pervasive traits of the world revealing a character to God. But some religions claim "special revelations," particular historical events or histories (as of the Hebrew people), and these are sometimes said to be more important than general revelations. Christianity makes an extraordinarily strong claim for the historical revelation of Christ, namely, that Christ Himself was wholly God, incarnate, and uniquely determinative of the meaning of history. Islam makes as nearly as strong a claim in saying that the Koran is divinely and literally inspired in the event of its reception by Mohammed. Judaism makes a more diffuse but still strong claim in its belief that the history of God's relationship with the Hebrews uniquely reveals God's personal character; God is not only a person (analogously), He has a definite personality. Hinduism and Buddhism, insofar as they claim historical events to be revelatory, at most say that God is *illustrated* in them, not constituted by them.

Now, special revelations are eminently empirical questions. One can say he "accepts" a cluster of events as revelatory "on faith." One can even carry out a "dogmatic" theology through the explication of beliefs premised on faith. But this is to ignore the seriousness of the question of *truth*. If an historical element is alleged to be revelatory, that is a claim of empirical fact and must be tested accordingly.

The empirical testing of such claims is extraordinarily complex. There are problems enough with the ordinary historical reporting of the events. But the revelatory claims usually also assert that some *effect* is made by the revelation, some new power or change in history. Encounter with the events, through historical rendering, is often said to have a self-authenticating quality. And people's response to revelations is surely as much a function of their readiness and of historical condition as of any coerciveness in the revelatory report. William James may be right in holding that some kind of evidence demands prior faith in order to be grasped. These factors combine to make empirical justifications very tenuous. Just about any claim can be explained away or made a function of something irrelevant.

On the other hand, certain massiveness of evidence simply cannot be ignored. The spiritual regeneration of Christian experience is not falsified by other religions, it seems to me. The Jews are still a united people despite dispersions which have destroyed the folk-integrity of all other competing groups. And the people of Allah conquered most of the world and still are the fastest growing religious group.

The most plausible logical move in a situation like this is to find some scheme for integrating the strengths of the world's great religions. This has been attempted from a variety of angles, from Schleiermacher to Panikkar, and I myself think it is the most promising tack. But whether it can succeed is an empirical matter. There is no intellectual integrity in asserting the pre-eminence of one tradition over the others without a thorough empirical investigation. Nor can we claim that they are compatible until we discover that in fact they are so.

III. PRACTICAL CONCLUSIONS

The comments in the previous section were about theoretical conclusions to be drawn about empirical theology from the premiss of the speculative hypothesis. The comments here are more practical.

A fundamental critical question must be raised about the entire procedure of the previous pages. Christianity may well be in the throes of a violent spiritual encounter with the world's other major religions. But at least the encounter is concrete and vital, not a matter of mere theory. Why then should anyone take seriously the suggestion that speculative philosophy has a contribution to make? In fact, had we not abandoned serious speculative philosophy long before we abandoned that cultural chauvinism which protects us from non-Western ideas? I want to offer several answers to this criticism.

First, reflection on the speculative level itself is part of concrete experience. To oppose thought to life is to leave the evolution of the human mind an inexplicable mystery.

Second, cultural traditions legitimately get bored with endeavors like metaphysics when they turn in upon themselves and become academic. This is a serious problem: when metaphysics fails to enlighten concrete life, it is judged to have no experiential meaning. But when a cultural tradition no longer can look only to itself, when it must orient itself to other traditions appearing on the scene as live options to be handed over, then metaphysics becomes once again a vital and imperative need. An intercultural encounter calls into question the basic images and themes of each culture, and a new set of images and themes is required. But the only control men have over the formation of such fundamental contours of culture is through very general speculation—metaphysics. Only through speculative philosophy is it possible to give a *critical* account of what is threatened and what reinforced in an intercultural encounter. Only speculative philosophy allows one's own and another's cultures to be compared. Only speculative philosophy allows cultural conflict to move from counterassertion (perhaps with bludgeons or bombs) to the adducing of reasons from a common perspective. Speculative philosophy is the hope of reason in the face of conflict which is ultimate, without the speculative perspective.

Third, speculative philosophy about God works. The growing concern for comparative cultural studies and Eastern religions has fed an increasing interest in speculative philosophy. Even if one has no taste for the hypothesis of God the creator, the school of speculative theology deriving from Whitehead is thriving, as are reinvigorated strands of Thomism, Existentialism, and Idealism. Our empirical studies of cultures are now sophisticated enough for us to be able to criticize and nourish these approaches to speculative philosophy from the standpoint of a variety of cultures.

From the perspective of the arguments of this paper, a tentative evaluation can be made of major trends in recent theology. Contrary to what liberals have said, the Scholastic tradition of philosophical or natural theology is the authentic progenitor of the speculative contribution to theology today. It should therefore be encouraged in its contemporary successors, primarily process theology and its neighboring foes (I count the theory of God the creator as a neighboring foe of process thought).

Contrary to what conservatives have said, the empirical emphasis of Protestant liberalism and, more recently, "spirit" theologies in Roman Catholicism are fundamentally correct. The empirical approaches to theology cover a wide range—Schleiermacher, Strauss, Bauer, Schweitzer, Ritschl, Harnack, Rauschenbusch, Bultmann, and Tillich, just to name some classic Protestant liberals. Not all are of equal value. But they are right in the belief that the intellectual integrity of religion rests with experience, be the experience feeling, texts, history, morals, cultural *Zeitgeist,* or existential concern. I would say that what this tradition needs now is a strong acculturation to non-Christian religions, a point Tillich made with force in his late work *Christianity and the Encounter of World Religions.*[28] Whether theology departments take up the challenge of history of religions is an interesting bellwether of their academic strength. Western *society* is absorbing non-Christian cultures, and "merely" Christian theology is fast becoming obsolete.

Retrospect. A speculative hypothesis about God as creator of all determinate things was presented with only a sketch of the dialectical reasons for believing it. But considerable evidence was provided that its main elements are illustrated by the major religions of the world. On one level, the empirical evidence counts toward the plausibility of the hypothesis, adding weight to its claims for being true and fruitful. On another level, the evidence demonstrates the benefits of believing the hypothesis. The hypothesis allows one to see the major religions in a theoretical comparative situation. It allows one to interpret their disagreements. And insofar as the hypothesis is plausible, it gives a clue to what is essential and what is "merely relative" in each religion, although this is a circular inference with respect to the evidence of religions (and I have not pressed the point here). After the discussion of the hypothesis, I elaborated the senses in which this particular hypothesis commits one to empirical theology. An alternative hypothesis, giving an independent determinate character to God or interpreting metaphysical principles to be ontologically necessary truths, would have much less work for empirical theology. The practical conclusion of my hypothesis, however, is that theologians should have a stiff but brief course in metaphysics and then proceed with their empirical studies. Philosophers, of course, should never cease to challenge the speculative hypothesis.

I have tried to develop my twin themes of the theological necessity of speculative thought and the religious necessity of empirical theology with a bold move: overly bold, no doubt. I have tried to demonstrate what ought to be done by first doing it (in capsule form) and then showing how neatly it puts things in their places, interpreting the interrelation of the world's major religions. There is no better argument that something is possible than a demonstration of an actual instance of it; and there is no better justification that something would be worthwhile doing than the doing of it and a demonstration of its actual benefits. Of course, this strategy puts my main themes in jeopardy. A person could reject my particular hypothesis but still be open to the main themes—he will be put off by my strategy here. But by the same token, a responsible effort to reject my particular hypothesis will of necessity involve the critic in speculative philosophy far enough to accept at least the first theme. And if his own hypothesis vitiates the empirical character of religion, the worst which can happen is a separation of philosophic life from religious life, a common enough condition anyway.

The encounter of Christianity with the world's other major religions is not a problem for Christianity alone. It is a problem for the other religions as well. And it is equally a problem for those people dissociated from all organized religions but seeking cultural means to express their religious sensibilities. But in all these cases, I believe a steadfast pursuit of speculative heights to be the best procedure for guaranteeing faithfulness to concrete experience.

NOTES

1. This is one of the themes of John E. Smith's fine book *Experience and God* (New York: Oxford University Press, 1968). See also his essay "The Experiential Foundations of Religion," *Reason and God* (New Haven: Yale University Press, 1961), pp. 173-83.

2. See, for instance, *The Book of Mencius*, 2A:6, 3A:5. There are many editions and translations of this book; one of the best is *A Source Book in Chinese Philosophy*, ed. Wing-tsit Chan (Princeton: Princeton University Press, 1963).

3. The twin themes of the practical importance of metaphysics and of the empirical foundation of important religious truths have found multifaceted expressions in the philosophy of Elizabeth G. Salmon, to whom this article and this book are dedicated. She has also maintained that metaphysics itself is based on experience, one of the main points defended in this article. Although

she must forgive the fact that my interpretations of the themes often differ from hers, my emphasis on their importance is intended as a sign of respect for the centrality of her thought.

4. The main dialectical argument is found in *God the Creator* (Chicago: University of Chicago Press, 1968). It is summarized in "Creation and the Trinity," *Theological Studies*, 30 (1969), 3-26, and "Can God Create Men and Address Them Too?" *Harvard Theological Review*, 61 (1968), 603-23.

5. The legitimacy of the distinction between cosmological and ontological causation is subject to much debate. Since it centers on the concept of God the creator, see Lewis Ford's "Whitehead's Categorial Derivation of Divine Existence," *Monist*, 54 (1970), 374-400; see also my "Whitehead on the One and the Many," *Southern Journal of Philosophy*, 7 (1969-70), 387-94, in which Whitehead is criticized for not making the distinction. *God the Creator* argues for the distinction in Chapters 5 and 7.

6. The defense is found in *God the Creator*, Chapter 3.

7. Hans Jonas has a fine treatment of many of the complexities of the history of the doctrine of creation *ex nihilo* in his "Jewish and Christian Elements in the Western Philosophical Tradition," in *Creation: The Impact of an Idea*, edd. Daniel O'Connor and Francis Oakley (New York: Scribner, 1969), pp. 241-58. It is interesting that, in discussing the Scotistic idea of creation (of which my hypothesis is a version), Professor Jonas argues that the doctrine that the divine intelligibles are products of the divine will leads to the relativizing of values to human will when faith in the divine will fades. Another way of looking at the contingency of the intelligibles and of all values, however, is to say that they are known only empirically, not *a priori*. To conclude, as so many do, that divine voluntarism entails conventionalism, is to presume that experience cannot be a source of important knowledge.

8. 1. Non-being then existed not nor being:
   There was no air, nor sky that is beyond it.
   What was concealed? Wherein? In whose protection?
   And was there deep unfathomable water?

   . . . .

   6. Who knows for certain? Who shall here declare it?
   Whence was it born, and whence came this creation?
   The gods were born after this world's creation:
   Then who can know from whence it has arisen?

   7. None knoweth whence creation has arisen;
   And whether he has or has not produced it:
   He who surveys it in the highest heaven.
   He only knows, or haply he may know not.

Hymn x. 129, *A Source Book in Indian Philosophy*, edd. Sarvepalli Radhakrishnan and Charles A. Moore (Princeton: Princeton University Press, 1957).

9. See for instance, the *Bṛhadāraṇyaka Upaniṣad*, ii, iii; or iii, viii.

10. This whole world the illusion-maker (*māyin*) projects out of this.
   And in it by illusion (*māyā*) the other is confined.

Now, one should know that Nature (Prakṛiti) is illusion (māyā),
And that the Mighty Lord (maheśvara) is the illusion-maker (māyin).
Śvetāśvatara Upaniṣad IV, i, 9-10, Radhakrishnan and Moore, op. cit.

11. See the Mādhyamika-śāstra by Nagarjuna, especially Chapter 1, in The Concept of Buddhist Nirvana, ed. Th. Stcherbatsky (London: Mouton, 1965).

12. Ibid., Chapter 25. See also Seng-chao's treatises, "The Immutability of Things" and "The Emptiness of the Unreal," in Chan, op. cit.

13. Compare Fa-tsang's "Treatise on the Golden Lion" in Chan, op. cit., for instance, with the Western doctrine that determination is by negation of the otherwise unlimited pure act.

14. See Nicolas Berdyaev's discussion of Jacob Böhme's contribution to the notion of freedom and creation in The Beginning and the End, trans. R. M. French (New York: Harper Torchbook, 1957), pp. 104-17.

15. Vedānta Sūtra I, i, 2, in Radhakrishnan and Moore, op. cit.

16. Śaṁkara's commentary to Vedānta Sūtra I, i, 2, also in Radhakrishnan and Moore, op. cit.

17. Nagarjuna in Stcherbatsky, op. cit., Seng-chao in Chan, op. cit.

18. The strictly logical exposition of the speculative hypothesis would be to say in the first proposition that determinate things are created and in the second that the creator is indeterminate and divine. I have chosen a different division, however, because of the lay of the evidence. The religious evidence for creation of the world makes reference to a creator, and so the creator must be included in a discussion of creation ex nihilo. But the character of the creator can be left vague until it is considered in a separate proposition.

19. David Burrell, for instance, argues this way in his "Religious Life and Understanding," Review of Metaphysics, 32 (1969), 690-95. The assumption that a self-defeating or contradictory statement is a "non-statement" is his; some other philosophers might want to reserve "non-statement" to refer to statements so ill-formed as to be unintelligible. A contradiction, after all, must be a fairly clear assertion if it can be recognized as contradictory.

20. The Tao (Way) that can be told of is not the eternal Tao;
The name that can be named is not the eternal name.
The Nameless is the origin of Heaven and Earth;
The Named is the mother of all things.
Therefore let there always be non-being so we may see their subtlety,
And let there always be being so we may see their outcome.
The two are the same,
But after they are produced, they have different names.

. . . .

Chan, op. cit., p. 139.

21. Tibetan Buddhism is perhaps the most picturesque form of Mahāyāna in terms of mythical beings and places. See the Tibetan Book of the Dead, ed. W. Y. Evans-Wentz (London: Oxford University Press, 1927). The editor's Introduction contains a splendid explanation of the three "bodies" or "kayas," pp. 10-18.

22. See, for instance, the glorification of Kriśna in the *Bhagavad-gītā*.

23. This theme is pressed in my "Creation and the Trinity," cited in note 4.

24. See William H. McNeill's *The Rise of the West* (Chicago: University of Chicago Press, 1963), pp. 157-66. See also Sabatino Moscati's *Ancient Semitic Civilizations* (New York: Capricorn, 1960).

25. This point is perhaps overstated by Oscar Cullman in *Christ and Time*, trans. Floyd V. Filson (rev. ed.; Philadelphia: Westminster, 1964), where he treats the Hellenic sense of time as cyclical. A superbly nuanced general study of Eastern people's sense of the disposition of the world is Hajime Nakamura's *Ways of Thinking of Eastern Peoples*, ed. Philip P. Wiener (Honolulu: East-West Center Press, 1964). If the comparison is not too simplistic, the Eastern time sense is symbolized by the everturning wheel of the mandala, the Western by the beams of the cross, representing life as an intersection of eternal action and linear history.

26. In this view of metaphysical hypotheses, I follow that of Charles S. Peirce expressed in his essay "A Neglected Argument for the Reality of God," in *The Collected Papers of Charles Sanders Peirce*, edd. Charles Hartshorne and Paul Weiss (Cambridge: The Belknap Press of Harvard University Press, 1935), 6.452-93.

27. I have attempted to justify the hypothesis as a kind of knowledge in Pt. II of *God the Creator*; Pt. III of that book used the hypothesis to interpret pervasive religious phenomena.

28. (New York: Columbia University Press, 1963).

Bibliographical Note

The best collections of philosophico-religious texts of Eastern thought are listed below. I regret that I know of no comparable volume of Islamic thought.

Chan, Wing-tsit (Ed.). *A Source Book in Chinese Philosophy*. Princeton: Princeton University Press, 1957.

The following books on comparative philosophico-religious ideas are generally helpful:

Dye, James W., and Forthman, William H. *Religions of the World*. New York: Appleton-Century-Crofts, 1967.

Eliade, Mercea. *From Primitives to Zen: A Thematic Sourcebook of the History of Religions*. New York: Harper & Row, 1967.

——. *The Sacred and the Profane: The Nature of Religion*. Trans. Willard R. Trask. New York: Harper & Row, 1957.

Noss, John B. *Man's Religions*. 4th ed. New York: Macmillan, 1969.

Otto, Rudolf. *The Idea of the Holy*. Trans. John W. Harvey. London: Oxford University Press, 1926.

Radhakrishnan, Sarvepalli. *Indian Philosophy*. 2 vols. London: Allen and Unwin, 1923.

II

'Vaguely like a Man':
The Theism of Charles S. Peirce

VINCENT G. POTTER, S.J.

PEIRCE'S THEISM IS NOT CALCULATED TO PLEASE many philosophers
—at least not at first sight. His theism, he says, is "sound pragmatism,"
and this is not likely to attract positivists who have adopted its maxim
as an expression of their own views concerning verification. His
theism, he says, is a consequence of anthropomorphism—a claim
not likely to delight either traditional theists or hardheaded scientists.
Finally, his theism is intrinsically infected with vagueness, a disease
which surely will be diagnosed as fatal by many analysts and logicians.
We have failed to remark perhaps the most disturbing claim of all:
Peirce's theism is supported by a form of the ontological argument!
This will perhaps please no one at all.

Yet there it is in all its outrageous boldness: a theism supported
by an "exact logician" trained in natural science; a theism which is
the consequence of pragmatism; a theism vague and anthropomorphic, and *therefore* indubitable in the strictest sense. These are
hard words and who among philosophers will hear them? The
point of this paper is to help the philosopher, if he is still willing to
read on, to understand the precise import of these shocking claims
and perhaps suggest at least that they are not so shocking—perhaps

too that in the end they are not so bad even if unusual and/or distasteful.

In a letter to William James (July 23, 1905), Peirce remarked that his own belief in theism was "good sound solid strong pragmatism" (8.262).[1] Three years later he published his well-known "Neglected Argument for the Reality of God" in the *Hibbert Journal* (6.452-493) where he gave a "poor sketch" of that argument and a mere "table of contents" of what would be required to show its validity. This poor sketch is in reality a rapid and terse outline of that philosophical view called "pragmaticism" which he had elaborated over the preceding half-century. The "table of contents" is nothing but a marshaling of the conclusions he had reached concerning the nature of reasoning worked out with so much labor over that same period.

In a short article, we cannot hope to do justice to Peirce's thought on this matter. We shall simply try here to expound some of his reflections which may serve as a propaedeutic to his well-known article in the hope that it will aid the reader first to understand the unusual kind of argument it is, and second to help focus properly critical evaluation. We shall not attempt an analysis of the argument itself; that alone would require an article or two. We restrict ourselves, then, to preliminaries: what Peirce had to say about God-talk in general and why in general he held what he did. Although this paper does not seek critical evaluation *in recto*, it does so *in obliquo* since it pretends not only to expound but also to explain and interpret. That explanation and interpretation intend to be a presentation of the truth of the matter as this writer sees it, while at the same time remaining faithful to Peirce. The presentation will consist of three parts: 1) traditional theism, 2) anthropomorphic theism, 3) vagueness.

I. TRADITIONAL THEISM

In a letter to William James (June 12, 1902), Peirce says that he has been reading Royce's *The World and the Individual* and finds it not in very good taste "to stuff it so full of the name of God" (8.277). The reason is that "the Absolute is strictly speaking only God, in a Pickwickian sense, that is, in a sense that has no effect" (8.277).

The point of this remark seems to be that, although it may be true that God is absolute, such a characterization is altogether too abstract and formal to make of God an object of belief. An object of belief in the strict sense according to Peirce must be such that it is capable of influencing human conduct. Peirce seems to think that Royce's absolute if not allowed other attributes would be precisely incapable of such influence because it would be too abstract and empty. It is God in a Pickwickian sense, in a sense which has no effect, and so, literally, is incapable of belief. The reality (or unreality) of God as merely "the Absolute" would make no difference to human conduct. Whatever attributes over and above "absoluteness" we decide "God" must have, they must be such as to show God to be intimately related to and "concerned with" what men do. To be an object of belief the reality of God must make a difference to human conduct. The meaning of "God," then, must be rooted in human experience and at the same time must indicate in some way that that reality is not confined to space and time. Let us consider how Peirce describes the absolute reality called "God."

In the opening lines of his article on the neglected argument Peirce defines the term "God" as *the* definable proper name signifying *ens necessarium* (6.452). This reality is not only necessary but also one, personal, not immanent in creation but creating the universe (5.496; 6.505-506), omniscient (6.508), omnipotent (6.509), infallible (6.510), not subject to time (4.67), and not finite (8.262). These attributes are recognizable as the traditional ones of theistic natural theology. What is different, however, in Peirce's description is that he will not allow that God exists, in the strict sense of that term, but rather that He is real (cf. 8.262). The reason is that existence strictly belongs to the category of secondness, of brute force or interaction. Whatever belongs to secondness must be capable of action and reaction and must therefore be spatio-temporal. Consequently, such a reality would be limited and finite. But this will not do for God, since He is the Creator of the three universes of which the actual—the realm of existents—is but one. God, then, must be said to be real (as opposed to unreal, fictitious, non-being) but not to exist.

The term of Peirce's argument, therefore, is a non-finite, necessary reality which can best be described in traditional theistic terms because such a description makes of that reality more than an abstract and empty Absolute. It makes of that reality something which would make a difference to human conduct if it were acknowledged as real. It is a conception which would arise from meditation upon human experience and which in turn would affect that experience insofar as it is subject to self-control. It was such considerations as these which led Peirce to try to write down a description of his argument:

> If God Really be, and be benign, then, in view of the generally conceded truth that religion, were it but proved, would be a good outweighing all others, we should naturally expect that there would be some Argument for His Reality that should be obvious to all minds, high and low alike, that should earnestly strive to find the truth of the matter; and that this Argument should present its conclusion, not as a proposition of metaphysical theology, but in a form directly applicable to the conduct of life, and full of nutrition for men's highest growth [6.457].

In a word, Peirce believes that there is no more adequate way for us to conceive of the adequate cause of the universe than as vaguely like a man (5.536). The theistic notion of God, then, is both anthropomorphic and vague. According to Peirce, it is precisely because that notion is anthropomorphic that it is believable and because it is vague that it is a notion of God.

2. ANTHROPOMORPHIC THEISM

Peirce's claim that theism must be anthropomorphic to be believable is, to say the least, unusual. One might have expected that a theist would try to avoid the charge of anthropomorphism as an objection to any theory of God. The medieval theologians were at pains to avoid precisely this sort of objection by developing at length a negative theology and a doctrine of analogous predication. Whether these attempts by some of the leading proponents of theism were successful or not is not the point here; what is important is the lengths to which defenders of theism have gone in order to avoid this sort of criticism. And yet Peirce not only does not reject the allegation, he seems to revel in it.

What, then, does he understand by anthropomorphism? Peirce contrasts his use of this term with Schiller's "humanism." Though humanism is allied with anthropomorphism and is in perfect harmony with pragmatism, it does not deal precisely with the same question since Schiller, in Peirce's view, identifies it with the "old humanism" which was not so much a scientific opinion as an aim. Pragmatism as a scientific opinion is best expressed by the term "anthropomorphism." The scientific opinion to which Peirce refers is of course the correct analysis of scientific method at which all his logical researches were directed. It is this analysis which implies theism.

> . . . if by metaphysics we mean the broadest positive truths of the psycho-physical universe . . . then the very fact that these problems can be solved by a logical maxim is proof enough that they do not belong to metaphysics but to "epistemology," an atrocious translation of *Erkenntnislehre* [5.496].

Among other things, *Erkenntnislehre* shows that man has powerful and accurate instincts besides reasoning. In fact, reasoning is nothing but a development of instinct and so is continuous with it. Instinct is more basic than reasoning, and no adequate account of reasoning and scientific research can be given without recognizing its role. This, of course, is not to say that reasoning is identical with instinct. It is not. But, according to Peirce, a correct analysis of scientific reasoning will show its roots in human instinct. Thus he can say:

> For those metaphysical questions which have such interest [human interest], the question of a future life and especially that of One Incomprehensible but Personal God, not immanent in but creating the universe, I, for one, heartily admit that a Humanism, *that does not pretend to be a science but only an instinct*, like a bird's power of flight, but purified by meditation, *is the most precious contribution that has been made to philosophy for ages* [5.496; italics mine].

Peirce argues that almost all human conceptions are at bottom anthropomorphic. This is true even of scientific hypotheses, and to say that an hypothesis is unscientific simply because it is anthropomorphic is an objection "of a very shallow kind, that arises from prejudices based upon much too narrow considerations" (5.47). According to Peirce, this is the objection of the nominalist. In opposition to these "much too narrow considerations," Peirce maintains that all man's knowledge, including all scientific and philosophical theories and hypotheses which can have any meaning, is based upon experience.

I hold . . . that man is so completely hemmed in by the bounds of his possible practical experience, his mind is so restricted to being the instrument of his needs, that he cannot, in the least, *mean* anything which transcends those limits [5.536].

All man's conceptions, then, are anthropomorphic in the sense that they depend upon the limits of his possible experience. But to say this is like passing a law forbidding man to jump over the moon; such a law would not prevent him from jumping as high as he could. Man will continue to try to conceive of a supreme and indeed transcendent cause or agency of the entire universe, but there will be no more adequate way of conceiving it than "as vaguely like a man." Furthermore, Peirce repeatedly recalls that the only satisfactory explanation of man's ability to form any hypothesis applicable to the universe is his affinity to the universe.

And in regard to any preference for one kind of theory over another, it is well to remember that every single truth of science is due to the affinity of the human soul to the soul of the universe, imperfect as that affinity no doubt is. To say, therefore, that a conception is one natural to man, which comes just about to the same thing as to say that it is anthropomorphic, is as high a recommendation as one could give to it in the eyes of an Exact Logician [5.47].

Peirce's anthropomorphism, therefore, is nothing other than his metaphysical realism.

They [the great realists] showed that the general is not capable of full actualization in the world of action and reaction but is of the nature of what is thought, but that our thinking only apprehends and does not create thought, and that that thought may and does as much govern outward things as it does our thinking [1.27].

The basic mistake of nominalism is that it violates the fundamental rule of exact logic—do not block the road to inquiry. By denying that anything is real except the actual, it at once renders all knowledge of the world inexplicable and posits an unknowable "thing-in-itself." It renders knowledge of the world inexplicable because all knowledge of the world involves generals. If generals are not real but only figments of the mind, then knowledge is not of the world. Rather it posits a mere "out-there-here-and-now" about which nothing can be said, conceived, or judged. It would be positing the utterly unintelligible and inexplicable as the ultimate explanation, thus cutting off all further questions and inquiry. For Peirce such a position turns out to be in the strictest sense meaningless in virtue of the pragmatic maxim.

> The elements of every concept enter into logical thought at the gate of perception and make their exit at the gate of purposive action and whatever cannot show its passports at both of those gates is to be arrested as unauthorized by reason [5.212].

Peirce's "anthropomorphism," it must be concluded, is but another name for his realistic pragmatism (pragmaticism).

3. VAGUENESS

Theism, it has been remarked, is only implied by anthropomorphism. The middle term, as it were, for this inference is to be found in Peirce's critical common-sensism, itself a consequence of pragmaticism (5.439). It is so, in our view, because it takes seriously the role of "instinctive mind" by which man has an affinity to nature (5.47) and to God (8.262; see 6.516).

> Our logically controlled thoughts compose a small part of the mind, the mere blossom of a vast complexus, which we may call instinctive mind, in which this man will not say he has *faith*, because that implies the conceivability of distrust, but upon which he builds as the very fact to which it is the whole business of his logic to be true [5.212].

This "instinctive mind" through which every concept enters into logical thought Peirce elsewhere calls "Insight . . . into Thirdnesses, the general elements, of Nature." Again he refers to it as a "faculty" which man must have because otherwise there would be no accounting for his undeniable ability to guess right among the millions of possible hypotheses often enough to allow him to make genuine discoveries (5.171ff.). This is man's *il lume naturale*, the natural disposition with which man comes into the world (see 1.80, 2.750, 5.47, 5.603-604, 6.10, 5.504). Ultimately, then, instinctive mind must consist of "*in posse* innate cognitive habits, which is all that anybody but John Locke ever meant by innate ideas" (5.504).

Instinctive mind, then, is "pre-scientific"; it is the ground of reasoning both as an activity and as a developed habit; it is the affinity of the mind to reality which makes any scientific inquiry possible. Insofar as science strives for greater and greater precision in its terms and concepts, instinctive mind will escape scientific analysis. It will always remain vague and indeterminate because it is the innate source and origin of reasoning itself whose function to a large extent is to analyze and make precise what it apprehends. No attempt to inquire scientifically into instinctive mind (no matter how useful and informative such investigation may prove to be) can be adequate to the reality so investigated. Something which is vague and indeterminate will always be "left over." Not only is this true of instinctive mind but of any reality investigated by science. The real is continuous and therefore intrinsically affected by vagueness and generality, both forms of indeterminateness; this is why the real is intelligible; why it must be said to be "mind-like"; and why, finally, there is any affinity between human minds and the universe.

The point we are trying to make is that for Peirce it is a serious mistake not to take vagueness seriously. It would be even a greater mistake to think that whatever remains vague after investigation can be disregarded as unreal. And perhaps the greatest mistake of all would be to think that in principle all vagueness can be eliminated even from science in the strictest sense. These errors in understanding human knowing are found in varying forms and degrees in the several nominalistic interpretations of inquiry. Peirce's pragmaticism was meant to avoid them. Critical common-sensism and "scholastic" realism, both consequences of pragmaticism, argue for vagueness and generality as essential ontological as well as logical categories.

In an attempt to show that there is nothing contradictory in holding a common-sensism which is at the same time critical, Peirce lists six characteristics which distinguish his position from the Scotch school. The fourth and most important of these he states as follows:

> By all odds, the most distinctive character of the Critical-Common-sensist, in contrast to the old Scotch philosopher [Reid], lies in his insistence that the acritically indubitable is invariably vague.
> Logicians have been at fault in giving Vagueness the go-by, so far as even to analyze it [5.446; see 5.505].

The recognition of vagueness as an important logical category is essential to Peirce's discussion of theism. Our ideas of the infinite are extremely vague, he writes to James, and become contradictory the moment we attempt to make them precise (8.262). It is true to say of God that He is omniscient and omnipotent if we leave these concepts vague (6.508-509). And yet these predicates "are not utterly unmeaning" for, as a matter of fact, they can be interpreted "in our religious adoration and the consequent effects upon conduct" (8.262). The vagueness of our notions of God, therefore, ought not for that reason to rule them out from rational belief. Indeed this vagueness acts as a corrective to anthropomorphism by negating the limitations of human experience and classification in the infinite reality. In a word, it is vagueness which allows our notions to be about God.

Vagueness is a form of indeterminateness. Generality is another. A subject is said to be determinate with respect to a character when that character is predicated of it universally and affirmatively. Such a subject of course would also be determinate with respect to the negative of such a character. In all other respects the subject is *indeterminate*. A sign is objectively *general* if it leaves it to the *interpreter* to supply further determinations. Thus, in the sentence "Man is mortal" the term "man" is objectively general because the answer to the question "Which man?" is "Any one you choose." A sign is objectively *vague* if it reserves *for some other possible sign* (and not for the interpreter) the function of completing the determination. Thus, in the sentence "This month a great event will happen," the term "great event" is objectively vague because the answer to the question "Which event?" is not "Any one you like" but rather "Let us wait and see" (5.447; 5.505). Now, every utterance leaves the right of further exposition to the utterer, and so every utterance is to that extent vague. Its vagueness is removed to the extent that the signs it uses are rendered general. According to Peirce it is usually the case that an affirmative predication covers generally every essential character of the predicate, while a negative predication vaguely denies some essential character (5.447). It turns out, therefore, that in every communication situation *absolute* determinateness and precision are not and cannot be attained.

. . . honest people, when not joking, intend to make the meaning of their words determinate, so that there shall be no latitude of interpretation at all. That is to say, the character of their meaning consists in the implications and the non-implications of their words; and they intend to fix what is implied and what is not implied. They believe that they succeed in doing so, and if their chat is about the theory of numbers, perhaps they may. But the further their topics are from such precise, or "abstract," subjects, the less possibility is there of such precision of speech [5.447; see also 2.357].

Another way of distinguishing vagueness and generality as two forms of indeterminateness is as follows: "anything is *general* in so far as the principle of excluded middle does not apply to it and is *vague* in so far as the principle of contradiction does not apply to it" (5.448; cf. 5.505). Thus, Peirce observes, a triangle in general is not isosceles, equilateral, or scalene. It is false neither that an animal (in a vague sense) is male, nor that an animal is female (5.505). Though no sign can be both vague and general in the same respect, still every sign is to some extent indeterminate and to that degree is both vague and general. The only way in which it could escape being either vague or general would be for it to be completely and absolutely determinate. According to Peirce this is simply not possible. Although every proposition actually asserted must refer to some non-general subject, still no communication between persons can be entirely non-vague. The reason for this, without going into detail, is that there is no such thing as a logical atom in the strict sense, that is, a term incapable of logical division (see 3.93). It follows, then, that none of our conceptions, even the most intellectual and scientific, is absolutely precise, that is, without some vagueness.

Peirce holds that our acritically indubitable beliefs are invariably vague. To submit such beliefs to criticism involves an attempt to render them more precise. To the extent that they are rendered more precise, Peirce admits that they are open to doubt. His point, however, is this: "Yet there are beliefs of which such a critical sifting invariably leaves a certain vague residue unaffected" (5.507). The question, then, is simply whether that vague residue itself would disappear under persevering attempts at precision.

But the answer . . . is that it is not because insufficient pains have been taken to precise the residuum, that it is vague: it is that it is vague intrinsically [5.508].

The example of such an indubitable belief offered by Peirce is that of order in nature. A host of critics have submitted to criticism every precise statement of that order which has been proposed. Each of these precise statements is open to doubt. "As precisely defined it can hardly be said to be absolutely indubitable considering how many thinkers there are who do not believe it" (5.508). All this shows, however, is that any precise statement of nature's order is open to doubt. In fact, it is the very precision which allows room for doubt and therefore for criticism. And yet for all that "who can think that there is *no* order in nature?" (5.508). For Peirce such a claim is literally unthinkable. Pure chaos cannot be thought; the notion of chaos itself is parasitical upon the notion of order; it is *relative* disorder, that is, relative to an order we expected to find or hoped to find. Any number of doubts can be cast upon this or that or the other characterization of nature's order, but there always remains a vague residue of that original belief which cannot be eliminated. This residue is indubitable and indeed acritical, but it is not indubitable precisely because it is acritical in the sense of simply not having been criticized. Rather it remains indubitable because it cannot be criticized since it remains essentially vague.

Peirce is convinced that there is a relatively fixed list of such original beliefs which is the same for all men. He tells us that he was not always so convinced but that experience and reflection have led him to this view. He admits to having always been strongly attracted by a form of common-sensism which holds that there is "no definite and fixed collection of opinions that are indubitable, but that criticism gradually pushed back each individual's indubitables, modifying the list, yet still leaving him beliefs indubitable at the time being" (5.509). A better understanding of vagueness, however, changed his mind. From very early on (at least from the paper "Some Consequences of Four Incapacities" in 1868), Peirce held that there is no first, indubitable proposition which occupies a privileged epistemic position. This basic criticism of what he took to be the "spirit of Cartesianism" is compatible with the position outlined in the preceding paragraph. Every proposition is indeed open to criticism, revision, and doubt to the extent that it is precise, i.e., non-vague. On the other hand, every proposition remains to some extent and in some respect vague. Otherwise it simply would not function as a symbol (see 2.357).

Every proposition, therefore, is to be interpreted in terms of another proposition and thus *ad infinitum*.

To the extent that the vagueness of a proposition is intrinsic to it, that proposition retains an element of the indubitable. Hence every proposition is open to revision both in the sense that it can always give way to a more adequate expression and in the sense that an erroneous proposition (i.e., a false proposition) can give way to a true one. Indubitables in the sense of primitive, original beliefs are indubitable because they remain intrinsically vague not only with respect to the individual logical subjects to which they refer but also with respect to the character or characters predicated of them. No amount of analysis will render those predicates absolutely precise and determinate since they will always carry the rider "vaguely like." This rider, of course, warns the hearer or reader that some unspecified character of that predicate does not apply to the subject, and so that the subject is also vaguely *unlike* the character applied to it. Some predicates, e.g., infinite, omnipotent, etc., carry this warning in themselves since they contain in their own comprehension the negation of some general predicate (non-vague in that respect).

Perhaps all of this is not well put, and an example might be worth a thousand vague and general explanations. Let us consider Peirce's own example: there is order in nature. The logical subject of this indubitable is a non-vague, non-general reality vaguely and generally characterized in the first place by the predicate "nature" and further specified by the vague and general predicate "order." What is intended in this proposition is not at all indefinite, and consequently the subject term partakes of the nature of an index in that it functions so as to force attention on its object. Still the logical subject of a symbol is not strictly an index because it indicates its object only as a result of being intended to do so (a true index is a sign independently of anyone's intending it to be). Since only a true index can be absolutely determinate and since the subject of a proposition is only *like* an index, the logical subject of our proposition is not absolutely non-vague. This sort of vagueness attaches to the logical subject of any proposition whatsoever.

This is what Peirce means by saying that there is no logical atom. Both predicates in our example are also vague and intrinsically so. "Nature" is vague because it is understood to be the denial of "artifact" and a collective term for all such non-artifacts. More precision can be accomplished only by indicating further what "nature" is not or by pointing to objects which comprise "nature" without being nature—natural objects. The positive content of that term remains imprecise although not empty on that account. "Order" is vague because it is a relational term and can be made precise only with respect to some standard of comparison antecedently specified. What this comes to is that this or that particular order might be non-vaguely indicated but not order as such. Similarly non-order is a relative term. It indicates the absence of some anticipated kind of order. But absolute non-order is literally unthinkable and cannot be even vaguely indicated. Since non-order is not real in any absolute sense at all, it has no positive content at all. It is pure negativity—the limit notion of "no thought at all." The proposition under consideration, then, is at least doubly vague, with respect to its subject and with respect to its predicates.[2] Its predicates are vague not because of any lack of diligence on the part of analysts but of their very nature (sic!). Order is unity amid multiplicity—one and many—and of course this is *the* paradox!

Belief in the God of theism is for Peirce an original belief. It is one of the indubitables in that relatively fixed list which is the same for all men. Doubts about God's reality or about the attributes which most aptly describe Him arise from attempts at precision. Every formula about God which claims to be non-vague is to that extent open to real doubt. The ultimate ground for such doubt is the fact that insofar as such formulae succeed in being precise they are false. An infinite being is not the sort of thing which can be precisely classified. If it were, then it would fall under a genus and so would entail the possibility of many Gods (8.262). Doubts about God's reality, therefore, are in fact doubts about various formulae meant to express that reality in relatively non-vague terms. Such doubts, however, are not about God's *reality*; indeed for Peirce such a doubt is impossible because belief in it is instinctive; it is an acritical indubitable in the sense already discussed. Doubt about it, according to Peirce, vanishes once it is recognized that all appropriate formulations of that reality are intrinsically vague. Thus Peirce claims that any argument for God's reality is really a form of the ontological argument.

NOTES

1. References to Peirce's works are taken from *Collected Papers of Charles Sanders Peirce*, vols. I-VI, edd. Charles Hartshorne and Paul Weiss (Cambridge: The Belknap Press of Harvard University Press, 1931-1935); vols. VII-VIII, ed. Arthur Burks (Cambridge: The Belknap Press of Harvard University Press, 1958). References are by volume and paragraph.

2. Peirce remarks that "indefiniteness and generality might primarily affect either the logical breadth or the logical depth of the sign to which it belongs" (5.448n). In the case of a proposition, logical breadth is the subject denoted and logical depth is the predicate asserted (5.471; see 2.394ff.).

12

God and the Search for Meaning

ROBERT O. JOHANN

IT IS NOT UNCOMMON TODAY to hear people talk of life or existence as meaningless. The purpose of this paper is to argue the opposite. As I shall try to show, even our anxiety about the meaning of life presupposes our prior involvement in a final order of meaning. If, nevertheless, life sometimes seems to be without meaning, it can only seem so because, on the level of explicit awareness, we have somehow lost touch with ourselves, somehow become estranged from ourselves. What is called for, then, is a reflective effort to recover that from which we have become separated. The following is such an effort at self-reflection, and what we shall find at its end is, not surprisingly, what today's man seems most to forget—the radically religious nature of genuinely human existence.

I

Before taking up the question of life's meaning as a whole, let us first try to distinguish between "meaningfulness" and "meaningless-ness" as these terms might be applied to any particular situation in which we find ourselves. As a first attempt, I shall suggest that a situation is experienced as meaningful if it is experienced as calling for one response on our part rather than another. Or, what comes to the same thing, a situation is meaningful to the extent that it provides us with grounds for choice. If there are no grounds in the situation for choosing between alternative ways of dealing with it, then to that extent it lacks meaning; it is meaning-less.

If we inspect this first proposal, it becomes apparent that according to it, no situation is "meaningful" in the absence of an agent. By itself, the situation just is what it is. Moreover, even in relation to an agent, a situation will not be meaningful unless the elements which comprise it can somehow be distinguished into plus and minus factors, resources to be capitalized, obstacles to be overcome or avoided. Without such a classification, the agent involved in the situation has no basis for choosing a course of action, i.e., no basis for being an agent.

What is it, then, in the light of which various facets of the situation cease to be neutral for the agent and become, instead, charged with positive or negative value? It can only be, I would suggest, the interest which the agent himself brings to the situation. The agent himself as interest-structure involved in the situation is the principle or standard of discrimination in terms of which situational factors may be adjudged as positive or negative, promotive or obstructive, and therefore as calling for one sort of response in preference to another.

Meaningfulness, therefore, in this first sense, is a matter of having the wherewithal for rationally deciding a course of action. To be meaningful, a situation must include within itself a norm or standard for its rational determination. This condition is met by the sheer presence in the situation of an agent who is aware of his own interests and the possible bearing of factors in the situation on the fulfillment of those interests. Wherever there is an interest-structure, there is a standard of meaning; and wherever this interest-structure is the object of awareness, there is a standard capable of being applied in a judgment determining the course of action called for. To be aware of oneself, therefore, as an interested agent is to be aware of the situation in which one finds himself as to that extent meaningful—i.e., as being the ways and means, positive and/or negative, for self-realization.

Clearly, this is a limited sense of "meaningfulness." It is simply a matter of "being relevant" to the agent's needs and purposes. And just as clearly, this limited sense is insufficient when we come to the question of "life's meaningfulness," or of "the meaning of existence." For we do not speak of life as meaningful merely because it provides the ways and means of fulfilling the particular interests we may bring to it, or because, in the light of such given interests, various courses of action recommend themselves and others do not. An agent, aware of his interests in a situation, is aware of them precisely as standards of selection and rejection. That is to say, he is aware of these interests as playing a determining role in the formation of his practical judgments and consequently on the style and shape of his life. For such an agent, then, the question about the suitability of his actual interests having so decisive a place inevitably arises. Just as the objective situation has to be appraised in the light of human interests if it is to become humanly meaningful and if the agent's response is to be grasped as rationally justified, so also, it would seem, must those interests which serve as standards for interpreting the situation be reflectively appraised if the agent's *allegiance to them* is to be more than blind and irrational. For, although it is true that one's commitment to a particular standard is *a priori* with respect to the judgments one makes on its basis, it is also true that such a commitment itself is a human and rational act only to the extent that it too is a matter of reflective assent. In other words, if one cannot justify the standards in the light of which one judges the situation and the actions to be taken in relation to it, then those judgments themselves remain ultimately unjustified. To have a situation as fully meaningful, therefore, means more than having it as grounding our choices from some limited and unquestioned perspective. It must also be had as grounding our choice of perspectives.

All this may perhaps be put another way. In a much-neglected essay, John Dewey makes the point that a practical (as distinct from a purely intellectual) judgment is always an act of self-determination.[1] In the act of judging what act to perform or what course to follow, the judger is really judging himself, i.e., determining the kind of agent he is to be. For in the case of a practical judgment, the character and interests of the agent have an intrinsic bearing on its content and must be made explicit if the judgment is to be warranted. That is to say: in such judgments, the disposition of the judger is a logical factor or condition, and not merely a practical one. This is not the case with purely intellectual judgments, i.e., judgments which seek to determine simply the objective possibilities of matter-of-fact connections in the situation under inquiry. Here character is only a practical condition. What this means is that, if one is going to inquire effectively, he must indeed bring to his effort certain dispositions, e.g., an overriding desire to judge truly, a readiness to be led by evidence alone in the formation of his judgments and not by any extraneous factors. Without such dispositions, he is unlikely to reach the truth of the matter. But, whereas dispositions of this kind are presupposed for any warranted judgments of the intellectual kind, they affect all alike and do not enter into the content of any one in particular. In a practical judgment, however, its specific content is determined expressly and consciously by reference to the judger's attitudes and interests, which function as the very basis for making the judgment. Thus, we are unable to judge an act as worth doing except in relation to the interest it promotes, and to approve the act as worthwhile on this basis is at one and the same time to approve the interest itself as one worth pursuing. In other words *judging* anything to be good, as distinct from merely finding it attractive or being drawn to it, involves not only the presence of an interest-structure but its *reflective ratification*. In his practical judgments, the agent not only weighs means in relation to ends already given; he re-commits (determines) himself to those ends, re-identifies himself with them, and by that very fact makes them his own and himself the kind of person he is. This is why a practical judgment is inevitably an act of self-determination. It is also why judgment of the meaning of a situation, i.e., the response it calls for, is incomplete—indeed, is not even possible—without at least an implicit appraisal of the standard (interest) by which that meaning is determined. If no appraisal of the standard is possible, then no practical judgments are possible. An agent incapable of rejecting a particular end (i.e., wholly determined to it) is controlled, not by judgment, but by impulse. But to act on impulse is precisely not to choose, much less to have grounds for choice.

This, it seems to me, is the basic shortcoming in Richard Taylor's recent inquiry into life's meaningfulness.[2] Taylor asserts that the plight of Sisyphus could have been a meaningful experience if the gods, in their mercy, had but instilled in him—e.g., by injecting some substance into his veins—a consuming passion for rolling stones up the hill. In such a case, even though the activity led to nothing beyond itself but was its own end, it would have been just what Sisyphus wanted to do. It would have been "meaningful" to him, i.e., subjectively. By the same token, our own lives can be said to be meaningful, not because they lead anywhere or because anything is finally accomplished, but simply because of the deep interest we have in what we find ourselves doing. We have, says Taylor, a kind of "inner compulsion" to be doing just the sort of things we do, and so our lives, though lacking any kind of objective meaning (i.e. as prescinding from our personal interests), are nonetheless "meaningful" to us.

The first thing to notice here is Taylor's assumption (one, unfortunately, widely shared) that an "objective" evaluation of our lives is one made in abstraction from our interests. This is simply false. For as we have seen, if the judger abstracts from every interest in the situation, no judgmental appraisal, objective or otherwise, can be made at all. The interests of the judger are precisely the standards for his evaluation of the situation, which is why I have insisted that they too must be justified if his judgments are to be deemed just. More importantly, however, Taylor's effort to redeem life's meaningfulness succeeds only in making it less than human. For any act which is based on compulsion, instead of reason, is to that extent not a human act. If our behavior is determined to be what it is, not by judgment, but simply by inner attractions and repulsions (*unexamined* interests, if you like), it is simply not human behavior. What Taylor has overlooked is that it is not enough that an act be aimed at an end for it to be human; the act must also be the agent's own, an aiming of himself at the end, an act of self-determination. A miraculous substance in his veins might account for a being's finding one thing attractive rather than another. But his grasp of it as something worthy of his allegiance and commitment can only be the fruit of judgment. Without examination and judgmental appraisal of the interests and drives in relation to which things in its environment attract or repel the living organism, organic activity is possible, to be sure, but we are still this side of human life.

But here the real difficulty arises. If the meaningfulness of a situation requires the appraisal and justification of the interests in the light of which it is interpreted, then where do we look for the standard in the light of which these interests themselves may be judged? It would seem that we have painted ourselves into a corner. For what could such a standard be but, on the basis of our own explanation, some further interest, whose acceptance as a standard will itself require justification, and so on, endlessly? In other words, unless we are already in reflective possession of some final standard of judgment, some absolutely inclusive interest whose very inclusiveness would proclaim it as self-justified and the ultimate basis of all possible evaluations, then we can never have any of our choices as finally grounded or justified. Our lives, then, however meaningful from some arbitrary and limited perspective, would indeed be finally meaningless. And, of course, this is what not a few philosophers have actually concluded, and what a good many more would have, had they only been consistent with their premisses. Is this conclusion inevitable?

II

So as not to waste time, let me say at the outset that I regard such a conclusion as not only not inevitable, but impossible. It is a practical contradiction. For if the statement "Life is ultimately meaningless" were true, it would mean that there were no final grounds for anything we do, including the making of such a statement. Its very content precludes such a judgment from being finally warranted. It should be regarded, therefore, not as a judgment but as a cry of despair about our ability to judge. And since such despair, although it may occur, cannot be reflectively justified (the same kind of contradiction would be involved in any effort to do so), let us not question our capacity to judge but rather try to discern what is implied in it.

We have said that any appraisal of a situation involves at the same time an appraisal of the interest in the light of which the situation is being interpreted. Any warranted appraisal, therefore, involves a reference to some final standard of appraisal. Assuming, then, as we must, that some of our appraisals can be warranted, the problem confronting us is to make explicit the final standard which makes this possible.

A beginning, I think, can be made if we first recall the distinction between judgment as an act and judgment as a content.[3] So much has been made of the latter by logicians and epistemologists that the former has been all but neglected—which has not a little to do with the problem we are now considering. To call judgment an act is to insist that judgments do not float in the void; that an instance of judgment occurs only where there is someone engaged in a specific kind of activity, that, namely, of judging. This means that in addition to any interest which the judger may be subjecting to appraisal in his judgment, there is already another interest at work, to wit, the interest leading the agent to perform this kind of act rather than another. For, conceivably, the agent could be doing something else—looking at television, washing the dishes, writing a letter. The fact that he chooses instead to engage in judging implies an awareness on his part, however obscure, of an interest which the act of judging fulfills. To be deliberately judging a situation instead of dealing with it in some other way is to be aware, at least implicitly, of the import of doing so, of the difference which such an act makes, and to be set on effecting that difference. In this light, the judgments we make have a role to play; they are means to an end and thus are able to be appraised and judged according as they promote or obstruct its attainment.

Now, without at this time specifying just what it is we aim at in judging—something we shall have to do if it is to be the basis for judging our judgments—there are already a number of things we can say about it. First of all, it itself is not the basis for distinguishing between judgments of fact and judgments of value. The difference between these two types of judgment lies, we have seen, not in the absence or presence of interest as a motive for the act of judging but in the absence or presence of interest as a determinant of *what* is judged (i.e., of judgment as content). Since the interest we are talking about is simply the interest in judging, the same interest presumably underlies all the judgments we make. This, however, is not to say that it affects them all in the same way. For, in judgments whose contents are determined by interests (i.e., value judgments), the interest in judging functions more than simply as a motive; it is also a logical factor. Let me explain.

If our judgments (as contents) are means for attaining the end aimed at in judging, then any judgment which is inconsistent or in conflict with this basic aim is self-defeating. To judge in a way which negates the aim of judgment is really not to be judging. Since, however, the only thing which *can* conflict with an aim or interest is another aim or interest, the possibility of inconsistency or conflict between what we judge and our interest in judging is limited to those cases in which the content itself is logically dependent on interest. This rules out all purely intellectual judgments but, at the same time, includes all practical ones. My interest in judging can have no logical bearing on what is already the case but is utterly revelant to the way in which I determine myself. Put another way: since the content of intellectual judgments is determinded in abstraction from the particular interests of the judger, no such judgments can conflict with the interest underlying their formation. By the same token, since a particular interest is intrinsic to the content of a value judgment, such a basic conflict is not only possible, but so long as positive steps are not taken to avoid it, the judgment itself as possibly self-defeating cannot claim our full assent. This means that we cannot hold our practical judgments as fully warranted until we have expressly formulated the interest implicit in the very act of judging and applied it as a standard for appraising their contents. On the other hand, since this interest, as the wellspring of all judgmental activity, is the source and ground of rationality, any value judgment which is found upon examination to be in accord with it needs nothing more to be accepted as fully rational and grounded.

If this is so, then even though we have not yet spelled out the nature of the final standard of judgment, we know where to look for it. It is not a question of whether there is anything which can serve in this capacity. It is only a question of how to put it in words—to which we shall address ourselves shortly. Right now it is important to see that such verbalization is crucial. For, so long as we are only implicitly aware of why we engage in judging or what we are aiming at when we do judge, we are utterly unable to defend our judgments, even to ourselves. In other words, reasons have to be expressly formulated if they are to function logically as reasons. Without such express formulation, the ultimate basis on which his decisions might rest remains reflectively unavailable to the judger, and although he

may persist in making judgments, these will lack final control. They
will, that is, even to the judger himself, be only partially rational
and not completely so. It is then that doubts arise about life's final
meaning—doubts which cannot be stilled. For in this state the judger
lacks on the reflective level the wherewithal to resolve them. He is,
on that level, literally out of touch with himself and the final source
of meaning.

Getting back in touch, however, is no easy matter. It demands,
so to speak, a work of second-order reflection, a reflection on reflection. The judger must, as it were, step behind himself and look
over his own shoulder as he judges the world around him, and try
at the same time to discern and describe the intentionality animating
his activity. Since this radical aim or intent is implicitly embodied
in every judgment he makes, he should be able to do this, and also to
recognize the extent to which the description he devises actually fits
what he is trying to describe. Indeed, recognition is what it is all
about, i.e., re-cognizing on the level of reflection what is already
cognized, but only implicitly, on the level of direct awareness. The
test of the reflective effort is how much self-recognition and self-
recovery it makes possible. It succeeds in the measure that the
judger recovers himself from his manifold judgments, newly recognizes what he has been up to, is newly at home and at one with
himself. Or, if you like, it succeeds when the re-cognition is such that
questions about life's meaningfulness are manifestly no longer pertinent. How much a given reflective formulation brings this about,
each judger must say for himself. But it is clear from what we have
seen already that any formulation must meet certain conditions.
What is proposed in the formulation must, that is, be such that it can
actually serve as a final standard of judgment and the controlling
commitment of judgers. Since it is this to which the judger is expected to give his explicit and total allegiance, it must be such as to
call for this kind of response. In other words, what is proposed as
the end at which judging aims cannot be anything partial, relative,
or conditioned. As the ground of all rational action, it cannot itself
stand in need of grounding or justification, but must be something
absolute, all-inclusive, and justified in and of itself. What this might
be we must now try to make clear.

III

One answer which immediately suggests itself is this: We engage in the activity of judging when we are interested precisely in *knowing*, or in *knowing the truth*. There is, to be sure, a sense in which this answer is incontestable. The sense in which it is so, however, depends on just how one interprets "knowing," or "knowing the truth." Is "knowing," for example, something final and complete in itself, the consummation of that "pure desire to know" which is the constitutive intentionality of the human spirit (à la Bernard Lonergan)? Or is "knowing" but a condition for the attainment of something beyond itself which is what we are really interested in when we seek to know? We can recall here the basic contention of John Macmurray that all knowledge is for the sake of action and all action is for the sake of friendship.[4] Or Dewey's thesis that "knowing" is *instrumental* to having gross, qualitative experience in a more secure, settled, and satisfactory way.[5] Again, if one says that the interest which judgment promotes is our interest in truth, everything depends on whether truth is viewed as a property assignable to judgments independently of the interest underlying the activity of judging, or whether, on the other hand, a judgment (as content) will be seen to be true only in the measure that it is grasped as fulfilling the interest which prompts the judgment as act. My point in all this is simply to indicate that the answer which first suggests itself is not as simple and straightforward as might at first appear. Let us, therefore, try to go about it another way. As we proceed, my own position regarding this first suggestion may, indirectly, be clarified.

Once again, then, how shall we explicate the interest which judgment as a kind of activity promotes? What are we trying to bring about when we engage in judging? Or perhaps more directly, just what are we doing when we are judging?

Taking the last form of the question first, I shall say that, whatever else we may be doing when judging, we are at least engaged in determining what can be properly or validly *said* of something. That is, we are lifting some aspect or element of experience from the realm of immediacy and are deliberately situating it in the realm of discourse and communication. To determine what can be said of something is to determine it expressly as something existing for *us*, something able to be dealt with in common, a possible focus of shared concern and conjoint action. This means that judgment is inconceivable as the act of a solitary entity. His very ability to judge presupposes that the would-be judger is already involved in a communicative relationship, already exists in mutual relation with other persons, is already an "I" correlative to a "you" in a world existing for both. It is thus *our* existence, and not mine alone, which is the matrix and source of judgmental activity.

But if the prior reality of the "we" is what makes judgment possible, the maintenance and development of the "we," i.e., of a genuinely common life, are what make judgment necessary. For "we" exist only where there is real consensus in action, i.e., where individual entities do not merely react to stimuli but freely moderate their behavior in accordance with mutually accepted rules for dealing with their environment and one another. Without rules on which we agree and which enable us effectively to coordinate our actions, there is no "we." Rules, however, are not part of the given; they are not something we stumble upon. Rules arise only insofar as they are deliberately instituted and the act which institutes them is precisely the act of judgment. Let us look at this a little more closely.

What I am suggesting is that the interest underlying judgment as act is an interest in the harmonious relation of persons, an interest in the achievement of a genuine "we." As Jurgen Habermas puts it in *Knowledge and Human Interests*, our very first judgment "expresses unequivocally the intention of universal and unconstrained consensus."[6] What we are trying to accomplish when we engage in judging is to determine common grounds for our ongoing common life. These common grounds include not only a common world of possibilities for conjoint action (the world of facts) but, just as importantly, common standards for appraising those possibilities and deciding on a joint course of action (the world of values). Inquiry leading to judgment is always a search for such common grounds. We give ourselves to inquiry, instead of acting directly, only in the absence of an accepted rule for interpreting and dealing with what confronts us. Inquiry, indeed, looks to the institution of such a rule. Rules, however, belong to the interpersonal domain. They are the ways and means for realizing the relation of persons. If I act merely on whim, I determine myself apart from you. But when I act in accordance with a rule, my act is more than mere self-expression; it is controlled by my interest in "you," my concern that "you" be an effective presence in my life. In every action based on judgment, *you* have a part.

This brings us, I think, to the heart of the matter. The interest which gives rise to judgment is, in the last analysis, an interest in "you" as the ground of my life. It is an interest in keeping myself, your partner, correlative to you in all my undertakings. For what I am present to when confronting you is not just another determinate factor in my surroundings, another limited item in my own private world. Facing you, I face being as boundless, as literally incomprehensible, unable to be confined or constrained within any limits. You are not there simply as something to which I attend. You are there as *attending to me*, questioning me, challenging me, inviting me to share in your life. You are being, not as determinate, but as determining, being as source, being as free initiative, being as transcending finiteness and limitation. Instead of being simply a part of my world, you are as enveloping both me and my world. In short, being-as-you, disclosed in every genuine encounter between persons, but not limited to or exhausted by any particular encounter, is Being as absolute value. To have my life confirmed by being-as-you (i.e., by You) is thus to have my life confirmed absolutely. Through Your accord, Your "yes" to me in what I do, my life becomes Your embodiment as well as my own and acquires infinite weight. As promotive of being-as-you, whatever I do has final import.

So formulated, the interest underlying the activity of judging is not so much an interest which I have (one, that is, among many) as an interest which I am. At the core of my being as person, I am a responsive relation to the other as You, to the other as enveloping presence. Living out this relation (which is living out my essential vocation as "I") requires that I regulate my conduct on the basis of shared meanings and common standards whose elaboration is the work of judgment. The act of judging thus finds its origin and test in our ongoing common life. Judgments required by this common life, i.e., necessary for the maintenance and development of my relation to being-as-you, have a worthy claim on assent. Judgments, on the other hand, inconsistent with this relationship, call for rejection. Thus my nature as person, the interest in You which I am, is the final standard of judgment implicit in the exercise of any judgment. And since to abide by this standard and fulfill this interest is to give body through my life to absolute value, a life of devotion to You is its own justification.

IV

We said at the outset that anxiety about life's final meaningfulness presupposes our prior involvement in a final order of meaning. How this is so should now be clear. For questioning and inquiry, no less than the judgments at which they aim, *presuppose* the communicative relationship, man's constitutive interest in being-as-you. As we have portrayed it, this responsive relation to You is the transcendental structure of human experience, the very ground of our humanity, implicated in all we do, although not necessarily regulative of (indeed, often distorted by) what we do. Here is precisely the problem. As Tillich puts it: "Man is able to ask because he is separated *from*, while participating *in*, what he is asking about."[7] If man were not already in responsive relation with Being, he could not raise the question of life's meaningfulness. But were he not also out of touch with this constitutive dimension of himself, he would not have to raise it. If life is to be had as meaningful, therefore, more is needed than that man be constituted by an interest in the absolute. His life must actually be regulated by that interest. This demands the express formulation and acceptance of the communicative relationship, in which Being alone as absolute value reveals itself, as the final standard and norm of human activity. Everything man does must be judged and controlled in terms of this standard, the promotion of You in the world. If it is not, if in place of real communication (i.e., the continual coming-to-terms with being-as-you) other interests are made central and life is organized around such goals as, say, conformity or productivity, then man's living is out of joint with the ground of his being and cannot make final sense. In other words, a life of which You are not the focus has no final focus.

And so, finally, we come to the other point suggested at the outset—the radically religious character of genuinely human existence. I have not, to be sure, used the word "God" up to now. But what is the idea of "being-as-you," the transcendent value in relation to which each of us is first constituted a person, but the idea of God? As disclosed in every encounter between persons but not confined by the particularities of any individual encounter, being-as-you is the universal ground of our very vocation as persons, our vocation to universal community. For I cannot be responsive to being-as-you (nor, by the same token, true to myself) unless I am open to any and every appeal. To be deaf to the cry of the other on any occasion is to be deaf to You. Only a universal love fulfills my responsibility as a person. Once again, however, what is the idea of a universal community in which responsiveness-to-You is the supreme regulative principle but the idea of God's kingdom on earth? Where You reign, is it anyone less than God who reigns? And where God has died and is no longer of any concern, is it not You and the reign of love which have succumbed to other concerns?

One of Martin Buber's contentions (in *A Believing Humanism*) is that our faith is founded on our humanity, and our humanity on our faith. If we take faith in the sense of reflective assent to an order of meaning antecedent to and underlying all rational inquiry, then it is indeed rooted in our vocation as persons and is a "yes" to that vocation. This is not, with Feuerbach, to reduce the divine to the human but, on the contrary, to grasp the human as essentially constituted by a relation to the divine. Faith is our "yes" to that relationship. But the other part of Buber's thesis, that our humanity has our faith for its foundation, is the part which needs stressing today. For if it is common to hear our age described as one of crisis and breakdown in the realm of meanings, the essentially religious character of this crisis is too often lost sight of. Modern man is perhaps too disenchanted with religion as he has known it to look in that direction for salvation. The idea of God as a threat to our humanity rather than as its ground is perhaps too widespread. Still, if man really is as we have described him, then the very humanity of man's life is radically dependent on the vitality of his faith. The meaning of being human is not itself a human invention, but something presupposed by all such inventions. It is a meaning to which we can only open our hearts and gratefully assent. That meaning, and the final ground of all meanings, is our being in relationship with You. The present crisis of meaninglessness is thus indeed a crisis of faith. It is because we have turned from You and centered our lives elsewhere that emptiness haunts us and normlessness prevails. For only as committed to You is man true to his own humanity, and only as focused on You is his life a truly human affair.

NOTES

1. See his "Logical Conditions of a Scientific Treatment of Morality" in *Problems of Men* (New York: Philosophical Library, 1946), esp. pp. 229-32.
2. See the last chapter in his *Good and Evil* (New York: Macmillan, 1970), esp. pp. 264-68.
3. See Dewey, *op. cit.*, p. 220.
4. See his *Self as Agent* (New York: Harper, 1957), p. 16.
5. This is a constant theme in Dewey's writings, but perhaps it is most thoroughly developed in *The Quest for Certainty* (New York: Capricorn, 1960) and in *Logic: The Theory of Inquiry* (New York: Holt, Rinehart & Winston, 1938).
6. See Jurgen Habermas, *Knowledge and Human Interests* (Boston: Beacon, 1971), p. 314.
7. See *The Courage to Be* (New Haven: Yale University Press, 1952), p. 48.

GOD KNOWABLE AND UNKNOWABLE

Edited by Robert J. Roth, S.J.

This collection of essays is intended
to be a contribution to the lively,
contemporary dialogue about God.
The great questions about His existence, nature, attributes, and relation
to the world are as challenging and
controversial as ever. This work,
then, represents the tradition of positive effort to ascend by reason to the
ultimate Mystery which is the source
of all being, meaning, and value.
The essays fall into two groups—
historical and speculative. The former, in effect, constitute a dialogue
between contemporary philosophers
and classical thinkers, and the picture which is painted is that of a
"God Knowable and Unknowable,"
a God of light and shadow, of clarity and obscurity. The latter are
problem-oriented, striving to come
to grips with old questions in their
new setting and to bridge the differ-